THE NEW POLITICAL ECONOMY
OF URBAN EDUCATION

Urban schools and urban contexts are being transformed by global forces of
privatization and markets and new articulations of race, class, and urban space.
This is the starting point for Pauline Lipman's analysis of the relationship
between contested education policies and the neoliberal economic, political,
and ideological processes that are reshaping cities in the United States and
around the globe.

Using Chicago as a case study of the interconnectedness of urban policies
on housing, economic development, racial containment, and education,
Lipman explores larger implications for equity, justice, and "the right to the
city." She synthesizes scholarship in critical geography, urban sociology and
anthropology, education policy, and critical analyses of race to develop a
powerful critique of market-based solutions to education and urban problems
and a hopeful alternative. By examining the cultural politics of why and how
neoliberal policies resonate with people's lived experience, Lipman pushes
the analysis toward a new educational and social paradigm rooted in radical
political and economic democracy.

Pauline Lipman is Professor of Educational Policy Studies in the College of
Education, University of Illinois-Chicago.

The Critical Social Thought Series
Edited by Michael W. Apple,
University of Wisconsin—Madison

THE NEW POLITICAL ECONOMY OF URBAN EDUCATION

Neoliberalism, Race, and the Right to the City

Pauline Lipman

Routledge
Taylor & Francis Group

NEW YORK AND LONDON

First published 2011
by Routledge
711 Third Avenue, New York, NY 10017

Simultaneously published in the UK
by Routledge
2 Park Square, Milton Park, Abingdon, Oxon OX14 4RN

Routledge is an imprint of the Taylor & Francis Group, an informa business

Library of Congress Cataloging in Publication Data
Lipman, Pauline, 1944–
    The new political economy of urban education : neoliberalism, race,
    and the right to the city / Pauline Lipman.
    p. cm. — (The critical social thought series)
    Includes index.
    1. Education, Urban—United States. 2. Multicultural education—
    Curricula—United States. 3. Education—Curricula—United States.
    4. Cultural pluralism—United States. 5. Toleration—United States.
    I. Title.
    LC5131.L555 2011
    370.9173'2—dc22
    2011000554

ISBN 13: 978-0-415-80223-9 (hbk)
ISBN 13: 978-0-415-80224-6 (pbk)
ISBN 13: 978-0-203-82180-0 (ebk)

Typeset in Bembo and Stone Sans by
EvS Communication Networx, Inc.

Printed and bound in the United States of America on acid-free paper by
Walsworth Publishing Company, Marceline, MO.

To the parents, young people, teachers, and community members who struggle against great odds with courage and dignity and tenacity for a just and enriching education and a better future for all of us.

CONTENTS

ACKNOWLEDGMENTS

I want to thank Michael Apple for his generous support and confidence in this project and for its inclusion in his important Critical Social Thought series. Catherine Bernard has been a superb editor. Her thoughtful reading of the manuscript and her advice greatly improved the book. I am also grateful for a fellowship at the Great Cities Institute at UIC and for research support from the Chicago Area Studies project. I want to thank Nathan Haines and Cristen Jenkins for their terrific research assistance, analysis, and collaboration.

This book is deeply influenced and inspired by so many people's thinking, theorizing, and collective action over these past six years. I want to especially acknowledge the perspectives and courage of Jitu Brown; Cheryl Johnson, Marguerite Jacob, and the Committee for Safe Passage and People for Community Recovery; Areceli Gonzalez, Maria Hernandez, Lily Gonzalez, Carmen Soto and all the parents of Carpenter, Peabody, Whittier, and Andersen Schools; the parents and youth in Altgeld Gardens; and all the other parents and teachers and young people who continue to fight so hard for a meaningful and just education and future for all children. I have worked closely with, and learned much from the Caucus of Rank and File Educators, the Grassroots Education Movement, the Teacher Activist Groups national network, and all my friends in Teachers for Social Justice. The wisdom and spirit of Aisha El-Amin, Berenice Salas, Astrid Suarez, and Allie Epstein help me keep going. A special thanks to Rhoda Rae Gutierrez whose constant support, friendship, collaboration, and, above all, clarity, have shaped my thinking and kept our projects on track for so many years.

I continue to learn so much from many colleagues, but I especially want to acknowledge the work and thinking of Tom Pedroni, Lois Weiner, David Hursh, Patrick Camagnian, Janet Smith, Rachel Weber, Bill Watkins, Jean

Anyon, Gloria Ladson-Billings, Jeannie Oakes, Rico Gutstein, Enora Brown, Stephen Haymes, Ken Saltman, Susan Robertson, Kalervo Gulson, and Michael Apple. The "counter hegemonics," our graduate student group, provide an intellectual home at UIC. Many people offered important insights and critical feedback on various drafts and parts of this book. I especially want to thank Rachel Weber, Tom Pedroni, Ruth Lupton, and Sandi Gutstein, who is not only a brilliant critic but an inspiration. My special thanks to Rico Gutstein, my partner, for his invaluable close critical reading of multiple drafts of the book, his unflagging support, excellent dinners, intellectual and political clarity, comradship, and love and to the rest of my beautiful, justice-loving family—Sandi, Jesse, Cristina, Malaya, and Kapua.

SERIES EDITOR INTRODUCTION

Certain books are published at exactly the correct time. Pauline Lipman's new volume, *The New Political Economy of Urban Education: Neoliberalism, Race, and the Right to the City*, is a powerful critical analysis of the dominant models of school reform that are being instituted throughout the United States and elsewhere. The word *elsewhere* is not simply an add-on here. I am writing this Introduction in London. Corporate models, choice policies, reductive accountability regimes, attacks on the public sector, and similar policies are very visible here, many of them drawn from the discourses and policies being put into place in the United States (see Apple, 2006).

Lipman is already well-known for her critical work on what is happening in urban education. Her earlier book, *High Stakes Education* (2004), is highly regarded, and justifiably so. Like this earlier book, Chicago becomes the paradigm case of the global project of reconstructing the city. But both the reach and the implications of *The New Political Economy of Urban Education* extend well beyond the confines of her analysis. First, at this writing the former Superintendent of Schools of Chicago is now the Secretary of Education for the United States. He is bringing the initiatives he tested out in Chicago to the national level, even though they have been subjected to serious criticism in the place where they originated.

Second, and perhaps of even greater import, Chicago is a "zone of experimentation," an experiment that has differential benefits for all of those who live there and attend its schools. But as a zone of experimentation, it provides a lens through which we can see other world cities, other places where who really has a right to the city is being struggled over right now.

Lipman starts her account with one school. And then through a powerful analysis, she extends outwards, showing the complex relations between her beginning story and the dynamics of class and race and urban political economies in which all such stories are embedded. The fact that she examines the interactions among class and race and places these dynamics side by side in their contradictory and tense sets of movements and struggles is significant. It makes this book a major contribution not only to our crucial deliberations of how school reform now works and should work. But it also contributes in essential ways to the growing literature on how critical researchers and educators are to understand the nature of what in critical race theory is called *intersectionality*, how multiple relations and dynamics of power interact in any real situation (see, e.g., Apple, Au, & Gandin, 2009; Gillborn, 2008; Leonardo, 2009).

Lipman is clear about what the book aims to do—and about what is at stake if the current neoliberal agenda is not contested. As she puts it:

The underlying problem and motivation for this [book] is how those of us working for economic and social justice and a democratic alternative to the present social order can better understand the dialectics of the present situation in order to transform it. How do we make sense of the story I began with—the closing of Andersen School, writ large, and the urban dynamics in which it is embedded? And how can we contest these injustices with greater potency and clarity than we have mustered so far? Understanding the political economy of urban education at the beginning of the 21st century is an important piece of the work of social transformation.

In analyzing this situation and showing the power of these questions, Lipman draws upon a rich set of traditions such as critical geography, political economy, cultural studies, and critical policy analysis. Indeed, her synthesis of these lenses gives added punch to her critical appraisal and hope for the future.

Lipman situates all of this in the history of neoliberalism, not only as a theory, but as a set of real policies that have real effects on the lives and experiences of real people in real communities, and in real schools. Just as importantly, unlike many other critical commentators on neoliberalism, she documents the central role that *race* has played and continues to play in these theories, policies, and effects. This is a crucial intervention, since neoliberalism—like liberalism itself (Mills, 1997)—is often dependent on an unacknowledged "constitutive outside," the source of pollution, the irrational, the "other" (Apple, 2006). As a number of people have argued, it is impossible to fully understand the meaning and effects of urban policies in education and so much else without placing that social construction we call "race" as a key element at the center of one's analysis. Lipman fully recognizes this. But it is not simply a rhetorical trope in this book. The constitutive power of race and of racializing structures and effects are constantly brought to the forefront in her detailed assessment of what now count as "reforms" in urban communities and in the schools they are meant to serve—and in the larger project of neoliberal depredations as a whole.

In doing all of this, Pauline Lipman joins with a select group of other fine writers who consistently document that daily life is often a source of struggle for many people. As Mike Davis, for example, reminds us, we do damage to reality by considering words such as *food, housing, jobs,* and *education* as nouns. Instead, we need to think of them as *verbs*, as things that require constant labor to obtain and to defend them (Davis, 2006). Vigilance and hard work are necessary if we are to counter the kinds of policies that are growing so powerful in current school reforms. Such vigilance and hard work can be found in the community-based protests that Lipman describes in this book. Indeed, dominant policies over all these things are contested by real people in real communities in many places. As I show in a number of recent books, we have much to learn from these struggles and from the people who engage in them (Apple, 2003, 2006, 2010). But a key point is in the words *constant labor* and *defend*: Schools as community resources and as sites of possible social transformation for everyone, and especially for those who are the least advantaged members of communities, need that constant labor to defend the gains that have been made and to push forward toward thicker versions of democracy than those proposed in the systems so nicely analyzed in Lipman's work.

We are living in a time when schools are seen as sites of profit (Ball, 2007; Burch, 2009), when the sense of the common good is withering, when policies with clear racializing effects are being instituted using the rhetoric of democracy, when urban (and rural) spaces are being reconstructed to benefit the most advantaged. When all of this is happening right now, we need to stand back and rethink what counts as truly substantive and democratic school reform. Lipman does this; but she also goes further. What makes Lipman's book such a powerful analysis and her vision so rich with real possibilities is her nearly unparalleled ability to connect the ongoing struggles in education with the necessary transformations and social movements that are being built right now both nationally and internationally.

Many people may talk about the importance of connecting what must be done in education with the larger critically democratic movements that are going on in the economy, in politics, and in culture. Lipman shows how it can be done. In the process, she provides us with ways of thinking locally and globally, of building connections across our differences, and of building alliances that can change our lives. Finally, her book gives us reasons for hope—not the rhetorical hope of political rhetoric, but reasons for optimism if we but act (see Williams, 1989). *The New Political Economy of Urban Education* is an essential book for making sense of what is happening and for pressing all of us to challenge the dominant "solutions" that are being instituted throughout the nation and the world.

Michael W. Apple
John Bascom Professor of Curriculum and Instruction and Educational Policy Studies
University of Wisconsin—Madison

References

Apple, M. W. (2006). *Educating the "right" way: Markets, standards, God, and education* (2nd ed.). New York: Routledge.

Apple, M. W. (Ed.). (2010). *Global crises, social justice, and education.* New York: Routledge.

Apple, M. W., Aasen, P., Cho, M. K., Gandin, L. A., Oliver, A., Sung, Y. K., Wong, T. H., et al. (2003). *The state and the politics of knowledge.* New York: Routledge.

Apple, M. W., Au, W., & Gandin, L. A. (Eds.). (2009). *The Routledge international handbook of critical education.* New York: Routledge.

Ball, S. (2007). *Education plc: Understanding private sector participation in public sector education.* New York: Routledge.

Burch, P. (2009). *Hidden markets: The new education privatization.* New York: Routledge.

Davis, M. (2006). *Planet of slums.* New York: Verso.

Gillborn, D. (2008). *Racism and education: Coincidence or conspiracy.* New York: Routledge.

Leonardo, Z. (2009). *Race, whiteness, and education.* New York: Routledge.

Lipman, P. (2004). *High stakes education.* New York: Routledge.

Mills, C. (1997). *The racial contract.* Ithaca: Cornell University Press.

Williams, R. (1989). *Resources of hope.* New York: Verso.

1

INTRODUCTION

The city has emerged in recent years as an indispensable concept for many of the struggles for social justice we are all engaged in—it's a place where theory meets practice, where the neighborhood organizes against global capitalism, where unequal divisions based on race and class can be mapped out block by block and contested, where the micropolitics of gender and sexual orientation are subject to metropolitan rearticulation, where every corner is a potential site of resistance and every vacant lot a commons to be reclaimed, and, most importantly, a place where all our diverse struggles and strategies have a chance of coming together into something greater.

(Call for Participation, The City from Below, 2009)

It is a warm spring evening in Chicago. We arrive at Andersen Elementary School balancing our bags of fruit and juice, *pan dulce*, paper cups, and napkins. These are provisions for the parents and kids camping out on the sidewalk. The official sign in the schoolyard says, "Andersen Elementary School—We're still here." But large White canvas banners draped above both entrances read "LaSalle Language Academy." They hang incongruously close to the inscription "Hans Christian Andersen Elementary School" engraved in the stone doorway when the school was built. At the other end of the block, a new three-story condominium building advertises "Penthouse for Sale." The gentrified Wicker Park neighborhood (now magically renamed "East Village") is hopping. It's the annual street festival and the trendy restaurants and bars are overflowing onto the street. Sidewalk cafes are jam-packed. The scene is thumping with the beat from the festival tent in the next block and the voices of 20-something high fashion revelers modeling high boots and short skirts.

On the sidewalk in front of Andersen, teacher-supporters and Latino/a families (mostly women) in red Andersen T-shirts have pitched four tents. A dozen posters drawn by the children are tied to the school fence. "Please help us. Save our school." "We love our school. Don't close our school." One girl, who is 8, persistently works the line of passersby to sign her petition. She has lots of experience. Her family is one of those who have been fighting for the school for over a year. Her teenage sister and a friend stand at the edge of the curb jiggling bigger signs, "Honk if you support Andersen parents." Many do. The families plan to camp out all night to, once again, bring attention to their pleas to keep open a successful neighborhood school which the mayor's appointed school board voted to phase out in 2008. Andersen was one of 18 Chicago schools closed or phased out that year. Most were turned over to charter school companies or to a corporate "turnaround" specialist. Anderson was converted to a highly selective magnet school that few Andersen students can or will attend.

★★★★★

In June 2009, I attended a national conference of grassroots education activists, youth, and teachers. We traded similar stories from Dallas, New York, New Orleans, Philadelphia, Detroit, and Chicago: Schools closed in Black and Latino/a neighborhoods, students transferred all over the city, charter school companies taking over, attacks on teacher unions, no real public participation, gentrification of African American and Latino/a working class neighborhoods and families pushed farther out of the city. Conversations coalesced around similar questions: Why is this happening? How is the privatization of urban schools related to the gentrification and economic polarization of our cities? How can we fight for truly quality education for low-income children of color in this new environment and what would that education look like? It is an uphill battle. Over the past 6 years, these questions have compelled me to try to better understand the political and economic forces influencing urban education at the beginning of the 21st century, and to write this book.

I live and work in Chicago, a vivid example of these transformations in education and in cities. The rise of Arne Duncan, CEO of Chicago Public Schools (CPS), to U.S. Secretary of Education in the Obama administration signifies the national expansion of an urban education program pioneered here. That program focuses on expanding education markets and employing market principles in urban school systems. It features mayoral control of school districts, closing "failing" public schools or handing them over to corporate-style "turnaround" organizations, expanding school "choice" and charter schools, instituting teacher incentive pay based on student test scores and diminishing the power of teacher unions, and enforcing top-down accountability and standards. Several cities have already put much of this agenda in motion, and the Obama administration calls Chicago the national model. Policy changes that enable market-based and mayoral-control strategies give states points in their competition for a portion of the $4.35 billion in federal stimulus dollars targeted for education (Duncan, 2009a; U.S. Department of Education, 2009b).

This is a rendition of the global project to gear education to "economic competitiveness" and to impose market discipline on all aspects of schooling (Abdi, Puplampu, & Sefa Dei, 2006; Apple, Kenway, & Singh, 2005; Compton & Weiner, 2008; Dale, 2000; Lauder, Brown, Dillabough, & Halsey, 2006; Obama, 2009; Rizvi & Lingard, 2009). Much has been written about this project, but in this book I am interested in its relationship to urban restructuring. Neither education nor urban scholars have much explored the new political economy of urban education and its relationship to the economic, political, and spatial changes that have redefined cities and their contestations (exceptions are Anyon, 2005; Butler with Robson, 2003, Cucchiara, 2008; Lipman, 2004, 2008a, 2008b, 2011; Lipman & Haines, 2007; Lupton & Turnstall, 2008; Pedroni, 2011; Smith & Stovall, 2008). In this book I hope to further this discussion.

The New Urban Sociology (Feagin, 1998) and the influential scholarship of critical geography (e.g., David Harvey, Neil Brenner, Nik Theodore, Neil Smith, and others) and critical theorists of race (Lipsitz, 2006b, 2007) bring to urban studies a focus on power and conflict, particularly the role of capital and race in the spatial structuring of the city and urban life. I have built on this work in this book to argue that education is both shaped by and deeply implicated in globalized political, economic, and ideological processes that have been redefining cities over the past 25 years. These processes coalesce in the neoliberal restructuring of the city, or neoliberal urbanism. The neoliberal city is an entrepreneurial city driven by market ideologies and the regulatory power of global finance. In *The New Political Economy of Urban Education*, I look to Chicago as a laboratory for the articulation of education policy and the contested neoliberal political and economic dynamics that shape U.S. cities and, to varying degrees, cities globally.

The underlying problem and motivation for this study is how those of us working for economic and social justice and a democratic alternative to the present social order can better understand the dialectics of the present situation. How do we make sense of the story I began with—the closing of Andersen School, writ large, and the urban dynamics in which it is embedded? And how can we contest these injustices with greater potency and clarity than we have mustered so far? Understanding the political economy of urban education is an important piece of the work of social transformation.

The City as Vantage Point

In *Social Justice and the City*, David Harvey (1973) argued that the city is "a vantage point from which to capture some salient features operating in society as a whole—it becomes as it were a mirror in which other aspects of society can be reflected." In particular, [Western] metropolitan cities are, "The locus of the accumulated contradictions of a society" (p. 16). They concentrate major cultural, financial, social, and political institutions in close proximity with concentrations of low-income, marginalized, and excluded people (p. 203).

This observation is particularly prescient today. For the first time in human history, more people live in urban than rural areas (Davis, 2006). Cities across the globe typify the contrasts of wealth and poverty, marginality and centrality, that Harvey pointed to over 35 years ago. These contradictions are magnified in gated communities and favelas, glittering downtown developments and decaying working class neighbourhoods, and a globally mobile elite is juxtaposed with contained low-income communities. Although urban contradictions play out differently in different contexts, they are produced by a global political, economic, and ideological project geared to capital accumulation through dispossession and exploitation. But the hegemonic alliances implicated in this project are also contradictory and have to be continually reconstructed (Apple, 2006) and, as I will show, the policies they develop create new contradictions. They mobilize support for the "good sense" (Gramsci, 1971) in markets and privatization but also open space for new progressive social alliances. Cities are highly contested. In the United States and Western Europe they are home to new social movements of squatters, informal workers, women, lesbians and gays, artists, undocumented migrants, and others, as well as to ethnocentrism and defense of race and class privilege. Although elites attempt to impose homogenized corporate culture, cities are vibrant cultural mixes and sites of creative experiments in alternative economies and social relations (Leitner, Peck, & Sheppard, 2007).

In *High Stakes Education* (Lipman, 2004), I explored the relationship of centralized education accountability to the global economic forces restructuring urban labor markets and urban space. My focus was the connection between education policy and the production of inequalities that typify the globally constituted city (N. Smith, 2002). I focused on Chicago, a center of global finance and business services and international tourism—one type of "global city" (N. Smith, 2002). Cities of this type require concentrations of high-paid professionals and managers and legions of low-paid service workers. I argued high stakes accountability and a system of stratified educational opportunities supported gentrification, dispossession of working class communities of color, and the production of a stratified labor force. That argument still holds.

But in the first decade of the 21st century, urban education shifted more sharply toward the market. Centralized accountability helped pave the way for a decisive move to privatization, "choice," charter schools, performance pay for teachers, and mayoral takeovers. At the same time, urban policy has been driven by the ideology of entrepreneurism and global competitiveness (N. Smith, 2002; Wilson, 2007). As I discuss in more detail in chapter 2, corporate influence and public–private partnerships, gentrification as a pivotal economic sector, privatization, and marketing of all aspects of the city are the order of the day and are generalized to a wide range of cities nationally and globally (e.g., Marcuse & Van Kempen, 2000; Swyngedouw, Moulaert, & Rodriguez 2004). The ways in which these practices take hold are fragmentary, evolving, contested, and highly contingent (Brenner & Theodore, 2002; Leitner, Peck, & Sheppard, 2007; Lingard, 2000). They are rooted in specific experiences of colonialism, imperialism, postcolonialism, social democracy, state welfarism, and social struggle. Yet their political and economic logics are globally integrated.

The "Right to the City"

Education, like housing, jobs, and health care, is a terrain of struggle over what philosopher Henri Lefebvre (1968/1996) called "the right to the city." For Lefebvre, writing in the midst of the 1968 revolutionary ferment in France, there wass something profoundly democratic and transformative about the right to the city. David Harvey (2003a) continues to emphasize that the right to the city includes, but is more than the right to housing, jobs, and public space and more than the right to participate in electoral democracy. It is a right to transform the city, to make it the city we wish to live in, and in the process transform our selves and how we live together:

> a right to change [the city] after our heart's desire…the right to remake ourselves by creating a qualitatively different kind of urban sociality is one of the most precious of all human rights…. We individually and collectively make the city through our daily actions and our political, intellectual and economic engagements. But, in return, the city makes us.
>
> (Harvey, 2003a, p. 939)

This dialectic of remaking the city and in the process remaking ourselves is the core of the struggle for the right to the city. It is both a "cry and a demand, a cry out of necessity and a demand for something more" (Marcuse, 2009, p. 190). But, as Marcuse points out, it is crucial to be clear that it is not a demand for everyone's right to the city—not the bankers and real estate speculators, the corporate media, nor their state collaborators—they already run the city in their own image. It is with those who are deprived, excluded, alienated, exploited and discontented that movements for the right to the city are concerned. In the words of the Right to the City movement,

> This right cannot be limited to people who own property in the cities or to legally recognized citizens; instead, it belongs to all urban residents: working class people, poor people, homeless people, youth, women, queer people, people of color, immigrants, all of us. The people of the city have the right to remain in their cities and to benefit from what the city has to

offer. Perhaps even more importantly, they have the right to democratically determine the future development of the city.

(Goldberg & Mananzala, 2008)

The right to the city is both concrete and metaphorical. It is about the struggle
to remake actual cities, but it is also a metaphor for social transformation, in
part because for Lefebvre the city is the concentrated expression of the social
contradictions of our time and of the human potential to remake the world,
and ourselves, differently. In this sense, it is part of an imperative to transform
oppressive and exploitative economic, political, and cultural arrangements and
to build a new social order based on the full development of human beings
in relationships of mutuality, respect, and collective well-being. This idea
animates my analysis and vision of urban education, and I return to it in the
conclusion. But a starting point is an understanding of the present order.

Neoliberalism

Neoliberalism has been the defining social paradigm of the past 30 years.
Neoliberalism is a particular, historically-generated state strategy to manage
the structural crisis of capitalism and provide new opportunities for capital
accumulation (Jones & Ward, 2002). Put simply, neoliberalism is an ensemble
of economic and social policies, forms of governance, and discourses and
ideologies that promote individual self-interest, unrestricted flows of capital,
deep reductions in the cost of labor, and sharp retrenchment of the public
sphere. Neoliberals champion privatization of social goods and withdrawal of
government from provision for social welfare on the premise that competitive
markets are more effective and efficient. Neoliberalism is not just "out there"
as a set of policies and explicit ideologies. It has developed as a new social
imaginary, a common sense about how we think about society and our place
in it. Charles Taylor (2003) describes a social imaginary as the way in which
ordinary people "imagine" their world—the common understandings, myths,
and stories that make possible generalized practices and the widely shared
legitimacy of a particular social order. In this sense, the power of neoliberalism
 lies in its saturation of social practices and consciousness, making it difficult to
think otherwise.

The Rise of Neoliberalism

The boom created by post-World War II rebuilding and government spending
produced an extended period of economic growth and relative stability in
the Western capitalist world and Japan. Governments adopted a variety of
social democratic (Western Europe), liberal democratic (United States), and
bureaucratic state forms (Japan) that fostered economic growth and social

welfare and forestalled more radical social transformations. In the United States, the federal government promoted "full" employment,[1] and social welfare policies initiated during the New Deal (e.g., social security, unemployment insurance) provided a safety net for the working class, though people of color did not benefit to the same degree as Whites (Barlow, 2003; Lipsitz, 1998). Government spending and capital's compromise with privileged sectors of organized labor—higher wages and benefits in exchange for relative labor peace and support for imperialism abroad (Ranney, 2004)[2]—fueled consumer spending. This coupled with a huge government-financed military–industrial complex stimulated economic growth. The state also intervened to manipulate the money supply in order to smooth out the ups and downs of business cycles. In Western Europe, the state internalized class conflicts. Trade unions and their political parties gained considerable influence in government and achieved a welfare state that provided universal public health care, a shortened work week, and substantial vacation and unemployment benefits.

This ensemble of state-interventionist policies is variously called Keynesianism, military Keynesianism, or the Keynesian Welfare Settlement (Harvey, 2005; Ranney & Wright, 2004). Clark and Newman (1997) argue that the welfare state hinged on two other settlements as well: an organizational settlement (bureaucratic administration of state services and valorization of professional knowledge) and a patriarchal and racialized social settlement (males as primary wage earners, women as unpaid household labor, and normalization of Eurocentric White lifestyles). The latter excluded many working women of color from these gendered social arrangements.

Some sectors of society benefited, but others did not. Large corporations experienced a period of relatively stable growth, and access to cheap raw materials from the Global South while Latin American and Asian authoritarian regimes, clients of Western imperialism, were shielded by the military power and influence of the United States and other Western capitalist states. Male and White unionized workers and the middle class gained. The masses of workers and peasants in countries dominated by imperialism did not (Leitner, Sheppard, Sziarto, & Maringanti, 2007), nor did the masses of working class women, poor people, people of color, and many nonunion workers in the United States gain to the same degree.[3] Although the welfare state settlement provided social benefits it also was bureaucratic and often unresponsive, especially to poor people, people of color, and women (Clarke & Newman, 1997). In short, the "golden age" of Keynesianism was rife with political and social contradictions and fissures (Leitner, Sheppard et al., 2007).

Fissures in the welfare state and a deep crisis of capital accumulation came to a head in the late 1960s and early 1970s. Poverty, racism, oppression of women, imperialism, and social alienation seething beneath the surface of economic growth and political stability erupted in the social movements of the 1960s and 1970s. In the United States and Britain, the welfare state was no match for energized movements of poor people, people of color, and women. The social order was rocked to its foundations as urban rebellions raged in cities across the United States, a radicalized movement against the Vietnam war began to challenge the system of imperialism, the Civil Rights Movement broadened to raise economic demands, and organizations of people of color embraced revolution. In 1967, Dr. Martin Luther King called for the transformation of a system based on the "triple evils" of racism, materialism, and war (Washington, 1986). He was assassinated a year later while supporting a Black workers' struggle in Memphis. The potential for these movements to merge was a strategic threat to the existing U.S. social order. National liberation movements in Latin America, Africa, and Asia and alliances of raw-materials-producing countries and anti-imperialist and prosocialist movements in the formerly colonized world threatened to end the pipeline of cheap raw materials and labor from the economically developing world (Ranney & Wright, 2004). A socialist government was elected in Chile. In France workers occupied factories and a revolutionary worker–student movement came close to gaining political power in 1968.[4] In Britain a wave of strikes threatened the capital–labor compromise. The United States was losing an imperialist war in Southeast Asia.

At the same time, in the United States and some parts of Western Europe, capitalism faced a stagnating productive sector coupled with the inability of Keynesianism to control inflation caused by prolonged government spending. The Keynesian strategy to manage crisis and sustain capital accumulation was played out (Foster & Magdoff, 2009; Gill, 2003; Harvey, 2005; Ranney & Wright, 2004). Neoliberal think tanks at the margins of public policy stepped forward to offer their prescriptions: Societies function best when individuals are free to pursue their interests in the market without government intervention. The benefits of policies to promote corporate growth (corporate tax cuts and lowered wages) will "trickle down" to benefit everyone. "Freedom," "choice," and "individual rights" are best guaranteed by the market. Thus, the role of government is to remove restrictions on trade and corporate investment, reduce corporate taxes and eliminate regulation of industry, limit the power of unions, turn public services and infrastructure over to the market, and withdraw from provision of social welfare. Education should be restructured to serve "human capital" development (Hursh, 2008).

Tested in the early 1970s in Chile under the Pinochet dictatorship, over the next three decades neoliberalism coalesced as a hegemonic global strategy, beginning in Britain and the United States in the late 1970s and 1980s (Harvey, 2005). Neoliberals (and neoconservatives in the United States) took advantage of the structural crisis to promote the rollback of the social welfare state and to give free reign to the "market." In an evolving process, across a variety of local settings, neoliberalism emerged as a national and global project (Gill, 2003; Harvey, 2005), albeit variegated, locally contingent, and characterized by contradictions, resistance, and alternative projects and discourses (Leitner,

Sheppard, et al., 2007). It gained traction, in part, because it was constructed as the only alternative to the crisis, but also because of the weaknesses of the welfare state (Clarke & Newman, 1997). Failures and exclusions of the welfare state gave rise to popular progressive movements but were also fertile ground for the construction of neoliberal hegemony, as I will argue in relation to charter schools and "choice."

Despite neoliberal theory of limited government, "actually existing neoliberalism" involved the active intervention of the state to dismantle Keynesian policies and institutions and create new institutional arrangements, political coalitions, and policy infrastructure conducive to privatization and capital accumulation (Brenner & Theodore, 2002; Peck & Tickell, 2002). In the 1970s and early 1980s, the UK and U.S. governments audaciously attacked key sectors of the labor movement, dismantled aspects of the welfare state, and deregulated the economy so capital could flow freely to new arenas for profitable investment (Peck & Tickell, 2007; Ranney, 2004).[5] In the United States, a hegemonic alliance of neoliberals, neoconservatives, and other sectors of the population (Apple, 2006) congealed to promote an agenda that allowed the rich to accumulate enormous wealth at the expense of the majority. Over time, despite widespread and persistent opposition, particularly in Western Europe where battles continue some governments succeeded in dismantling aspects of the Keynesian state, defusing political crises, and diverting and diffusing the progressive social movements of previous decades.[6]

Foster and Magdoff (2009) note, "The ideal situation for capitalists is to be able to invest and sell where and when they want, to move money and products in and out of countries and to repatriate profits at will" (p. 41). Globally, an unfolding strategy of privatization and deregulation of trade and flows of capital opened up new arenas for capitalist investment. In the 1980s, the World Bank and International Monetary Fund imposed "structural adjustment" on economically developing countries, mandating privatization of state-owned industries, wage controls, and user fees for public services in exchange for loans (Harvey, 2003b). (Similar "shock therapy" was administered to post-Soviet Eastern European economies.) And free trade agreements in the 1990s, such as the North American Free Trade Agreement (NAFTA), undermined local agriculture and manufacturing, wrecking sustainability of developing economies, increasing their indebtedness to the world's biggest banks, and setting off a "race to the bottom" that drove down wages globally (Bello, 2002). In a new round of "accumulation by dispossession" (Harvey, 2003b), virtually all of human society and the natural environment was fair game for private investment and profit. With deregulation of national economies there was also a rescaling of economic activity and governance to the local, regional, and global scales with significant implications for cities, as we shall see in chapter 2. As states, led by the USA, deregulated financial transactions, global capital employed new financial instruments and forms of financial speculation and debt as a principle strategy to maximize profit. This enriched a small group of transnational investors (Ranney & Wright, 2004), and weighed down consumers with household and personal debt. In short, counter to neoliberal theory, a constellation of neoliberal economic policies and practices produced a massive transfer of wealth upward to a tiny group of global superrich, benefited a top sector of professionals and managers, and widened economic inequality within and between countries on a world scale (Jomo & Baudot, 2007; Polet, 2001; Wolff, 2002). In 2005, the United Nations Human Development Group reported that the annual income of the world's richest 500 people is greater than that of the poorest 416 million (p. 37).

However, neoliberalization as a hegemonic process is contingent, contested, and partial (Brenner & Theodore, 2002). For example, parts of the welfare state have been more difficult to dismantle in France than in some other European countries for political and historical reasons. The state itself is a contested arena. State interventions are cobbled together, designed and redesigned to manage crises and fix their own failures. Hegemony is continually contested and has to be reconstructed and renewed (Williams, 1978). Moreover the state must manage competing demands for capital accumulation, legitimation, and social control (Jones & Ward, 2002), as I illustrate in subsequent chapters with reference to education. The neoliberal project, like the welfare state that preceded it, is rife with contradictions and fissures that give rise to global social movements and alliances of all types and progressive political alternatives and projects (Santos interviewed by Dale & Robertson, 2004), as well as right wing nationalist movements. The current failure of markets and deregulation has brought to the fore weaknesses of the neoliberal strategy, creating an opening for alternative progressive agendas and alliances. I return to this in the conclusion of the book.

An Ideological Project to "Change the Soul"

Neoliberalism is an ideological project to reconstruct values, social relations, and social identities—to produce a new social imaginary. In this book I argue that education policies are both embedded in a neoliberal social imaginary and are a means to reshape social relations and social identities. In the mid-1970s, neoliberal theorist Friedrich von Hayek declared that the battle for ideas was central, but it would take at least a generation for neoliberal ideology to defeat Marxism, socialism, and the welfare state (cited in Harvey, 2005).

Thus began an assault on collectivity, social responsibility, equality, and solidarity that had some salience in the Keynesian period. Neoliberals redefined democracy as choice in the marketplace and freedom as personal freedom to consume (Harvey, 2005). Private property is sacrosanct. Competitive individualism is a virtue and personal accountability replaces government responsibility

for collective social welfare, summed up in British Prime Minister Margaret
Thatcher's famous pronouncement:

> there is no such thing as society. There are individual men and women, and
> there are families. And no government can do anything except through
> people, and people must look to themselves first. It's our duty to look after
> ourselves and then, also to look after our neighbour. People have got the
> entitlements too much in mind, without the obligations.
>
> (Thatcher, 1987)

The neoliberal project is not only to change how we think, but who we
are. As Thatcher put it, "Economics are the method, but the object is to
change the soul" (cited in Harvey, 2005, p. 23). Transforming subjectivities is
dialectically related to restructuring social policies, and education is a critical
piece. Policies are, in part, discourses—values, practices, ways of talking and
acting—that shape consciousness and produce social identities. Discourses
"systematically form the objects of which they speak" (Ball, 1994, p. 21).
One of the clearest articulations of this is in Stephen Ball's writings on the
"renorming and revaluing" of schooling. Ball (2001a) has noted that market-
driven policies constitute a "new moral environment," a form of "commercial
civilization," and a "culture of self-interest" (p. xxxiv). These practices entail
new social relations and produce a new meaning of being a teacher or student
or administrator or parent that is grounded in a coercive and market-oriented
culture (Woods & Jeffrey, 2002).

The Keynesian welfare state framed people as citizens with certain civil
rights and the state as responsible for a minimal level of social well-being.
Although the welfare state was deeply exclusionary, there were grounds to
collectively fight to extend civil rights. Claims could legitimately be made on
the state. In the neoliberal social imaginary, rather than "citizens" with rights,
we are consumers of services. People are "empowered" by taking advantage
of opportunities in the market, such as school choice and private pension
investments. One improves one's life situation by becoming an "entrepreneur
of oneself," (cultivating the image, persona, resumé that enhances one's
competitive position in the marketplace of "human capital).

Although deeply ideological, neoliberalism gains legitimacy by positing
postideological politics: "There Is No Alternative" to the neoliberal order;
we have reached the "end of history," the end of ideological conflict,
with the universal evolution of societies in the direction of capitalism
and Western liberal democracy as its political form (Fukuyama, 1992).
Neoliberals naturalize market forms, processes, and ways of thinking as the
only way to organize society (Leitner, Peck, & Sheppard, 2007). Neoliberal
policy discourses are thus "politically neutral," based on technical criteria
of "efficiency" and "effectiveness" thereby excluding discussion of values,

philosophy, and social interests. Pragmatism or doing "what works," is the order of the day, allowing those in power to dismiss criticism as politically motivated, ideologically driven, and change resistant. Discourses of change are mobilized to naturalize certain kinds of change and to paint the opposition as defenders of the status quo. President Obama evoked this trope when he contended criticism of his neoliberal Race to the Top federal education program "reflects a general resistance to change. We get comfortable with the status quo" (Obama, 2010).

The Centrality of Race

Cultural politics of class, race, ethnicity, and gender have played out in various ways to further and contest the neoliberal project (Body-Gendrot, 1993; Duggan, 2003; Goldberg, 1993; Gulson, 2008; Keith, 1993; Saito, 2009; E. Wilson, 2001). In the United States, a 400-year legacy of White supremacy has been pivotal to the country's development, the triumph of capitalism, and more recently, to advance the neoliberal agenda (Barlow, 2003; D. Wilson, 2006). The cultural politics of race are central to constructing consent for privatizing public goods, including schools. As Haymes (1995) argues, the "… concepts 'public' and 'private' are racialized metaphors. Private is equated with being 'good' and 'white' and that which is public with being 'bad' and 'Black'" (p. 20). Racism is the ideological soil for appeals to individual responsibility and ending "dependency" on the state. Constructing people of color as the undeserving poor (lazy, pathological, and welfare dependent) provides policy makers with a rationale to restructure or eliminate government-funded social programs and to diminish state responsibility for social welfare (M. Katz, 1989). In particular, the "inner city" and the public institutions with which it is identified are pathologized in a racially coded morality discourse that legitimates their dismantling. This racialized logic justifies privatization of public housing, schools, and health clinics and gentrification through dispossession of urban Black communities (D. Wilson, 2006).

At the same time, neoliberals frame the post-Civil rights era as "colorblind," relieving the state and the general public of responsibility for ameliorating racial inequality and oppression. This "postracial society" frame conveniently denies structural and ideological bases of persistent racial disparities in income, wealth, employment, access to higher education, health, life span, academic achievement, and other aspects of social life and well-being. Individual effort and entrepreneurship and personal accountability are the path to success. This paves the way for cultural explanations of poverty and race-neutral policies and furthers market solutions and disinvestment in the public sphere. Deracialization is the "silent partner of the market" (Brown, 2007). This is apparent in education with the rollback of affirmative action, the revival of "culture of poverty" explanations for educational failure (Payne, 1998/2005), and individual "choice" and vouchers as the way to obtain equitable education.

I argue throughout this book that disinvestment in African American and Latino/a working class communities and schools created the basis for gentrification and displacement of community residents and dispossession of their schools. Conditions for neoliberal urban restructuring were set by post-World War II racial segregation and policies that led to White flight, disinvestment in "inner cities," and urban decline. Segregation and structural racism allowed Whites to "shift the burden of inequality and poverty to people of color" and "poisoned" U.S. politics by undermining interracial coalitions (Goldsmith, 2002). In turn, neoliberal restructuring has intensified structural inequality based on race. While some people of color gained greater access to education and employment, and a few amassed wealth in the boom years of the 1990s, the vast majority bore the brunt of deindustrialization, cuts in social welfare, attacks on unions, and intensified policing. Racial inequality in income is greater today than 40 years ago. For example, between 1980 and 2004, the hourly wage gap in Illinois between White workers and Latino/a workers widened by 24%, and the gap between Whites and Blacks widened by 162% (Heartland Alliance, 2006). In the restructured economy of Illinois, people of color are concentrated in low-wage service jobs, including day labor where immigrants are more than five times as likely as nonimmigrants to be employed (ARC, 2007). Moreover, people of color have been hardest hit by the current economic crisis.

From Government to Governance

The "triumph of market ideology" is coupled with an erosion of the idea that informed citizens should make decisions based on the general welfare. The shift from *government* by elected state bodies and a degree of democratic accountability to *governance* by experts and managers and decision making by judicial authority and executive order is central to neoliberal policy making. "Increasingly, public debate and dialogue over key policy issues have been replaced by an instrumental-strategic form of governance emphasizing economic efficiency, individual responsibility, low taxes, and user fees—the 'public citizen' replaced by the 'strategic consumer'" (Miller, 2007, p. 225). Public–private partnerships, appointed managers, and publicly unaccountable bodies comprised of appointed state and corporate leaders make decisions about urban development, transportation, schools, and other public infrastructure using business rationales. In these arrangements, the state acts as an agent of capital (Hackworth, 2007). At the grassroots level, neoliberal versions of "participation" take the form of appointed advisory boards with no decision-making power and tightly regulated public hearings where the public may air grievances and opinions but decisions are made elsewhere and are based on "efficiency" (see examples in Bennett, Smith, & Wright, 2007; Lipman & Haines, 2007).

Coercion is the other face of neoliberal governance—from the coercive pressures of transnational institutions, such as the International Monetary Fund and World Trade Organization, to violent suppression of labor organizing in Central America and Colombia and teacher unions in Mexico, to restrictions on civil liberties in the United States, Britain, and other "democracies." To manage the social contradictions produced by neoliberalism, the state intensifies surveillance, punishment, and incarceration to maintain order in society (Wacquant, 2001). These contradictions also create opportunities to deflect anger onto immigrants, people of color, and "dangerous others," as with the post-9/11 "War on Terror."

Policing and incarceration is a key strategy to politically contain and manage the surplus labor of communities of color in the United States (Gilmore, 2007a; Parenti, 1999). Over the past 30 years, the neoliberal state expanded police powers and enacted new penal laws that disproportionately targeted African Americans, Latino/as, and immigrants, nearly tripling the U.S. prison population (Pew, 2008).[7] Aggressive urban policing to make the city "safe" for the middle class, made famous by New York Mayor Giuliani in the 1990s, has become a central feature of the neoliberal city (N. Smith, 1996) and has been exported globally (Fyfe, 2004). This is mirrored in schools by zero tolerance discipline that disproportionately punishes and excludes low-income students of color, contributing to the "school to prison pipeline" (Robbins, 2008). Certainly, strategies of persuasion and consent persist through, for example, a curriculum of official knowledge, the power of global corporate media, and social processes that produce self-regulating persons. But the point is to recognize in education and other social spheres the implications of a politics of coercion that may supplant as well as operate alongside the politics of consent.

Neoliberalism and Education

Much has been written about neoliberalism and education (e.g., Apple, 2006; Ball, 1994, 2004; Compton & Weiner, 2008; Dale, 1989–1990; Gewirtz, 2002; Hursh, 2008; Molnar, 1996; Rizvi & Lingard, 2009; Saltman, 2007). My intention is to build on this work to examine the intertwining of neoliberal education policy and the restructuring of the city. As a brief summary here, the neoliberal agenda is to bring education, along with other public sectors, in line with the goals of capital accumulation and managerial governance and administration. U.S. education policy has always juggled tensions between labor market preparation and democratic citizenship, but the neoliberal turn marks a sharp shift to "human capital development" as the primary goal. In this framework, education is a private good, an investment one makes in one's child or oneself to "add value" to better compete in the labor market, not a social good for development of individuals and society as a whole.

This ideology and the economic logics in which it is rooted have produced a global convergence of policies rooted in neoliberal values, albeit mediated by specific national histories—including colonial histories, policy arrangements, relative strength of social forces, and local traditions and values (Ball, 2001; Dale, 2000; Rizvi & Lingard, 2009; Robertson, Bonal, & Dale, 2002). But the overarching theme is that schooling is to be dominated by the knowledge and skills privileged in the (stratified) economy, and teachers and schools are to be held accountable to standards and performance targets (Rizvi & Lingard, 2009). On the assumption that the private sector is more efficient and productive than the public sector, neoliberal policy promotes education markets and privatization. Privately operated but publicly funded charter schools (USA) or academies (UK) and their global counterparts, private school vouchers, and privatized education services have opened up a whole new arena for capital accumulation (Burch, 2009; Saltman, 2007). School administration is geared to management techniques designed to meet production targets (e.g., test scores). Teaching and learning are driven by performance indicators such as benchmark scores, narrowing the curriculum and producing a new regulatory culture of "performativity and fabrication" (Ball, 2004). Teacher unions are also under attack. The result is a "global assault on teaching, teachers, and their unions" (Compton & Weiner, 2008) and on public education.

Methodology

In a germinal book on urban education, Gerald Grace (1984) argued against the prevailing instrumental "policy science" approach to the study of urban education problems in the USA and Britain. Drawing on sociologist C. Wright Mill's critique of "abstracted empiricism," Grace rejected policy science's "technical and immediately realizable" within-the-system solutions to urban education problems abstracted from the urban context (p. 32). He proposed a "critical policy scholarship" that situates urban education in the social, economic, political, and cultural contexts shaping the city. Critical policy scholarship illuminates the material and cultural struggles in which schooling is located and is generative of social action toward social justice (p. 41). An underlying assumption is that policy is an expression of values arising out of specific interests and relations of power. Grace notes that framework requires a multidisciplinary approach that draws on urban studies as well as urban sociology. In a somewhat similar vein, Rury and Mirel (1997) argue that "[E]ducational researchers [in the U.S.] too often accept the urban environment as a given natural setting, rather than one that has itself been determined by larger economic and political processes" (p. 85). What is needed, they argue, is a political economy of urban education that examines the contested dynamics of power and wealth that shape the urban context, their historical dimensions, and how they are articulated spatially. Rury and Mirel propose that we place questions of power, particularly the role of capital and race in structuring urban space, at the center of the research agenda.

To examine intersections of education and urban development, I respond to Rury and Mirel's call and build on Grace's critical framework and extend his multidisciplinary method to bring in scholarship in critical urban studies and spatial theory. Spatial restructuring of urban education and its relationship to neoliberal urban development is illuminated by the work of critical geographers who treat space as a constitutive aspect of capital accumulation (Harvey 2005; N. Smith 1996). Investment and disinvestment in schools, class and race-based funding inequities, and policies that engineer student social mix are all implicated in this process. Cultural geographers also attend to ways power is reproduced (and contested) and daily life is regulated through socially produced meanings about specific places (Keith & Pile, 1993; Soja, 1999); for example, the racialized social construction of "bad neighborhoods." This cultural lens is useful in examining how contested representations of urban schools are implicated in claims on the city. Examining the racialization of space is crucial to my analysis, particularly the work of scholars who foreground racial oppression and its integral relationship to urban restructuring (e.g., Haymes, 1995; Lipsitz, 2006b, 2007; Wilson, 2006).

I explore the interplay of structural and ideological forces in contested urban development and education policy through several interrelated strands of analysis: (a) The relationship of education policy to neoliberal urban development, gentrification, and displacement of working class and low income communities and the lived experience of these policies. (b) The cultural politics of race, particularly the pathologization of Black urban poverty as ideological ground to warrant dismantling homes and schools and advocating mixed-income solutions to poverty and failing urban schools. (c) Processes of constructing consent for neoliberal education policies through the actions of "grassroots" actors, not just elites, but also marginalized parents and teachers acting in conditions not of their own making. This builds on Gramsci's (1971) theory of the construction of hegemony and the work of Apple (1996), Pedroni (2007), and others. (d) Neoliberal forms of governance and how they expand the space for various corporate actors, philanthropists, and civic organizations to shape and steer education and urban policy.

Finally, I discuss the way forward for education and cities, particularly in light of the current structural crisis of capitalism and the emergence of new social paradigms in the Global South. Much has changed since I began this book and we cannot proceed with "business as usual" critiques of neoliberalism. Radical ruptures open a space for transformative solutions. The crisis has provoked me to open a conversation on new terrain—the need to move beyond capitalism and the role that education might play.

Activist Scholarship and My Data

I align myself with a tradition of activist scholarship that links critical research, social action, and social movements. I adopt Charles Hale's (2008) definition of activist scholarship as scholarship that is aligned with an organized group in struggle. It is both collaborative and politically engaged. A basic assumption is that research and political engagement enrich each other, and that "knowledge is vital to social action" (Hale, 2008; see also Emihovich, 2005). More broadly, activist scholarship develops a structural and cultural critique that challenges dominant groups and ideologies and aims to contribute to a public conversation about policy (Foley, 2008; Mehan, 2008).

For the past 6 years I have been immersed in ethnographic and collaborative research and action with youth, teachers, and community members against neoliberalization of education in Chicago and nationally. I have been critiquing dominant policies and ideologies, aiming to contribute to a public conversation about policy, collaborating with parents and teachers to bring in the voices and perspectives of those left out of the dominant discourse, and trying to produce knowledge vital to their struggles. I grapple with the dialectic of research and social transformation as do others who are engaged in this work. That is, how can research help reconstruct the field of ideological and material struggle (Gilmore, 2007b)? What is the relationship of researcher and social movements? And how does social struggle create and transform knowledge (Lipsitz, 2007)?

I work alongside teachers, youth, and communities of color as we contest neoliberal education policies and their impact on children and schools and the city in which we live, and I study these issues. Sometimes activism and scholarship are conflated, sometimes not. Some of my research projects are collaborations with community organizations and aim to strategically bring to light the experiences of working class African American and Latino/a parents and students and their teachers, which are often made invisible in public discussion about dominant education policies (e.g., Lipman, Person, & Kenwood Oakland Community Organization, 2007). I also collaborate with other scholars to examine the evidence for education policies and make this research available to schools and community activists to "speak truth to power" (Fleming, Greenlee, Gutstein, Lipman, & Smith, 2009; Greenlee, Hudspeth, Lipman, D. A. Smith, & J. Smith, 2008). I hope to contribute to a public conversation about policy by speaking to and writing for a broad audience as well as an academic one (J. Brown, Gutstein, & Lipman, 2009; Lipman, 2008b). Some of what I study is not for publication at all, but gets folded into the strategies that we pursue to get some justice. Often I put my researcher role aside. But the epistemologies and perspectives of the people with whom I work in solidarity deeply inform my understandings.

My analysis is based on research reports and archival documents on federal housing policy, urban development, and urban education nationally and in Chicago and on the ethnographic research, collaboration, and activism with communities and teachers described above. My data include a variety of documentary and participant observation data collected in public meetings of teachers, union and education activists, parents, community organizers, and youth, and in official public hearings. Data also include formal interviews with teachers, parents, and school staff. From July 2004 to the present (June 2010), I have attended and participated in relevant monthly school board meetings and numerous community hearings and discussions around the city, rallies and pickets, press conferences, community and teacher meetings and forums. I have also attended regular coalition meetings, planning meetings, three congressional task force meetings, and several meetings with top school district officials. I have had ongoing conversations and discussions with community organization members, teachers, parents, school staff, local school council members, a citywide parent organization, and representatives of teacher and school employee unions, school reform organizations, community-based research groups, and community leaders. Although I did not collect data in these private and informal settings, my understanding deepened and interpretations percolated and jelled as we brought our various perspectives, experiences, and wisdom to bear on the challenge of getting just education policies in the city.

I have been deeply influenced and enlightened by the theories and analyses of the people I join forces with—those most affected and least heard. Their voices are threaded throughout this book in an attempt to capture the desires, hopes, heart aches, and wisdom of those who live in and fight to remake the schools and city more in their own image. Here I heed Apple's (2006) advice to "reposition" empirical research: "the best way to understand what any set of institutions, policies, and practices does, is to see it from the standpoint of those who have the least power" (p. 229).

Three coauthored reports also contribute to this book. In 2006, I collaborated with a colleague and an African American community organization to formally interview parents, teachers, administrators, school staff, and students on the effects of school closings in the Midsouth area of Chicago. The initial report we coauthored was used by community organizations, local school councils, and others concerned about effects of school closings and displacement (Lipman, Person, & Kenwood Oakland Community Organization, 2007). In 2008 and 2009, I coauthored reports on school closings and neighborhood effects (Fleming et al., 2009; Greenlee et al., 2008). These were presented at press conferences and to the Board of Education and parents and teachers used them to challenge school closings. Throughout the book, but especially in chapters 3 through 6,

I intersperse vignettes drawn largely from my observations and participation. The vignettes are meant to bring to life experiences of education and urban restructuring. They add depth to an analysis that might otherwise miss the texture of contests over policy and power. I hope they convey something of the scenes, panoramas, and social geography of these contests. As a participant, sometimes the voice is my own, expressing my own experiences and reminding the reader that I am located inside this story too.

In practice, activist scholarship involves wearing many hats and sometimes explicitly taking off the researcher hat to put on the activist chapeau and vice versa. As a White woman professional, it also requires negotiating boundaries of race, class, gender, and privilege—and a lot of humility. I won't pretend it's not difficult. I am reminded of Santos's (2002) admonition to the intellectual to keep "a constant epistemological and political vigilance on [her]self lest [her] help becomes useless or even counterproductive" (p. 1085). In the end, my thinking is deeply indebted to the intellectual and practical leadership of the community activists, teachers, parents, and youth I join with.

Chicago and the Dynamics of Neoliberal Urbanism

Understanding political economy of urban education requires examining how education, economic and political structures, and ideologies are intertwined *in actual cities*. I turn to Chicago as a case of neoliberal urbanism and draw parallels with other U.S. cities. I do not claim that Chicago is *representative* nor that we can *generalize* from it to other U.S. cities and urban school districts. "Actually existing neoliberalisms" (Brenner & Theodore, 2002) are path dependent and variegated. However, a case study can reveal broader processes, mechanisms, and dynamics (Lofland & Lofland, 1995; Small, 2009) through which urban restructuring and education policy and practice are intertwined, shaped, and reshaped. These broader processes, mechanisms, and dynamics are my topic. In this sense, this study follows the path of previous examinations of specific cities that demonstrated the role of racial segregation and deindustrialization in shaping urban education in previous decades (Rury & Mirel, 1997).

Chicago is more than a rich example. It is incubator, test case, and model for the neoliberal urban education agenda. Chicago is where big city mayors go to see how to restructure their school systems. It was Arne Duncan's prototype on his national road show to promote school closings and education markets after he was appointed U.S. Secretary of Education in 2008. Chicago is also a prominent case of the transformation of the industrial, Keynesian, racially segregated, city to the entrepreneurial postwelfare city. Throughout the book, I show that social processes which are blatant in Chicago, a global metropolis, define cities and urban school districts elsewhere. I draw parallels between Chicago and other cities, but it is up to other researchers to examine how these processes play out concretely in their contexts (see Buras, Randels, Salaam,

& Students at the Center, 2010; Butler with Robson, 2003; Cucciara, 2008; Gulson, 2008; Lupton & Turnstall, 2008; Pedroni, 2011, for examples).

Organization of the Book

It is striking that at a moment when neoliberal policies have precipitated the deepest capitalist crisis since the Great Depression, neoliberalization of education is moving full steam ahead. While there is much talk about the need to reregulate markets and government has intervened to recapitalize failing banks and corporations, the national education program is for more markets and privatization. Education is open territory for neoliberal experimentation, and cities are policy labs. In the following chapters I examine the political, economic, and ideological dynamics at work.

In chapter 2, I summarize key features of neoliberal urban restructuring and describe Chicago as a "zone of experimentation" (Peck & Tickell, 2007) for neoliberal urban policy. I review Chicago's recent education policies that have played a vanguard role in promoting and legitimating a neoliberal urban education agenda. In chapter 3, I examine the lynchpin of these policies— education markets and the role of top-down, high stakes accountability in laying the groundwork. I analyze Chicago's Renaissance 2010 education policy as exemplar of policies unfolding in New Orleans, New York, Philadelphia, Detroit, and other cities. I argue that this national agenda is linked to a larger program to privatize public services and restructure urban space to serve investors. Chicago exemplifies the dynamic interplay of education policy, gentrification, and racial displacement. The failures of Chicago's education policies and their contestation also illustrate the potential for new alliances to reinvigorate and reframe public education.

Chapter 4 looks critically at the notion that mixed-income schools in newly constructed mixed-income communities are generative of educational equality and social justice. The chapter examines the relationship of education to federal policy to dismantle public housing, relocate tenants, and build market-driven mixed-income developments with mixed-income schools. I argue that although mixed-income strategies propose to reduce poverty and produce class integration and educational improvement, they can best be understood in relation to strategies to restructure the city for capital accumulation and racial containment and exclusion. The chapter links the racialized cultural politics underpinning this project to broader neoliberal cultural politics that posit behavioral explanations for structural inequality.

Chapter 5, written with Cristen Jenkins, explores the shift from government to governance through a focus on the role of corporate venture philanthropy in restructuring urban education and the intervention of philanthropies in the terrain of urban social struggle. The decline in federal funding and growth in public–private partnerships opened new opportunities for powerful corporate foundations to influence public policy. This chapter outlines how venture philanthropists have become part of the "shadow state" (Wolch, 1990), playing key roles in setting urban policy and performing government functions without public accountability. Through an analysis of four projects funded by the Gates Foundation, the chapter demonstrates how philanthropists attempt to strategically fund market reforms, co-opt democratic projects, and mobilize grassroots support for their initiatives, but also how contested these mobilizations may be.

Chapter 6 complicates critiques of neoliberalism by examining the cultural politics of charter schools and choice. I am interested in ways in which education markets resonate with teachers and parents, particularly parents of color, who are fed up with the failures of public schools to educate their children appropriately. Drawing on Gramsci's analysis of the construction of hegemony, I examine neoliberalism as a process that mobilizes social movements of marginalized people to its agenda and appeals to a common sense partly rooted in the exclusions and unresponsiveness of welfare state public institutions. Listening to teachers and parents, I argue for the "good sense" (Gramsci, 1971) in their tactical choice of charter schools in the face of the disinvestment, disrespect, and stultifying curricula they have experienced in public schools in their communities, particularly in the absence of alternatives that take seriously the urgent concerns and desires of those whom the public school system has failed. This chapter points to the need to reframe public education.

In the concluding chapter, I take up the challenge to theorize how educators and education activists should respond to the present social conjuncture—a deep structural crisis of capitalism, waning legitimacy of the state, and the emergence of alternative social paradigms. Since I began this book the ground has shifted under our feet. This provoked me to move beyond critiquing neoliberalism and offering modest steps toward an invigorated public education and city. Instead, I discuss the implications of the crisis for the city and education, and join others who see this social conjuncture as opportunity and necessity to talk about the possibility of a democratic socialist alternative, the essence of the "right to the city." This is a modest contribution to the national dialogue about the role of education and progressive education movements in shaping "the world we wish to see" (Amin, 2008).

2

NEOLIBERAL URBANISM AND EDUCATION POLICY

[C]ities (including their suburban peripheries) have become increasingly important geographical targets and institutional laboratories for a variety of neoliberal policy experiments, from place-marketing and local booster-ism, enterprise zones, tax abatements, urban development corporations, and public–private partnerships to workfare policies, property redevelopment schemes, new strategies of social control, policing and surveillance and a host of other institutional modifications within the local state apparatus. The overarching goal of such experiments is to mobilize city space as an arena both for market-oriented economic growth and for elite consumption practices.

The manifestations of destructively creative neoliberalization are evident across the urban landscape: the razing of lower income neighborhoods to make way for speculative development; the extension of market rents and housing vouchers; the increased reliance by municipalities on instruments of private finance; the privatization of schools; the administration of workfare programs; the mobilization of entrepreneurial discourses emphasizing reinvestment and rejuvenation; and so forth.

(Peck, Brenner, & Theodore, 2008)

U.S. public schools sit in cities that look quite different from the way they did 20 years ago. Neoliberal policies that facilitated perhaps the greatest concentration of wealth in the fewest hands in history have reshaped urban areas. In this book, I argue that educational policy is constitutive of urban restructuring processes described by Peck, Brenner, and Theodore above. This chapter begins by summarizing the motivating factors and characteristics of neoliberal urbanism.

I develop this summary through the illustrative case of Chicago, a "laboratory" for neoliberal policy experiments. I then review Chicago's recent history of education reform. This sets the stage for the rest of the book where I look more deeply at core neoliberal education initiatives and their interconnection with urban restructuring. I draw particularly on the work of critical urban scholars who elaborate the dynamic relationship between political economy and cultural politics and its spatial dimensions.

Neoliberal Urbanism and "Glocalized" Political, Economic, and Social Relations

Business leaders have historically played a major role in the development of U.S. cities. City governments provided physical infrastructure and subsides for industrial development and corporate headquarters, gave corporations tax subsidies, furthered corporate interests through zoning and other policies, and promulgated anti-labor policies. Of course, these policies were contested, sometimes with great militancy, and there were real gains as with rent stabilization, free admission to city universities, and benefits for public employee unions. Urban development projects that displaced working class communities and people of color also have a long history going back to "slum clearance" of immigrant settlements at the beginning of the 20th century, urban renewal from the 1940s through 1970s, construction of public housing to contain African Americans, construction of freeways that bisected working class communities and communities of color. Nor is the replacement of working class housing and neighborhoods by upper middle and upper class residents new. So what is different about neoliberal urbanism and what are its motivating forces?

Each era of capitalist development presents the state with new tasks (Ranney & Wright, 2004) and is associated with privileging specific geographic scales, places, and territories for capital accumulation over others (Brenner & Theodore, 2002). Over the past 30 years, cities and large urbanized areas have become fundamental geographical units in the spatial reorganization of the international division of labor. In a new global–local configuration, cities and metro regions compete directly in the global economy for investment, tourism, and production facilities. Brenner and Theodore (2002) provide a helpful explanation: During the Keynesian period, the national scale was the preeminent locus of capital accumulation and regulation of political and economic life, with industrial regions, like the U.S. Midwest and the British Midlands, functioning as the backbone of their national economies. But a constellation of global political–economic transformations beginning in the 1970s fractured the relationship between national mass production and consumption on which the Keynesian state was based. Over the next 20 years there was a rescaling of economic activity in which cities took on new economic roles and functions in relation to the global economy.[1] "Glocalization" signifies this dynamic interplay of the global and local in the creation of new political, social, and economic relations. Brenner and Theodore (2002) summarize:

> the geographies of actually existing neoliberalism are characterized by a dynamic transformation of capitalist territorial organization from the nationally configured frameworks that prevailed during the Fordist-Keynesian period to an increasingly "globalized" configuration of global-national-local interactions in which no single scale serves as the primary pivot for accumulation, regulation, or socio-political struggle.
>
> (p. 363)

A number of political and economic factors motivated these "glocalization" changes (Brenner & Theodore, 2002; Hackworth, 2007; Harvey, 2001, 2005; N. Smith, 2002): a) Declining profits and deindustrialization of economic engines, such as the U.S. Midwest, and increased global competition pushed corporations to relocate production to huge metropolitan areas such as São Paulo and Bangkok. These new "production hearths" of the global economy (Smith) are tied economically to cities in the Global North by a web of financial connections, production outsourcing, and labor migrations. b) The breakup of the Bretton Woods convention allowed the value of national currencies to float in global currency markets, which weakened nation-states' regulation of their economies. c) In the United States, neoliberal theories of "lean government" and devolution of powers to local government, justified cuts in federal funding to cities. This imposed fiscal constraints on local governments and delinked them from national government. As cities competed directly in the global economy, urban entrepreneurship, "space marketing" (Harvey, 2001), and market rule became the driving ideologies in city government. d) At the same time liberalization of global finance coupled with cuts in federal funding for cities made debt financing central to the operation of city governments, further integrating them into, and subjecting them to the regulation of global financial markets.

Gentrification is an example. Whereas previous waves of gentrification, for example, beginning in the 1960s, were housing-based, localized to certain cities, relatively confined to specific neighborhoods, and a marginal sector of urban economies, gentrification at the end of the 20th century and beyond is much wider in scope and far more economically significant (N. Smith, 2002). Aggressive promotion of real estate development, particularly downtown megaplexes and gentrification of neighborhoods, is a global urban strategy. Generalized to cities of all sizes, this wave of gentrification is characterized by gentrification complexes of housing, recreation, and consumption financed by consortia of local, national, and global investors and facilitated by the state. Redevelopment of London's docklands, marketization of public housing in

Sydney, and gentrification of working class Paris are examples (Darcy & J. Smith, 2008; Swyngedouw, Moulaert, & Rodriguez, 2004). This new wave of gentrification has become a pivotal economic sector and an "unassailable capital accumulation strategy for competing urban economies" (N. Smith, 2002, p. 96). It serves as a key opportunity for profitable investment, a key source of revenue for cities, and a principal tool for marketing the city to the upper middle class.

Across quite different contexts, cities are driven by these global–local neoliberal logics and marked by new geographies of social and spatial exclusion. Zones of extreme poverty characterized by informal labor and housing (street selling, part-time jobs, favelas, squatters, homeless encampments) and in-migrations of displaced workers and farmers (Davis, 2006; Marcuse & Van Kempen, 2000; Sassen, 2006; Valle & Torres, 2000) are juxtaposed with enclaves of hyperaffluence in cities as diverse as Mumbai, São Paulo, Beijing, and Los Angeles. Megacities, with populations up to 20 million (e.g., Mexico City) are magnets for millions of dispossessed and unemployed farmers and workers (Davis, 2006).[2] In global cities of North America, Europe, and parts of Asia and the Global South, glittering corporate skyscrapers, gated communities, condominium developments, refurbished mansions, and luxury zones for the rich contrast with disinvested working class, low-income, and immigrant enclaves. In short, the urban landscape is littered with the debris of "accumulation by dispossession," what Mike Davis (2005) graphically calls "a planet of slums."

Social control has always been a function of urban government to control labor organizing, social movements, and urban rebellions, and to enforce racial segregation, defend private property, and diffuse social conflict and resistance. But aggressive policing and racialized containment are specific features of the neoliberal state's management of potential resistance and social disintegration due to cuts in social welfare and magnified urban inequalities. It is part of a strategy to "return" the city to the (White) middle and upper middle class. This strategy was pioneered by New York Mayor Giuliani's aggressive "stop and frisk," "zero tolerance" policing. Mitchell (2003) describes these tactics, branded as "quality of life" policing, aimed at "the most oppressed—workers and 'welfare mothers,' immigrants and gays, people of color and homeless people, squatters, anyone who demonstrates in public. They are excoriated for having stolen New York from a white middle class that sees the city as its birthright" (p. 1). Cities across the United States and globally went on to import Giuliani's tactics, often marketed and advised by the ex-mayor and his police chief (Lawyer's Committee for Human Rights, 2003; Mountz & Curran, 2009; Rushing, 2009). Meanwhile, gated communities, corporate plazas, and high-end shopping malls operate as zones of spatialized "exclusionary citizenship" (MacLeod, 2002), backed up by the policing arm of the state and private security. And those displaced by gentrification are pushed to the outskirts of the city and beyond by de facto racial segregation in housing and inflated housing and rental markets.

Nonetheless, neoliberalization is marked by tensions, contestations, and contingencies. Each local state has to juggle often contradictory tasks of support for capital accumulation, social control, and legitimation. The state internalizes conflicts among these social, economic, and political agendas and ideologies, and has to adjust policy to deal with the contradictions, setbacks, and social costs of neoliberalism (Jones & Ward, 2002). For example, while public housing has been pulled down across the U.S., it has been largely preserved in New York because of the particular alignment of social forces and history of the city (Hackworth, 2007). Neoliberal policies have also spawned diverse oppositional cultural and political projects and alternative forms of social organization and uses of public space, e.g., community gardens, co-ops (Leitner, Peck, & Sheppard, 2007). Yet, as a whole, they have succeeded in reshaping cities and urban policy discourses and have set in motion new forms of economic, social, and spatial inequality, marginality, and exclusion.

Neoliberal governance, economic strategies, and ideologies are the "drivers of urban change" (Hackworth, 2007, p.2). From New York to Madrid to São Paulo to Glasgow, cities deploy neoliberal strategies to assist capital accumulation and racial/ethnic/class exclusion—all discursively legitimated by the supposedly indisputable logics of "effective governance," "global competition," and the need to attract capital and prevent capital flight. Drawing on discourses of "regeneration" and "rebirth," city governments facilitate large scale projects such as museum complexes, downtown development, and gentrification of the inner-city and working class neighborhoods beyond the center city, pushing out the people who live there. To cover costs of social reproduction and infrastructure, the local state relies on debt financing, subjecting it to regulation by bond rating agencies. Subsidizing capital to relocate and invest in the city, reducing government subsidies for social welfare and privatizing public health, education, transportation, and public housing are axiomatic (Hackworth, 2007; Swyngedouw, Moulaert, & Rodriguez, 2004). Government has become "governance," deploying managerial discourses and embracing public–private partnerships that integrate corporations and corporate philanthropists into city policy making without public accountability. Surveillance, zero-tolerance policing, and containment of immigrants, homeless people, low-income communities of color, and the poorest residents of the city are the order of the day (Mitchell, 2003; N. Smith, 1996).

In the following sections, I draw particularly on Chicago to unpack neoliberal urbanism. Chicago's transition from industrial powerhouse to neoliberal city illustrates the changing role of the urban state and restructuring of the urban economy. The city also illustrates intertwined logics of White supremacy and neoliberal urbanism in the U.S. The roots of this transition are in post-World War II urban change.

From Industrial City to White Flight and Growth Machine

Chicago's steel mills, manufacturing industries, and agricultural processing plants, and its role as a national transportation hub, made it a major force in the postwar economic boom. It was also home to major corporate headquarters, and the Chicago Board of Trade and Chicago Mercantile Exchange put the city at the center of national agriculture marketing and commodity speculation. However, in the 1950s the contradictions bubbling beneath the surface of the welfare state settlement began to surface. Higher wages earned by White workers (and some unionized workers of color) led to demand for better housing and schools. At the same time, there was a postwar migration of African Americans from the South and secondarily Latino/as from Mexico and the South West to northern cities. Real estate practices that provoked "panic" home sales by playing on White racist fears set off mass White working class and middle class flight to the suburbs. The exodus was facilitated by a national strategy of government subsidies for home ownership, particularly for Whites after World War II (Lipsitz, 1998), and the construction of the national highway system. The growth of new suburban housing was accompanied by a boom in retail outlets, and cheaper land outside the city encouraged the growth of suburban manufacturing, further fueling migration out of the city.

The suburban boom had devastating economic consequences for the urban core. As Whites left central cities, African Americans and Latino/as and other immigrants filled their place. But because of racism in the trade unions and in hiring, the new workers earned lower wages and fewer benefits than Whites. They also faced segregated housing markets forcing them into neighborhoods with inferior schools. As African Americans and Latino/as moved into housing vacated by Whites, landlords took advantage of racial segregation to subdivide properties and neglect building maintenance. All this instigated falling property values. The end result was huge losses of municipal revenue from property taxes and disinvestment in the urban core (Ranney & Wright, 2004). These developments set conditions for neoliberal urbanism.

Yet central areas of Chicago and other cities retained corporate headquarters that could not be abandoned by city government. To rebuild the urban tax base, from the late 1950s through mid-1970s, Chicago along with some other cities embarked on a "growth machine" strategy of downtown development and corporate subsidies (Logan & Molotch, 1987). In Chicago, this was driven by a powerful coalition of banks and financial institutions in league with real estate developers, major corporations, the Chicago Federation of Labor, and Mayor Richard J. Daley's Democratic Party machine. This alliance shaped city development, land use policies, and real estate markets. Feagin (1998) and Ranney and Wright (2004) outline the key elements of the Chicago strategy: expansion of the central business district, racial containment through slum clearance and construction of public housing, multiple municipal tax authorities to mask fiscal crises, and deflection of African American resistance through cooptation of Black politicians into the city's political machine.

Chicago's growth machine agenda was concretized in the 1973 *Chicago 21 Plan* produced by the Commercial Club of Chicago (CCC), an over-100-year-old organization of the city's leading corporate, financial, philanthropic, and civic leaders (see Shipps, 2006 for a history of the CCC.) The introduction to *Chicago 21 Plan* was written by Mayor Daley. The *21 Plan* proposed a far-reaching redevelopment of the downtown (the "Loop"), lakeshore, and surrounding area to attract corporate headquarters, expand the Chicago branch of the University of Illinois, and attract middle-class consumers back to the downtown. The plan was realized, despite resistance, over a period of more than two decades by demolishing African American and other working class neighborhoods that stood in the way (Lipman, 2004; Rast, 1999) and by morphing into neoliberal urbanism.

Through the 1970s and 1980s, the growth machine strategy provided massive public subsidies to corporate, banking, and real estate interests while squeezing out small and medium manufacturers and working class residential areas near downtown. Rast (1999, p. 24) reported that medium and small manufacturers in and around downtown provided 115,000 jobs in 1970, 23% of the city's total manufacturing jobs at the time. They were replaced by corporate headquarters and up-scale residential developments. Thousands of good paying working class jobs were lost, contributing to overall deindustrialization. From 1967 to 1990, Chicago manufacturing jobs shrank from 546,500 (nearly 41% of all local jobs) to 216,190 (18% of jobs) (Betancur & Gills, 2000, p. 27). They were mostly replaced with lower paying service jobs or work in the informal economy. Working class neighborhoods were gentrified or cleared for construction of the University of Illinois's Chicago campus (Rast, 1999; Squires, Bennett, McCourt, & Nyden, 1987). The mayor's Democratic Party machine eliminated potential opposition and funnelled city resources to corporate center development through zoning ordinances, tax policies, publicly financed infrastructure improvements, federal Urban Development Action Grants, and financial incentives (Rast, 1999).

In cities across the United States, the Keynesian urban state, supported by federal funding and industrial production and based on racial containment, began to falter as cities were hit with Black rebellions in the 1960s, deindustrialization, effects of the global capitalist crisis of the 1970s, and then federal revenue cuts. In Chicago, this set the stage for the election of the city's first Black mayor, Harold Washington, in 1983. In his brief tenure Washington tried to implement a less corporate-centered economic development strategy. Although he continued to work with the city's corporate leaders, Washington supported community economic development, especially in working class communities of color, modernization of manufacturing, and alliances with community organizations, and pushed for continued federal assistance (Clavel

& Kleniewsky, 1990). But Washington, like other Black urban mayors (e.g., in Detroit, Atlanta, Newark, Gary, Indiana) faced a dramatically changing global economy. When he died unexpectedly in 1987, Chicago, like other U.S. cities was transitioning to the neoliberal world order, including loss of living wage jobs, hyperconsumption stimulated by expanded credit, and financialization of all aspects of the economy, including urban government (Betancur & Gills, 2000; Ranney & Wright, 2004). Over the next two decades, the wealthiest Chicago residents and upwardly mobile professionals did extremely well from these policies while the majority of working class and poor people saw a decline in income and living standards (Michel cited in Ranney &Wright, 2004).

Neoliberal Restructuring

In the United States, the 1990s marked an important phase of deregulation of capital and transition to neoliberal urban governance. The ideological manifesto for this transition was the Republican Party's 1994 *Contract with America,* which prioritized individual liberty, economic opportunity, limited government, personal responsibility, and national security (Hackworth, 2007, p.15). The *Contract* set the terms for a massive rollback of Keynsian state welfare programs and the devolution of federal responsibility for social welfare to city government. This was intertwined with transformations in the global economy outlined above.

As I described in chapter 1, actually existing neoliberalism involves the intervention of the state on the side of capital, first to destroy existing institutional arrangements, and then to create a new infrastructure for capital accumulation. Peck and Tickell (2002) describe the two phases as "rollback" and "rollout" neoliberalism. Rollback includes destruction of Keynesian artifacts (e.g., public housing, free or nearly free public universities), policies (e.g., redistributive welfare, labor protections), agreements (e.g., federal redistribution of revenue to cities, labor contracts that include fully funded benefits), and institutions (e.g., U.S. Department of Housing and Urban Development as provider of housing). Roll out neoliberalism then creates new practices and institutions or reconstructs existing ones to serve capital accumulation, particularly to create markets in areas where they don't exist, such as public housing, public schools, public infrastructure, and retirement funds (Harvey, 2005). Thus the neoliberal state is noninterventionist when it comes to regulating capital (except when stability of the system is at stake)[3] and providing for social welfare, but interventionist when it comes to ensuring the rule of markets and favorable conditions for capital accumulation. Below I outline some of these state strategies in Chicago.

Marketing the City for Investment and Consumption

The election of Richard M. Daley (former Mayor Richard J. Daley's son) as mayor in 1989 hearlded the neoliberal era in Chicago. In the 1990s, the construction of new skyscrapers, luxury condominiums, and entertainment venues made Chicago's downtown a destination for the affluent and the global business set. Chicago's ubiquitous new boulevard flowerbeds, "magnificent mile" luxury shopping zone, and revitalized parks are all part of the city's place marketing strategy. The cultural and food scene and nonstop festivals and stunning lakefront have turned the city of big shoulders into an international tourist destination and a hip place to live, work, and relax for those who live there (Judd, 2003). The icon of downtown beatification is Millennium Park, a $475 million, 24.5 acre park, garden, and performance space, built through a public–private partnership with major corporations and banks. Achieving world city status in a global environment of culture and leisure marketing requires contracting world famous architects and designers. Millennium Park was designed by global architectural icon, Frank Gehry and internationally famous landscape architects, and features the signature Cloud Gate sculpture by British artist Anish Kapoor. How does the city pay for such lavishness?

Bond rating agencies, such as Standard and Poor's and Moody's, the gatekeepers of global capital markets, are a central institutional force on neoliberal urban governance (Hackworth, 2007). Their role can be traced to reduced federal funding for cities in the rollback phase when the federal government slashed funds but increased local responsibility for social welfare, such as public housing. Tougher crime laws put additional demands on municipal budgets for police and jails. Driven by market ideology and to make up for federal cuts, local governments, including Chicago, turned to property and real estate taxes, debt financing, and financialization (Hackworth; N. Smith, 2002; Weber, 2002). Municipal debt, in the form of municipal bonds and other securities generated through real estate tax revenues and other taxes, is traded in the global financial markets (see Weber, 2002, for a full discussion). As a result, cities are especially vulnerable to the decisions of bond rating agencies, which place considerable constraints on city governments, giving finance capital tremendous influence over urban policies (Ranney & Wright, 2004). (A low bond rating signals to investors that the city's credit is shaky.) According to the logic of neoliberal urban governance, anything that hurts investment is "bad" for bond ratings and therefore "bad" urban policy.

Despite its discursive force (Wilson, 2006), there are contestations and internal contradictions in the neoliberal urbanist project. For example, in 2008, a coalition of unions and community organizations fought for a living wage ordinance; there was both support and opposition from corporate and community organizations for Chicago's 2016 Olympic bid (which lost in the final round); and the mayor's privatization of parking meters (a lucrative deal for investors and a temporary crisis solution) also cost him politically. Education policy has been a lightening rod for opposition to privatization and the policies have produced new sets of problems requiring new initiatives, as I describe in the next chapter.

Gentrification: A Pivotal Sector in Urban Economies

In the early 1980s I lived in Lakeview, a primarily working class racially mixed Chicago North Side neighborhood. My neighbors were factory and office workers with a smattering of teachers and social workers. My landlord next door had worked at a neighborhood factory from the age of 16 until he retired. I taught part time at an alternative school for adults on Chicago's West Side and worked at the unemployment office. Across the street from the three-flat brick apartment building where I lived was a small factory where my downstairs neighbor had worked for almost 40 years. We were just down the block from the "el" (elevated train station) and everything we needed was right around the corner or within easy walking distance: the dry cleaner, Tony's fruit and vegetable market, the Model butcher shop, Tony's mother's Italian grocery open on Friday and Saturday only (she made the best giardiniera and could give you a recipe for anything), Mr. Ramos's corner store where the kids too often tried to steal candy on their way home from school, Grobe's pharmacy, the branch library, the Jewel supermarket, two local department stores, a new Filipino restaurant next door to the Mexican restaurant, and on and on. In the summer we sat out on our stoops while the kids played up and down the sidewalk. We were just six blocks from the Chicago Cubs Wrigley field and could hear the roar of the crowd when a batter hit one over the fence.

It wasn't idyllic: the kids had fights; there was a crew of neighborhood toughs (not really a gang); people came home tired from hard, unrewarding, underpaid jobs; there were landlord "issues" and "silent" racism. But it was basically a stable neighborhood with all its contradictions, and we mostly looked out for each other and each others' kids.

I moved to New York in 1983 and didn't come back to visit until 1989. I heard the neighborhood had been "revitalized," but when I got off the el I could hardly believe my eyes. Lakeview was now prime real estate marketed to a new "creative class" of young upwardly mobile professionals. New cookie-cutter condominiums replaced some of the wood frame houses. The apartments where my friends Lydia, Chris, and Lionel had lived with their families had upgraded windows, new siding and front porches, wrought iron fences with locked gates, and had gone condo. The convenience store on the corner was now the Red Tomato, a chic restaurant with exposed brick walls. The Model Market, Tony's, his mother's store, Grobe's, the Balikbayan restaurant, the bowling alley, the small factory across the street—all gone. By the time I moved back to Chicago in the mid-1990s, my old neighborhood was a ritzy shopping and restaurant destination. My vintage apartment building, a brick three-flat with floor to ceiling windows, hardwood floors, in excellent condition though not remodelled, had been leveled along with my landlord's modest frame house next door. A giant condominium spanned both lots.

Renamed "Wrigleyville," the neighborhood is part of a huge swath of gentrification taking over much of the North Side spreading west to one of the few remaining (and only multiracial) public housing complexes, now slated for demolition. The complex is a collection of brick low-rise buildings in a leafy area on the Chicago River. Mostly gone are the factories and working class neighborhoods that comprised this part of Chicago.

What happened to Lakeview is repeated across the United States with new urban geographies of class and race exclusion, inequality, and contestation. Gentrification—the appropriation of working class and low-income neighborhoods and their "revitalization" for a new middle class clientele—is a pivotal urban strategy (Fainstein & Judd, 2001; Hackworth, 2007; N. Smith, 2002) and a central agent in the production of spatial inequality, displacement, and homelessness. African American neighborhoods that were disinvested of public and commercial infrastructure, including public housing, now sprout high-profile gentrification complexes. Badly maintained and subdivided, but architecturally significant, brownstones and mansions are reborn as million dollar single-family homes. Formerly stable working class and mixed-income neighborhoods are now coveted addresses of converted lofts and condo developments. New streetscapes festooned with flowers, boulevards, and wrought iron fences set off trendy shops and restaurants where mom and pop stores operated.

The consortia of global, national, and local capital (N. Smith, 2002), real estate developers, and public–private partnerships driving these projects are enabled by city government subsidies and policies. Reliance on property tax revenues to fund public services and to back up municipal bonds, makes cities more dependent on, and active subsidizers and facilitators of real estate markets. For example, the state absorbs risks and land development costs that would otherwise be born by developers, essentially giving them public land and funneling tax dollars to support development (Weber, 2002). In turn, real estate is a key speculative activity (e.g., condo "flipping"), with holdings in real estate transformed into financial instruments which are traded in the financial markets.[4] The consequences of all this for low-income and working class people can be disastrous as real estate speculation pushes up property values and property taxes and leads to displacement of public housing residents and working class renters and home owners.

Yet other, primarily African American, neighborhoods are monuments to disinvestment and public neglect with no full service grocery store or bank and few public resources. Some parts of Chicago's South and West Sides, dotted with overgrown vacant lots—scars of disinvestment that followed African American rebellions in the 1960s—are heavily policed cauldrons of social frustration. Other, crowded, bustling working class immigrant neighborhoods are also sites of cultural contestation. African, Latino/a, Asian, and Middle Eastern immigrant communities are at once policed and contained, commodified as ethnic tourist attractions and aestheticized diversity, and are bases to pressure the city for multicultural policies (Zukin, 2002).

Harvey (2001) argues that this spatial reordering of the city is located in the spatial logics of capital: "The inner contradictions of capitalism are expressed through the restless formation and re-formation of geographical landscapes" (p. 333). The territorial organization of capital—the physical location of production facilities, the built environment of cities, places of consumption— is devalued in one place (through deindustrialization, disinvestment, neglect) and rebuilt elsewhere in order to establish a "new locational grid" for capital accumulation (Brenner & Theodore, 2002, p. 8). The urban built environment is "junked, abandoned, destroyed and selectively reconstructed" (Weber, 2002, p. 174) when potential land values provoke a new round of reinvestment. Harvey summarizes the inherent logic of this process, "Capitalism perpetually strives, therefore, to create a social and physical landscape in its own image and requisite to its own needs at a particular point in time, only just as certainly to undermine, disrupt and even destroy that landscape at a later point in time" (p. 333). The reterritorialization of capital is always uneven as some geographical areas are under- or undeveloped while others are overdeveloped, which produces shifting geographies of inequality, centrality, and marginalization.

A Racialized Urban Imaginary of "Blight" and "Revitalization"

Neoliberalism reframes how we think about the city—who has a right to live there, what constitutes a "good" neighborhood, and what kinds of economic development are possible and necessary. Cultural geographers (Keith & Pile, 1993, 1993b; Soja, 1999) draw our attention to ways in which power is reproduced and daily life is regulated through cultural domination of space: Space is both "the 'perceived space' of material spatial practices and the 'conceived space' of symbolic representations and epistemologies.... Every lived space is simultaneously lived and imagined" (Soja, 1999, p. 74). Part of what is unfolding in the city is a contest over the meanings, desires, representations, and cultural practices that constitute the places where people live, congregate, and make meaning. As Miriam Greenberg puts it, cities are "produced not only materially and geographically but also in the social imagination and through changing modes of cultural representation" (2000, p. 228).

Urban "blight," "renaissance," and "revitalization" are constructed representations, an "urban imaginary" that shapes the meaning of the city and its attraction for capital and high paid labor. The value of buildings and whole neighborhoods is discursively constructed. Obsolescence is naturalized, and the market is framed as a neutral arbiter of value, determining what is obsolete and should be destroyed. Weber (2002) argues obsolescence is an "alibi" used to validate the destruction of the built environment for capital accumulation.

The state plays a key role by strategically declaring some areas "blighted" as a precondition for their seizure under eminent domain, for state-assisted private real estate redevelopment, and for gentrification.[5] She describes how this works:

> Because the presence or absence of value is far from straightforward, states attempt to create a convergence of thinking around such critical issues as the economic life of buildings, the priority given to different components of value, the sources of devaluation, and interrelationships between buildings and neighborhoods.

(p. 524)

In the United States and elsewhere, the cycle of neglect, racial containment, and redevelopment of central cities is justified by the pathologizing racial discourse of the "ghetto" (Gulson, 2007; Moynihan, 1965). Urban "blight" as a discursive category is applied selectively to areas of the city that have been abandoned by capital and public investment; generally they are African American, Latino/a, or immigrant (Weber, 2002; D. Wilson, 2006). Drawing on metaphors of disease and hygiene, Chicago officials and corporate media pathologize African American and Latino/a neighborhoods and public housing, calling for them to be "cleaned out" and "revitalized" (Grossman & Leroux, 2006). This follows a pattern epitomized by late 1980s gentrification of New York's Lower East Side, a working class, racially mixed area of the city—an emblematic tale of the racialized coding of a neighborhood as an "urban frontier" by developers and city officials (N. Smith, 1996). This framing facilitated marketing the area to hip young urban professionals as an "edgy" location open to "urban pioneers," a practice repeated across U.S. cities.

Negative representations of the "inner city" are nevertheless contested politically and culturally and in practices of everyday life. Weber notes that some organizing and lawsuits to stop urban renewal in the 1950s were successful partly because they challenged the scientific and legal basis of blight, "unhinging the signifier from the referent" (p. 181). Black and Latino/a working class communities may be pathologized in the media and by social policy discourses, but Haymes (1995) argues, to people who live there, they are also spaces of collective identity, survival, and cultural resistance. As I argue in chapters 3 and 4, displacement from schools and communities is more than physical disruption. It breaks a web of human connections in which the social and cultural practices of daily life are rooted, race and class identities are formed, and community is constituted.

Tax Increment Financing

Tax Increment Financing (TIF) is one of the most powerful tools employed by municipal governments in the United States to foster and facilitate market-driven urban development (Weber, 2002, 2003). The city declares an area "blighted" and unlikely to be developed without government subsidy. Once declared a TIF district, property tax revenues for schools, libraries, parks, and other public works are frozen at their current level for 23 years, and growth in revenues above this level is put in a TIF fund for economic development. The city also turns projected increments in property taxes into securities called developer notes (short-term debt instruments) which provide developers with short-term financing for their projects (Rachel Weber, personal communication, July 28, 2010). In this way the city entices investors to areas of greatest potential growth. TIF opens up land for development of tourist attractions, city beautification projects, housing and gentrification projects, and retail. It also allows the state to acquire property through eminent domain or property tax arrears and turn it over to private investors.

In the early 1990s, state legislatures expanded the use of TIFs, and under Mayor Daley, Chicago has made TIF a centerpiece of its development strategy.[6] TIF funds have been used to subsidize hundreds of Chicago's major real estate projects by providing support for developers and to front for infrastructure costs such as new streets and sewers. One of the most dramatic examples is the demolition of thousands of units of public housing to free huge tracts of valuable land for sale to developers (J. L. Smith, 2006) pushing out thousands of African American families. By the end of 2008, Chicago had 161 TIF districts, covering almost 30% of the city land area (Weber, 2009), including parts of downtown Chicago and areas already undergoing aggressive real estate development. (The discursive construction of "blight" to create TIF zones was brought home to me when my busy Chicago neighborhood commercial corner, hub of a bustling mixed-income interracial community, was declared blighted and "TIFed.") As of winter 2010, Mayor Daley controlled a TIF slush fund of over $1 billion (Joravsky & Dumke, 2009) with little transparency about where the money was spent (Joravsky, 2009).

TIF has become a major source of municipal debt financing. Municipal and state debt in the United States increased 55% between 2000 and 2005 to $1.85 trillion; approximately $1.13 trillion was local debt (Weber, 2009). The city repackages TIF funds into financial instruments (e.g., TIF bonds) which are traded in global capital markets, as Chicago did with TIF funds for the redevelopment of the Cabrini Green housing project (Weber, 2002). City government is so dependent on integration with financial markets that it has become a "risk management state" focused on limiting its financial vulnerability and improving investor confidence (Hackworth, 2007; Weber, 2009). TIF is a major component as the city pledges future TIF increments (projected gains in property taxes) as security on bonds or other financial products.[7]

This strategy has important implications for schools.[8] Because TIFs divert tax revenues from schools and other public infrastructure, they can contribute to disinvestment in low-income neighborhoods. On the other hand, TIF funds may be used to build new schools, but this is a political decision driven by juggling potentially competing demands for capital accumulation, legitimation, and social control. For example, in 2006, Mayor Daley launched a plan to use $600 million in TIF funds as part of a $1.5 billion plan for new school construction. But, because TIF gives the mayor more influence over the expenditure of tax revenues, it dedemocratizes city budgeting and decisions such as where new schools should be built. When schools are built, the projects are overseen by the Public Building Commission, appointed by the mayor, a body with little transparency about how schools are prioritized for funding. The city can also transfer funds from one TIF district to fund school construction in an adjacent TIF district without community input. The link between school construction and real estate development is illustrated by the fact that new schools built with TIF funds require a hearing before the City Council's Committee on Housing and Real Estate (Joravsky, 2008).

University as Real Estate Developer

The entrepreneurial university is another key actor in the acquisition and development of urban real estate, partnering with city and private investors to redevelop "inner city areas" (Perry & Wiewel, 2005). Yale is a primary player in the redevelopment of New Haven, CT. Johns Hopkins plays a similar role in East Baltimore, as does Columbia University in New York City (Harvey 2008). The University of Pennsylvania's 30-year expansion plan includes the 2007 acquisition of the U.S. Postal Service's Philadelphia facility on a 24-acre parcel of land near downtown. The construction of the University of Illinois-Chicago (UIC), which displaced a multiethnic working class community, was a central piece of the *Chicago 21 Plan*. Today, the University is a central player in the redevelopment of two of the largest gentrification complexes in Chicago: the $750 million University Village complex and the $450 million federally and locally subsidized mixed-income Roosevelt Square development of 2,441 homes (one third for public housing residents) covering 35 city blocks on the city's near West side. The two developments entailed the dismantling and reconstruction of ABLA Homes, the second largest public housing complex in Chicago, destruction of low-income rental housing, and dropping the wrecking ball on the historic Maxwell Street business district which wiped out a working class commercial hub and source of jobs for nearby residents.

University Village illustrates the role of the university in gentrification in collaboration with finance capital, real estate developers, and city government. To accomplish the $750 million, 14-acre University Village project, UIC bought up additional land to supplement the parcels it owned and sold the total package to developers for $17.8 million. As of December 2008, the developers had sold 837 homes for a total of $312 million. To help finance the project, UIC borrowed $332.5 million, and the city created a TIF district to provide $75 to $100 million for public improvements such as streets, sewers, and sidewalks (Novak & Fusco, 2009). The Roosevelt Square project was also lubricated by $9.7 million in TIF funded subsidies to developers. These university/developer/city driven projects have displaced thousands of primarily African American public housing residents, renters, and small businesses. The university's expansion and development projects are also a major impetus for the gentrification of Pilsen, a working class Mexican immigrant community south of the university (Betancur, 2005). UIC also took over the operation of a neighborhood elementary school and is partnering with the Noble Network of Charter Schools to operate the new UIC College Prep Charter High School with a focus on health sciences.

The University of Chicago's expansion into the African American South Side Woodlawn neighborhood and the Illinois Institute of Technology's central role in the massive Midsouth development project on the site of several miles of now-demolished public housing high-rises are other examples. In each case, the university is both an anchor and a key player in real estate development and place marketing. The University of Chicago's network of charter schools is a selling point for middle-class families looking to buy homes in the gentrified Midsouth area. I return to these issues in chapters 3, 4, and 6.

Markets and Privatization

On December 4, 2008, the Chicago City Council approved Mayor Daley's plan to lease the city's parking meters for 75 years to LLC, a division of the Wall Street investment firm Morgan Stanley. In return LLC made a one-time payment of nearly $1.2 billion. Immediately, the City Council quadrupled the parking meter rate from 25 cents to $1 an hour with an increase to $2 by 2013 and extended meter hours from 8 a.m. to 9 p.m. in every neighborhood, 7 days a week. Downtown fees jumped from $3 to $3.50 an hour and will go to $6.50 by 2013 when Chicago will have some of the highest parking meter rates in the United States. A City press release explained, "Under this creative agreement, we will use funds from the parking meter lease to help balance our budget this year" (City of Chicago, 2009). In the following weeks, hundreds of acts of sabotage were reported as the city's residents applied superglue and baseball bats to LLC's meters.

Then on July 1, 2009, Daley announced that every lakefront curb and parking lot bordering the lake would be parking metered to help fund the Chicago Park district. "The lake" is where we go for birthday parties, family picnics, volley ball games, barbeques, and just to chill (Chicago's east border is Lake Michigan). The Lake is where the counterpoint of many accents and the vibrancy of people coming from many lands or from right here in the city come together, even mingle. Lakefront parks are fragrant with the scent of *arrrachera* on the grill mingling with hot dogs, barbeque, and Vietnamese spring rolls. In a time of economic recession, which for too many in the park is all the time, the Lake is free, the park is free, and the parking *was* free. You might have to walk a little with your baskets and coolers, your grill and blankets and strollers and speakers, but you can spend the day. The lake is where the tensions of trying to live in the city with too little money and too few services and too much stress can be put on hold for a few mellow hours. From most of the lake vantage points you can get a view of the mass of skyscrapers clustered in the "loop," a beautiful view though a constant reminder of the power and wealth concentrated there. But at the lake you mostly see the "real Chicago"—the faces of the city's globalized working class.

Stripping cities of federal funds laid the groundwork for municipal governments to privatize public institutions and infrastructure. Across the United States, city governments have contracted out public services to private companies, leased public infrastructure such as roads and bridges to corporate investors, and entered into public–private partnerships that semiprivatize public institutions and public goods. While privatization is naturalized by discourses of the "inefficient" and "ineffective" public sector, it also resonates with popular dissatisfaction at unresponsive and disinvested public institutions and infrastructure. (I take up this point especially in chapter 6.)

Mayor Daley has presided over some of the most high-profile privatizations of public infrastructure in the United States. In 2004, the Chicago City Council approved Daley's lease of the Chicago Skyway toll bridge for 99 years to Cintra Macquarie Consortium, a transnational investment firm, for $1.82 billion.[9] In 2008, the City Council approved the lease of the city's parking meters to LLC, followed by a proposal to privatize Midway Airport in a $2.52 billion deal. The city also outsourced trash pickup service and some police functions to private companies and privatized parking at O'Hare airport, city parking enforcement, street resurfacing, engineering, purchasing, vehicle towing, and delinquent tax collections. The Mayor and City Council have handed over public goods to private companies with little public discussion or oversight, and contracted with corporations to commercially brand public infrastructure. Chicago's White Sox baseball stadium is now "Cellular Field," joining Minute Maid Park, HP Pavillion, and other branded sports venues across the country. Chicago's spectacular Millennium Park is a public–private partnership, owned by the city but cofinanced by corporate donors whose names are sprinkled throughout. Although it is a beautiful addition to the lakefront, it was built without real public discussion about priorities, and is sometimes closed for corporate events.

But perhaps the most significant changes in the social geography of the city's working class neighborhoods are the result of privatization of public housing and schools. In the next sections, I summarize these initiatives, situating education markets in Chicago in the recent history of education policy.

From Local Democracy to High Stakes Accountability

In 1988, the Illinois state legislature passed the Chicago School Reform Act. The law established unprecedented community participation in school governance through elected Local School Councils (LSCs), the majority of whose members were parents. LSCs have the power to hire and fire principals, approve annual school improvement plans, and allocate the school's discretionary budget (Federal Title 1 and State Chapter 1 funds), which can be substantial. But the law also gave the mayor authority to appoint an Interim School Board (Daley chose seven business and civic leaders), and a School Finance Authority (made up of business leaders) gained oversight of the school district central office and the Board (Bryk, Sebring, Kerbow, Rollow, & Easton, 1998; G. A. Hess, 1991; Katz, Fine, & Simon, 1997; Kyle & Kantowicz, 1992).

The 1988 reform reflected the relative strength of organized groups in civil society and their proactive response to the longstanding failure of the state to improve education. Washington's election in 1983 and reelection in 1987 as the first Black mayor of Chicago demonstrated not only the power of an organized Black electorate but the strength of a coalition of African Americans, Latino/as, and progressive Whites as a social force in the city. The 1988 reform was, in many ways, a culmination of African American parents, students, and teachers' mass movements for quality education in the 1960s (see Danns, 2002) and Latino/a struggles for equitable and bilingual education in the 1970s into the 1980s (Kyle & Kantowicz, 1992), and they were the backbone of community and parent groups that led the reform.

They formed a tactical alliance with business interests concerned about the city's economic competitiveness. Although parent and community groups,[10] with support from Washington, were a key force (Kyle & Kantowicz, 1992), the 1988 law was the product of a pragmatic alliance which included the Commercial Club of Chicago, school reform groups, and Republican legislators from rural districts. Corporate leaders saw LSCs as a form of site-based management aligned with new business management strategies. The law also increased corporate influence through the mayor's appointees and the School Finance Authority (Shipps, Kahne, & Smylie, 1999). School reformers hoped LSCs would unleash innovations in curriculum and instruction. Grassroots community activists and parents saw LSCs as a way for African American, Latino/a, and low-income parents to have a real say about their schools in a system plagued with endemic racism and persistent failure to educate their children (Kyle & Kantowitz, 1992; Orfield, 1990).

The 1988 reform energized broad grassroots participation in school reform, especially in the early years (*Catalyst*, 1990, 1991; Katz et al., 1997). Although LSCs institutionalized significant power for parents and community members in local schools, from the beginning they lacked the resources to truly improve schools that had historically been underresourced and underserved. The 1988 reform essentially devolved responsibility without sufficient funds and support for LSC members to fully develop the knowledge and skills they needed, and what supports were put in place have been steadily eroded. For example, in 2008, CPS assigned just seven people to support the hundreds of LSCs across the city (Field notes, LSC Summit, August 2008). Some argue the 1988 law also diminished the collective political power of parents and community members vis-à-vis the central administration by decentralizing community voices (Shipps, 1997). However, LSCs are a potent vehicle for local communities to contend for a share of city resources shape their schools, and to organize politically around other issues, including opposition to Daley's downtown development and displacement of working class people. LSCs continue although they have been overall weakened by each of the subsequent reforms, as I explain below.

The 1995 Reform: Accountability and Differentiated Schooling

The 1995 school reform grew out of a changing urban economy and shift in the relation of social forces. By 1995, the insurgent grassroots movement that put Washington in the mayor's office was divided and weakened. Richard M. Daley, who was elected mayor in 1989, was fully aligned with the Commercial Club's global competitiveness agenda. A key component was reforming public education.

Daley and corporate leaders were impatient with the pace of school reform, CPS's fiscal instability, and ongoing contention with the Chicago Teachers' Union (CTU) (Shipps, 1997). This time they took charge. Their agenda coincided with the desire of a new Republican majority in the state legislature to weaken the CTU. The state legislature put the mayor in control of the schools, with full authority to appoint the school board and CEO (replacing the superintendent). CPS has the largest budget and the most employees of any public agency in the state, and mayoral control supplied Daley with a huge source of funds with which to allocate contracts and gain leverage over labor. But most important, public education was an arena to institute policies supportive of his larger urban agenda.

The Daley-appointed school board was composed of banking and corporate leaders and headed up by Daley's Chief of Staff. Daley appointed Paul Vallas, his budget director, as CEO. Thus began a corporate regime at CPS which has been copied in cities across the country. Vallas launched a system of top-down accountability, based on standardized tests, put hundreds of schools on probation under central office oversight, and retained in grade thousands of students who did not meet test score benchmarks. He also further differentiated and stratified schooling by creating new selective enrollment magnet schools in gentrifying and wealthy areas, and military, scripted instruction, and basic education high schools (for students who failed standardized tests), all in African American and Latino/a low-income neighborhoods (Lipman, 2004). Despite some public opposition,[11] Vallas won praise for balancing the district's budget and for his tough, results-oriented style. He used his public relations savvy to roll out a "good-news media campaign" to bolster support for his policies (Shipps, 2006), but his accountability regime also resonated with some parents fed up with schools that were not educating their children. *Crain's Chicago Business* voiced its approval by naming him Executive of the Year in 1998. In a move that was as symbolic as instrumental, CPS moved its headquarters from the South Side to a renovated space downtown, near City Hall.

The 1995 reform spawned a revolving door of top-down accountability-driven interventions, including centrally mandated and directed programs, staff development, curriculum, pedagogy, budgetary and administrative decisions, and teacher monitoring. As I have written elsewhere, although these interventions produced more cohesive curricula and academic standards in some schools, overall they had deleterious consequences. They encouraged test-driven teaching, undermined culturally relevant and critical pedagogy, and demoralized teachers (Lipman, 2004). In the district as a whole, there were gains in test scores (Rosenkrantz, 2002), although these were questionable since the district changed tests and the state lowered benchmarks. (Chicago's scores on the National Assessment of Educational Progress, the "gold standard" of national tests, have improved only slightly and in some cases remained essentially flat, NAEP, 2003–2009.) In spring 2001, Vallas and Chico resigned and Daley appointed the Vice President of AT&T and real estate developer, Michael Scott, Board President and Arne Duncan, Vallas's Deputy Chief of Staff, as CEO. Duncan continued the Vallas program. But in 2004, accountability was overlaid with a major plan to close schools and expand charter schools, a market plan that would be a model for the Obama administration's urban education agenda.

Renaissance 2010

The failure of CPS to dramatically improve its performance on standardized tests and the punishing years of school probation and high stakes top-down accountability left many communities fed up. Charter schools were proliferating around the country and market ideologies had taken hold in education. Punitive consequences of repeated failure to meet adequate yearly progress benchmarks under No Child Left Behind (NCLB) loomed. A school district in danger of state receivership or restructuring under NCLB would undermine the city's bond ratings. For those entrenched in neoliberal market logics, the time was ripe to reshape public education in Chicago.

In June 2003, the Commercial Club's Civic Committee issued, *Left Behind*, a report that called for closing "failing" public schools and opening at least

100 new charter schools to "increase parental choice" and put "competitive pressure" on chronically failing neighborhood schools. Bemoaning Chicago's slow progress in raising test scores, the report echoed neoliberal theorist Milton Freedman's (1962) claim that school improvement is stymied because public schools are a monopoly. The Club's solution was to inject competition through the market. They also blamed LSCs and the teacher's union for obstructing reform.

On June 24, 2004, at an event hosted by the Commercial Club, Mayor Daley announced *Renaissance 2010* (Ren2010). The plan called for closing 60 to 70 public schools and opening 100 new schools by 2010, two-thirds to be charter or contract schools (similar to charters) publicly funded but privately operated by outside vendors with nonunion teachers and without mandatory LSCs. In *Left Behind* and in CPS Ren2010 press releases and public statements, flexibility and innovation are linked to removing obstacles in union contracts and limiting LSCs.[12] As of 2009, the plan was running ahead of schedule with 59 schools closed, consolidated, or phased out and 92 new schools opened (including 46 charter schools, 15 contract schools, and 31 performance schools). There are also six military schools, one for every branch of the armed services. This is the first stage of an overhaul of a large part of the school system citywide (Bluestein, 2005). In 2008, CPS began talking about expanding to "Renaissance 2015."

But the plan has been beset with contradictions and contention. CPS has been forced to continually defend and rework the plan in response to public criticism, community and teacher resistance, and the negative consequences of the policy. In 2009 the CCC issued a scathing follow-up report, *Still Left Behind* (Civic Committee), which debunked CPS's claims of rising test scores. The report called on CPS to step up the pace of replacing public schools with charter schools and revealed cracks and friction in the state–corporate coalition behind Ren2010.

In the next section, I briefly summarize another central initiative, the destruction and marketization of public housing in Chicago. The overlap of this policy with Ren2010 suggests the strategic role of education in making the built environment more attractive to real estate capital.

Neoliberal Housing Policy: The Plan for Transformation

In 2000, Chicago launched a $1.6 billion transformation of public housing—the Plan for Transformation (PFT). One of the most extensive revamps of public housing in the United States, the PFT has nearly completed demolition of 22,000 units of high-rise public housing, including all the remaining "family" units of three, four, and five bedrooms. On paper, the units are to be renovated or replaced, but, as I discuss in chapters 3 and 4, many are being rebuilt as mixed-income developments with a far smaller number of units reserved for public housing tenants than the original complexes (Bennett, Smith, & Wright, 2006). The PFT is a local implementation of the federal 1992 Housing Opportunities for People Everywhere Act (HOPE VI). HOPE VI devolved federal responsibility for public housing to local authorities and replaced government housing provision with privatized management of public units. The Act calls for revitalizing or demolishing "distressed" units and relocating public housing residents in scattered site housing or giving them vouchers in the private housing market, and developing mixed-income developments through public–private partnerships. A key revision in 1995 eliminated the requirement of one-to-one replacement, meaning displaced residents are not guaranteed return to new or rehabbed units. Public housing is one of the few remaining obstacles to gentrification, and this revision eliminated a significant barrier to opening up public housing sites to large-scale private market-rate development (Hackworth, 2007).

The national impact of Chicago's PFT was summed up by the MacArthur Foundation, which provided $50 million in support, including loan guarantees for investors: "Chicago … has the potential to demonstrate, at scale, the impact of mixed-income housing on neighborhood revitalization" (MacArthur, 2005). Viewed through the lens of neoliberal urbanism, the PFT is part of a development agenda which merges local, national, and transnational capital, in partnership with city government. In the following chapters I examine the interrelationship of housing and education policy, as illustrated by HOPE VI and Ren2010 in Chicago. Table 2.1 presents a chronology of their overlapping implementation.

Table 2.1 Chronology of Housing and School Transformation in Chicago

	Housing Policy/action	School Policy/action
1992	HOPE VI	
1995	HOPE VI Rescissions Act: eliminate 1-1 replacement	Mayoral takeover of CPS
1997		High stakes testing and accountability policies instituted
1998	HOPE VI Quality Housing and Work Responsibility Act: work and background checks	
2000	CHA Plan for Transformation launched demolition of public housing	
2003		Commercial Club of Chicago proposes school transformation
2004		Renaissance 2010 launched
2004–2009	Plan for Transformation continues	CPS Closes/ opens schools annually

Looking Ahead: The Intersection of Housing and Education Policies

Chicago's aggressive support for capital accumulation and corporate involvement in city decision making extends to incentives to developers and corporate and financial interests, public–private partnerships, the city's bid for the 2016 Olympics, efforts to control labor, and privatization of public assets. If downtown development and gentrification are the "icons of the neoliberal city" (Hackworth, 2007, p. 78), Chicago epitomizes this agenda.

In the following two chapters I argue that housing and education policy are intertwined in neoliberal urban restructuring. I argue that education policy is both driven by, and helps shape, gentrification and the regulation and displacement of low-income communities of color. Education is integral to housing markets and cultural representations of the city, which are used to market it to mobile capital and labor (Greenberg, 2000). The next chapter examines Ren2010 more deeply as an illustration of the relationship of closing schools to the displacement and disempowerment of low-income communities of color and the spatial restructuring of the city. It reveals how mayoral control of schools can facilitate bending education policy to neoliberal urban and education agendas.

3

DISMANTLING PUBLIC SCHOOLS, DISPLACING AFRICAN AMERICANS AND LATINO/AS

Secretary of Education, Arne Duncan: I think it's a real new day in Detroit. There's a governor who cares and is passionate, a brand new mayor who's willing to take this over and stand up and be held accountable. We want to do everything we can to be a good partner. [But] marginal gains are not what we need. We need an absolutely fundamental overhaul, radical new thinking, open to ideas that are controversial and hard and tough. If there's the political courage to challenge the status quo, not only are there stimulus dollars, but we have competitive (federal) grants…. But the city has to be willing to do some things very, very differently.

Reporter: Can you give an example?

Duncan: I'm a big believer in choice and competition. You need to have strong charter schools with real accountability. You need to be willing to turn around schools that have chronically failed. By that I mean, move adults out, move in new teams to work with those children.

(Duncan, 2009b)

In this chapter I begin with a discussion of the privatization of urban public schools in post-Katrina New Orleans. Then I focus on Chicago's Renaissance 2010 (Ren2010), which has become another model for market-driven urban school reform in the United States. Ren2010 is a powerful illustration of the intersection of neoliberal urban governance and education policy. I argue that education policy is implicated in the political economic processes that produce gentrification and displacement of mostly low-income communities of color. Like the marketization of public housing, education markets contribute to restructuring of urban space. My analysis points to the centrality of race in the knitting together of education policy and neoliberal urban development. Throughout, I try to capture the dialectic of a centralized policy confronted by popular resistance. In chapter 6, I also look at why these policies have resonance with some parents and teachers fed up with the persistent problems of urban public schools and how market ideologies are materialized through their responses.

Urban Schools: A Laboratory for Neoliberal Restructuring

A Nation at Risk (1983), released in the early years of the Reagan administration, was the opening salvo of the neoliberal education agenda. This report and the spate of subsequent reports sponsored by business organizations and corporate think tanks shifted education discourse toward U.S. economic competitiveness and "human capital development" (Berliner & Biddle, 1997). Thus unfolded two decades of restructuring public education through new forms of top-down, punitive accountability and prescriptive standards, increased business involvement, and school leadership redefined as (corporate) managerialism. Systems of centralized accountability based on high stakes tests were tested and elaborated through the Texas Achievement Assessment System in the 1990s (McNeil, 2000) and Chicago's 1995 accountability policies (Lipman, 2004), culminating in the federal No Child Left Behind (NCLB) law of 2002. The predictable failure of school districts to meet NCLB targets set the stage for corporate and state actors to move the discourse of education markets from a side role in urban education to the main event.

Policy makers justify these moves by a narrative of unaccountable teachers and schools and unresponsive and change-resistant public institutions. There is a lot of truth to this account for some parents and community advocates who have been fighting persistent battles to get real change in their public schools (Pedroni, 2007).

Ameliorative reforms of the 1960s and 1970s, made as concessions to the powerful social movements of the time, had some positive impact on educational equity. But too often they were weak renditions of original demands; for example, transitional bilingual education programs that were underfunded and understaffed and more assimilative than affirmative. Worse, compensatory programs directed to low-income students of color were often predicated on a deficit model and designed by those outside the community, enacting a colonial framework of "we know what is best for you" (King, 2005b). Nor did social welfare programs, such as the War on Poverty, substantially address the education debt (Ladson-Billings, 2005) owed African American and other oppressed communities for generations of compounded inequalities and educational injustices and disrespect. Abysmally low graduation rates, inequitable education opportunities, and the school-to-prison pipeline have persisted.

Sandwiched between the push for market-based accountability, on the one hand, and the problems and exclusions of public education, on the other, this binary obscures root causes of the problem. While disaggregated achievement data (e.g., No Child Left Behind) make transparent who is succeeding academically, even on narrow measures, the accountability discourse obscures the underlying structural and ideological roots of the disparities in urban public schools: grossly inequitable allocation of resources, Eurocentric and racist curricula, racial segregation, criminalization, lack of space for genuine participation of communities most affected, and cultural marginalization and psychic assault on working class students of color. Moreover, it glosses over the failure of public policy to address poverty and racial inequality and decades of disinvestment in physical, economic, and social infrastructure in areas of the city where African Americans and other people of color live (Anyon, 2005; King, 2005a). This clearly calls for a new vision of the public, a new "social imaginary" that offers new possibilities for a democratic, inclusive, equitable, and just public education. I take up this theme in the concluding chapter, but here I want to examine the market-driven response.

The logics of global economic competition, choice, and markets and the conversion of small school and charter school movements into instruments of the market are rapidly changing the face of urban school districts (Apple, 2006; Ball, 2007; Saltman, 2007). Urban schools are wound up in privatization, public–private partnerships, demands for union "flexibility," teacher merit pay schemes, and mayoral takeovers, along with high stakes testing and restricted democracy. Mayoral control, appointed school boards, corporate CEOs running urban school districts, direct involvement of corporate actors and corporate philanthropies dictating school district policies—these are the features of neoliberal governance dominating urban school districts. There are also new forms of racial containment and regulation of students of color (public military schools, strict discipline schools, zero tolerance discipline policies) alongside commodification of "diversity" for urban place marketing (e.g., selective public schools with a focus on "world language" or "global studies").

The laboratories for this agenda have been several large urban school districts where disinvestment and persistent racial gaps in educational achievement and graduation rates provide a warrant for a radical shift in the governing and provision of education. New York, Chicago, and New Orleans have all boldly experimented with neoliberal governance and markets. Chicago has been in the forefront with its high stakes accountability policies followed by Renaissance 2010 school closings and charter school expansion. Mayoral control is a critical tool to restructure school systems from the top with minimal public "interference." New York's Mayor Bloomberg used mayoral control to institute corporate management practices in the city's public school system (Traver, 2006). The devastation of Hurricane Katrina and the forced exodus of much of New Orleans' working class Black population opened an opportunity to reconstruct the city's school system across the board along neoliberal principles, from the top. In the face of the effects of the current economic crisis on cities, the stipulations of U.S. government economic stimulus funds for education are pressing Detroit, Philadelphia, Los Angeles, and other urban school districts to follow suit. In both New Orleans and Chicago, the neoliberal education policy complex converges with, extends, even leads neoliberal urban restructuring in a nexus of privatization of public goods, constriction of democracy, corporate domination, public–private partnerships, gentrification, and governance by unelected semipublic bodies. In both cities, structural and ideological racism are integral to this project. In the following sections of this chapter I examine this process and draw out its national implications.

New Orleans: Feasting on Disaster[1]

> Don't come back to new Orleans if you don't intend to fight! The only way that we are going to be able to come back is to fight for justice every step of the way!
>
> (Organizer Endesha Jukali in direct action to open up the St. Bernard Housing Development in New Orleans for its residents in April 2006, quoted in Quigley, 2006)

Nowhere has rollback and rollout neoliberalism been accomplished with such a single powerful blow as in hurricane-devastated New Orleans. In the words of George Lipsitz (2006b), the aftermath of the hurricane ushered in an orgy of "legalized looting to enable corporations to profit from the misfortunes of poor people. Just as he did with the occupation of Iraq, Bush viewed the emergency in New Orleans as an excuse for an exercise in social engineering and an opportunity to implement the free market fundamentalism that is not yet politically palatable in the rest of the country" (p. 452). Rollback neoliberalism and over a century of White supremacist public policy ripened up the city for corporate takeover and the purge of working class African Americans. Before Hurricane Katrina, one-third of the population lived below the poverty line; 80% of them were African American. More than half of the Black households in the city did not have a car. And the Bush administration slashed the U.S. Army Corps of Engineers' New Orleans District budget for shoring up levees by 44% in line with overall government cuts for public services (M. Parenti, 2005). The result? At least 1,282 Louisiana residents died as a result of the hurricane and failed evacuation, and 8 months after it struck 987 people were still missing (Quigley, 2006).

This set the stage for the crimes committed in New Orleans *since the hurricane,* animated by twin logics of capital accumulation and White supremacy. Immediately following the disaster, the Bush administration declared the entire Gulf Coast a taxpayer subsidized "enterprise zone" (Lipsitz, 2006b), meaning it suspended the Davis Bacon Act requiring contractors to pay prevailing wages for the cleanup, doled out billions of dollars in no-bid contracts, and eliminated federal fuel pollution standards in the area. The entire city was put under military control, including by the notorious for-hire Blackwater security forces used in Iraq. The mayor appointed an official commission to oversee rebuilding, headed by venture capitalist Joseph C. Canizaro who hailed the hurricane disaster as an "opportunity" to rebuild the city on new terms (Rivlin, 2005). Thus began quick restoration of the tourist sectors and middle class areas, and privatization of public services. Through an ensemble of strategic policies and deliberate government inaction, New Orleans officials promoted state-led gentrification of poor Black areas. Low-income evacuees were dispersed across the country, often separated from their families or warehoused in toxic trailers while their homes in the lower ninth ward and other historic African American working class areas were left to decay with no help for rebuilding. And despite militant and sustained resident protests, the state locked up and then seized undamaged public housing for new market rate development.

If New Orleans was open territory for "legalized corporate looting," education was at the leading edge. Just weeks after the hurricane the state of Louisiana took over 100 public schools and began a process of turning over millions of dollars of taxpayer money to private organizations to run them. The state fired all 4,500 public school teachers, broke the city's powerful Black-led teachers' union, and dismantled the school system's administrative infrastructure (Dingerson, 2008; Saltman, 2007). Right wing foundations quickly issued reports calling for vouchers and President Bush proposed $1.9 billion for K-12 students with $488 million targeted for national vouchers (to be used in schools anywhere). An influential report by the Urban Institute (Hill & Hannaway, 2006), hailed New Orleans as an opportunity for a grand experiment to decentralize and privatize the school system through vouchers and charter schools. Less than a month after the hurricane devastated the city, the U.S. Department of Education gave the state of Louisiana $20.9 million to reopen existing charter schools and open new ones, and 9 months later the department gave the state an additional $23.9 million for new charter schools, most in New Orleans. Prior to Katrina, there were only five charter schools in the city. Of the 55 schools opened in New Orleans in 2006–2007, 31 were public charter schools (Alexander, 2007). Before Katrina hit in August 2005, there were 63,000 students in New Orleans public schools; about 24,000 began classes there in the fall of 2008 (Dingerson, 2008). All this was done by fiat by the governor, guided by think tanks such as the Urban Institute and backed by corporate foundations such as the Gates Foundation. Excluded were the voices of working class African American and Latino/a parents, students, teachers, and community members, many of whom had been literally excluded from the city itself by redevelopment policies that made it impossible to return (Buras et al., 2010).

It would be hard to deny that New Orleans' schools were in desperate need of resources and transformation before the hurricane. In 1997, per pupil school funding was 16% lower than the average of poorly funded urban districts nationally (Saltman, 2007, p. 22). This reflects the long term pattern of disinvestment in inner city areas and its intensification due to federal funding cuts in the 1980s and urban entrepreneurism that followed. But, as in other cities, there were also strengths to build upon—schools that were responsive to children's cultures and identities, that were a core of their communities, and that spoke to aspirations for a more equitable and just future (Buras et al., 2010). The disaster might have been an occasion for a creative, democratic process of reinvigorating public education. Instead, the state at all levels, in alliance with local and national corporate interests and think tanks took advantage of the chaos wreaked by Katrina and the exodus of low-income working class African Americans from the city to dismantle public schools. This was a strategic move to exclude poor people from the city altogether because they not only had no homes to return to, they had no schools. The goal was a Whiter, more middle class, more capital and developer friendly New Orleans minus its historic Black working class and other low-income communities of color and their persistent struggle for dignity and self-determination (Buras, 2007; Lipsitz, 2006b). This was made plain by Orleans Parish School Board Member Jimmy Fahrenholtz: "I wanted to tear this system apart two years ago," but with Katrina, "A lot of our bad employees won't come back. A lot of our bad citizens won't come back.... This can be a turning point.... We can change the whole face of this city if we do it correctly" (quoted in Gray, 2005).

New Orleans is an extreme case of the coordination of education, housing, and urban development policy to "make the built environment more flexible and responsive to the investment criteria of real estate capital" (Weber, 2002, p.173). It makes clear the intersecting logics of capital and race at the heart of the neoliberal urban agenda in the United States. George Lipsitz (2006b) captures the dynamic intersection of capital accumulation and the dispossession of African Americans (and other people of color):

> The desires of the rich in respect to the rebuilding of New Orleans found direct expression in the words of Alphonso Jackson, George Bush's Secretary of Housing and Urban Development and one of those Black conservatives who usually claims that discrimination has ended and that the time for color blind policies has begun. Yet Jackson's approach to New Orleans was expressly color conscious. "New Orleans is not going to be as black as it was for a long time, if ever again," Jackson predicted. "I'm telling you, as HUD Secretary and having been a developer and a planner, that's how it's going to be" (Rodriguez & Minaya, 2005). Jackson did not specify exactly which principles of planning and development require the removal of Black people from cities where they are the majority of the population.

(p. 453)

Chicago's Renaissance 2010: Contested Policy

The Carpenter school community crowded the lobby of Chicago Public School Headquarters waiting for the chance to respond to the district's recommendations to phase out our school. The hearing taking place just before Carpenter's was for nearby Peabody Elementary, another neighborhood school in West Town slated for closing. As parents, teachers, and community members from Peabody descended in the elevators from the 5th floor chambers, they were met with applause and cheers of encouragement. "Go Peabody!" "We support you!" Peabody parents responded in turn, "Go Carpenter!" "Speak from the heart!" And speak from the heart we did: parents and grandparents, students and teachers, administrators and community members; in English and in Spanish, with the support of translators and sign language interpreters; some in small courageous voices and others in louder and more desperate tones. Carpenter packed the public seating area of the chambers, opposite the conspicuous, empty chairs reserved for [unelected] CPS board members. Still we persisted for hours into the night, filing in turn to the podium, many in the company of entire families, with one singular message: Please save our school.

(Fleming et al., 2009)

Mayor Daley and Arne Duncan, CEO of CPS, promoted Ren2010 as a market solution for failing schools and a way to develop mixed-income schools in mixed-income communities. As I outlined in the last chapter, the Ren2010 plan proposed to close at least 60 Chicago public schools and open 100 new schools, one-third charter, one-third contract (privately run schools that operate much like charter schools),[2] and one-third CPS "Performance Schools" (public schools with 5-year performance contracts and subject to Ren2010 policies). But the plan was beset with contradictions and conflict from the beginning and over the years the Board has had to continually reconstruct its agenda, modifying and mutating its provisions. Ren2010 began with an educational rationale for closing "failing schools." But forced to react to community protest and negative publicity about the spikes in violence and student mobility that accompanied closing schools and transferring students to schools across neighborhoods and gang lines, in 2006, CPS added the school "turnaround" strategy. Modeled on business turnarounds, the students stay in the school but CPS fires all adults and turns the management of the school over to an outside "turnaround specialist" that hires new staff, installs its own program, and runs the school. Ren2010 was also extended to consolidate and phase out low-enrollment schools, including very successful neighborhood schools, on the grounds of improving "efficiency" and "cost effectiveness." This also shifted the Ren2010 discourse to a purely technical one of "enrollment to capacity ratios."

Swirling at the surface of public contention, private conversations, and media accounts have been issues of educational equity, class inequalities in the city, race, gentrification, democratic community participation, student safety, individual choice, and the role of teacher unions. On the one side, CPS leaders, the mayor, and the Commercial Club contend Ren2010 creates "options" and "choice," promotes innovation, and raises achievement. As Ren2010 got underway, Board President and developer Michael Scott said, "We can't wait to rescue these schools from an educational wasteland" (Field notes, Board of Education meeting, September 22, 2004). Defending against community claims that Ren2010 is tied to real estate development and displacement of low-income African Americans, the CPS Senior Policy Advisor for Ren2010 in 2004 insisted "it has nothing to do with gentrification" (Field notes, Community Hearing, North Lawndale, November 15, 2004). On the other hand, opposed parents, students, teachers, and community residents claim the plan accelerates gentrification, destabilizes African American and Latino/a schools and communities, harms low-income children of color and homeless children in particular, eliminates local democracy, weakens unions, and privatizes schools. They are particularly insistent that Ren2010 was devised and continues to be implemented without community participation (Midsouth Fact Sheet, n.d.; Chicagoans United for Education press conference, July 1, 2004). Yet there were, and are, other parents and teachers who, in a context of desperately needed change defend the plan or are not so sure.

"Set Up for Failure": Accountability without Resources

Chicago is an advanced example of the relationship of high stakes accountability and education markets (Karp, 2002). The stage for Ren2010 was set by an accountability regime that normalized labeling, sorting, and classifying schools, and meting out penalties without regard for inequities in resources, opportunity to learn, teachers' ideologies, cultural marginalization in curriculum and instruction, the social context of the school, or the strengths children bring to the school setting.[3] Labeling and sorting schools was a necessary condition to identify those to be closed under Ren2010, to turn them over to private operators, and more recently to use their students' test scores to evaluate teachers. Under NCLB this ranking and sorting process lays the groundwork for a national privatization agenda.

But the "failure" of Chicago schools, even on narrow measures of standardized tests, is a product of the education debt owed the schools and their communities. High stakes accountability, has, in many cases, compounded that debt with a revolving door of mandated programs and punitive interventions that narrow the curriculum to test preparation and produce an exodus of some of the strongest teachers (Lipman, 2004; Valenzuela, 2005; Valli & Buesi, 2007). At the same time, teachers and community members point out that the schools have not been given the resources to succeed. Parents and educators in Chicago's Midsouth area where 20 of 22 schools were initially set to be closed, said they were "set up for failure" (Lipman, Person, & KOCO, 2007). A community leader testifying before the Board of Education in 2004 said, "You can't separate the failure in these schools from what's been done to them by CPS" (School Board meeting, September 22, 2004).

At nearly every school board meeting parents and teachers come to complain about the urgent need for repairs to broken and outmoded heating systems, windows, plumbing, roofs, elevators and more. Some schools lack up-to-date technology and science labs and some are dramatically overcrowded with up to three shifts in high schools, over 40 students in a class, and classes held in cafeterias. In Fall 2010, parents in the Mexican community of Pilson staged a 43 day sit in to win a school library. During the sit in, CPS revealed that 160 other elementary schools do not have libraries. Teachers and administrators in some schools report that over the past few years they have had cuts in support staff even while receiving displaced students from closed schools.

Booker elementary school (a pseudonym) is an example. In February 2005, CPS announced it was closing Booker as a failing school under Ren2010, despite community protest that children as young as 5 years old would have to walk over a mile to the designated transfer school. According to teachers, in 2000 the school struggled without books and supplies that had been destroyed in the chaos of building renovations. Over 5 years, the school was sent a string of probation partners, and when Booker was finally assigned an effective principal, she was sent to the school on one day's notice. Until 2001, some students had books so old they had their parents' names in them, but when the school finally got new textbooks with a new curriculum, teachers received little or no professional development. From 2001 on, the school experienced a very high turnover of staff (Points, 2005; teacher interview, September 2005) coupled with a very high student mobility rate. The "failure" of this school and others like it in Chicago and across the United States cannot be disentangled from these conditions or from the instability and economic impoverishment and public disinvestment visited on working class communities, especially communities of color. The disinvestment in schools is integral to disinvestment in African American and Latino/a neighborhoods (Kozol, 1992; Orfield, 1990).

Closing Public Schools, Harming African American and Latino/a Students

Negative consequences of Ren2010 should be instructive for other cities. In 2009 there were 92 Ren2010 schools, and over three-fourths of those that were nonselective were charter or contract schools (some multiple franchises of charter school chains), with the remainder selective enrollment or military schools.[4] In short very few neighborhood public schools have been created through Ren2010. Charter, contract, and military schools are concentrated in low-income communities of color while several neighborhood schools in gentrifying areas were turned into selective enrollment schools that largely exclude neighborhood children.

Across African American communities, schools have been closed for low achievement even when lower performing schools in other neighborhoods were not. Others, particularly in Latino/a communities, have been closed for low enrollment despite evidence to the contrary (see Fleming et al., 2009; Greenlee et al., 2008). These closings eliminate schools that are anchors in their communities. In some neighborhoods, charter schools recruit students from public schools, reducing their enrollment and siphoning off their funds, forcing cuts in staff, and potentially setting them up to be closed (personal communication of teachers and community organizers, 2008, 2009, 2010). School closings have resulted in increased mobility and greater neighborhood instability as children are transferred out of their neighborhoods, with elementary children forced to cross dangerous intersections and high school students forced to cross gang lines (Lipman, Person, & KOCO, 2007). This is a consistent theme in parent protests:

> Why should our children have to go out of their community? They have to cross heavy traffic and there is no safe way to go. Also, bullets have no names. Who is to say our children are safe coming and going? Head start kids? Kindergarten kids? In the winter, in below-zero temperatures? So where does justice come in? This is why we're protesting, doing all this walking, candlelight vigils. They [CPS] don't want to take responsibility. But we do. We care for our children.
>
> (quoted in Fleming et al., 2009, p. 23)

The student mobility and danger produced by closing schools and transferring students have been devastating. Some students in the Midsouth area were transferred to as many as four schools in 3 years as one school after another was closed, and receiving schools were destabilized by the influx of dislocated students (Lipman, Person, & KOCO, 2007). There were spikes in violence in high schools and some elementary schools. This was in the context of rising discipline incidents citywide from 5,762 in 2006–2007, to 12,058 in 2007–2008, to 15,094 in 2008–2009 (Karp, 2009). Yet CPS consistently failed to heed the warnings of parents and community members who predicted the closings would be a hazard for their children.

Moreover, in general, Ren2010 has not improved students' educational opportunities. Most displaced students from public housing units were reassigned to schools academically and demographically similar to those they left, with 84% attending schools with below the average district test scores and 44% in schools on probation for low test scores (*Catalyst Chicago*, 2007).

Displaced elementary students in general transferred from one low-performing school to another with virtually no effect on student achievement (Gwynne & de la Torre, 2009).[5] Because most of the closed schools have been in African American communities where there are heaviest concentrations of African American educators, these teachers have been particularly affected. According to the Caucus of Rank and File Educators, more than 2,000 African American teachers and over 100 principals and administrators lost their jobs (Schmidt, 2009).

Schools are also far more complicated than test scores. Certainly, there are schools that need urgent and radical action. Yet, school staff and parents in closed schools or those in jeopardy of being closed narrate a history of disinvestment, including reduction of support staff, poor facilities, and lack of up-to-date technology and science labs, failure of CPS to make building repairs, an influx of displaced students from closed schools, and so on (Lipman, Person, & KOCO, 2007). Some schools had taken new initiatives and showed steady improvement on the Board's measures only to be closed anyway. Others were centers of stability and support in neighborhoods destabilized by gentrification, home foreclosures, poverty, and disinvestment (Fleming et al., 2009). In some cases, parents, grandparents, aunts, and uncles of current students had attended the school. The narratives suggest a strategic process of devalorizing public schools in specific communities, contradicting the supposed neutrality of the "market" and its putative superiority to the public sector.

These are reasons why the policy has provoked public controversy and community resistance not seen in relation to Chicago school policy in nearly two decades. Ren2010 is a major topic at almost every Board of Education meeting. Each year, parents and children, mostly African American and Latino/a, and their teachers fill buses, compile elaborate binders documenting their school's actual enrollment and achievement, and pack the Board of Education chambers to argue that their school should not be closed. Parents, teachers, and children who have never before engaged in any sort of protest emerge as grassroots community organizers, speakers, and leaders. In January and February 2009, a grassroots coalition of parents, teachers, and community organizations led two large marches through downtown Chicago, picketed, and held neighborhood candlelight vigils, community meetings, and press conferences, and camped out in subfreezing weather in front of the Board of Education to dramatize their opposition to Ren2010. Yet their victory was modest; they were able to prevent the Board's proposed closing of 6 of 22 schools.

However, as research has begun to unravel some of CPS's claims about Ren2010's success (Gwynne & de la Torre, 2009) and the effectiveness and equity of charter schools (Frankenberg, Siegel-Hawley, & Wang, 2010; Center for Research on Education Outcomes, 2009), and as the counternarrative of Chicago parents and teachers has circulated nationally (e.g., Brown, Gutstein,

& Lipman, 2009), the contradictions of the policy and years of sustained community opposition have opened cracks in the dominant discourse. In July 2010, a policy framework proposed by seven national civil rights organizations (Civil Rights Framework, 2010), followed with a report by a national coalition of 18 community organizations (Communities for Excellent Public Schools, 2010), signaled a challenge to NCLB and the privatization agenda. In proposing their own framework for reauthorization of the Elementary and Secondary Education Act, the civil rights groups shifted the discourse from markets, high stakes standardized tests, and measurement of outcomes to input of equitable resources ("common resource opportunity standards") and from imposed school closings to community engagement in school reform. And, reclaiming the discourse of change, the coalition of community organizations announced, "The question is not whether to intervene in our schools, but rather, what interventions offer the best promise for successful and sustainable school transformation?" Repositioning community as collective actors, the report rejects the turnaround strategy and proposes school transformation based on community participation. Two days later, President Obama responded by resorting to the trope that those who opposed his agenda were "resistant" to "change" (Obama, 2010). A month earlier, the Chicago Teachers Union elected a progressive leadership on a platform of vigorous opposition to education privatization, turnarounds, school closings, top-down accountability, and high stakes testing. The election of this barely 2-year old caucus is an indication of the disaffection of Chicago teachers with the CPS agenda.

Renaissance 2010 and Neoliberal Urbanism

Notes from the 80th floor:

> The Commercial Club of Chicago Renaissance Schools Fund Symposium: "Free to Choose, Free to Succeed: The New Market of Public Education," May 5, 2008. The Symposium is in the MidAmerica Club on the 80th floor of the AON building, a corporate fortress jutting out into Lake Michigan in downtown Chicago. It is a clear day and I can see the entire lake shoreline south to Indiana. From the commanding heights of this exclusive corporate club where global financial deals are struck and high level public–private partnerships are forged, people on the street below look like ants. The lavish chandeliered conference room is packed with CEOs, CPS officials, charter school operators, representatives of national and statewide charter school associations, school officials from various cities, program officers of national philanthropies, and the press. CEO of CPS, Arne Duncan, welcomes the approximately 300 attendees by heralding "a new day" for education in Chicago. Under Renaissance 2010, CPS is becoming a "portfolio manager of schools."

> (Field notes, May 5, 2008)

Public–Private Partnerships

In the context of reduced federal revenues to cities, capital leverages its financial power to shape urban agendas through public–private partnerships. This is a key aspect of the neoliberalization of cities. These partnerships introduce markets in the funding and delivery of local services and integrate corporate actors in local "regeneration" projects. They create new institutional amalgamations of the state and business to oversee and develop economic and social policy (Jones & Ward, 2002, p. 138).

Public–private partnerships are also a mechanism for capital–state collaboration to reshape the landscape of urban education. An example is the partnership of the School District of Philadelphia and Center City District (CCD), a powerful business improvement district whose board of directors includes major corporate, banking, and investment firms. The CCD's stated mission is to revitalize the Center City area to attract middle and upper income families and increase the city's "economic competitiveness." In 2004, the CCD launched the Center City Schools Initiative to create a separate Center City school choice region within the school district with its own administrative structure. The plan included a new admissions policy that gave families within the region priority, a marketing campaign, improvement of schools to make them more "marketable," and partnerships with museums and other downtown institutions (Gold, Simon, Cucchiara, Mitchell, & Riffer, 2007). Another example, as I discuss in chapter 5, is the role of corporate venture philanthropy in setting urban education agendas by leveraging their funding of "cutting edge" urban initiatives.

The Commercial Club of Chicago's (CCC) collaboration with Chicago Public Schools in the design, implementation, and funding of Ren2010 is a high level public–private partnership to steer education in Chicago. Established in the 1870s to promote the interests of Chicago's corporate elite, the CCC has a long history of influencing the city's education policies (Shipps, 2006; Wrigley, 1982). Over the past 25 years, the CCC has promoted education policies geared to repositioning the city in the changing global economy. The role of education in developing the local workforce to serve "economic competitiveness" is a central concern of the CCC's 1984 long-term strategic plan, *Make No Little Plans: Jobs for Metropolitan Chicago* (Commercial Club, 1984) and its 1998 update, *Metropolis 2020* (E. Johnson, 1998). In its 2003 report, *Left Behind*, the CCC put forward an argument for a radical shift toward education markets. In *Still Left Behind* (2009), which calls for speeding up marketization of public schools, the CCC notes that education has been a "consistent focus" of its Civic Committee. It outlines its central role in the "1988 Chicago School Reform Law, 1995 Chicago School Reform Law (putting the Mayor in charge of the schools), 1996 Quality First (standards and criterion based assessment) and charter schools, 1997 School Reform and Funding, and 2004 CPS's Renaissance 2010" (p. 1).

Since 2003, the CCC has helped frame a discourse that denigrates public schools and promotes markets and choice. In *Left Behind* (Commercial Club of Chicago, Civic Committee/Education Committee, 2003), the CCC argues for opening up public education to a market of education providers, weakening unions, and strengthening centralized management. Echoing neoliberal theorist Milton Friedman (1962), the report argues that the problem with public education is that it is a "monopoly" and "competition—which is the engine of American productivity generally—is the key to improved performance of our public schools" (p. 55). The report goes on to say that although vouchers are the CCC's "preferred" solution, "the political climate in Illinois seems hostile," so the best way to create competition and provide consumer "choice" is to fund charter schools and expand the charter school market. Thus the report calls for "at least 100 charter schools located predominantly in inner-city neighborhoods..." (p. 55). *Still Left Behind* also contends that the reason Chicago school reform hasn't worked is because of "the constraints of the city wide teachers' union contract" (p. 13) and the inefficient meddling of parents and community members through local school councils which make the system "unmanageable" (p. 51). Mayor Daley's announcement of Ren2010, at a CCC event a year later, echoed the CCC's market discourse: "This model will generate competition and allow for innovation. It will bring in outside partners who want to get into the business of education. It offers the opportunity to break the mold. It gives parents more options and will shake up the system" (CPS Press Release, 2004b). This discourse now permeates CPS. At a symposium sponsored by the CCC, the Director of the CPS Office of New Schools claimed, "the monopoly is over." Let "different doorways open into the monopoly" (Field notes, May 6, 2008).

Ren2010 is an aggressive partnership of capital and the state. The CCC's Civic Committee created the Renaissance Schools Fund (RSF) (initially called New Schools for Chicago), to raise $50 million for the project and oversee its direction. The RSF is comprised of a small group of powerful corporate and banking CEOs joined by top CPS officials.[6] The partnership is a funding and policy setting body and concretely oversees implementation. The Chief Operating Officer of the RSF summed up the relationship, noting that the RSF is "engaged at a detailed level" and has a "close working relationship with CPS." "The Renaissance Schools Fund and CPS go through the whole process together" (Field notes, RSF Symposium, May 6, 2008). This unelected body selects and evaluates Ren2010 schools and trains new school operators, while distributing Commercial Club funds to the schools (Cholo, 2005; Rossi, 2004b).

However, the reality of differential funding belies the rhetoric of free markets and open competition. Some Ren2010 schools receive a large infusion of private funds, and the RSF and CPS tout their "success" as evidence that Ren2010 is working and that charter schools are better than public schools (Field notes, May 5, 2005). For example, Legacy Charter School, founded by a leading international corporate law firm in which Don Lubin, Chairman of the Board of RSF, is a partner, received a $1 million cash contribution from the firm in its first year for planning and operating expenses, and continues to receive funds and management support from the firm. This is on top of the public tax dollars it gets from CPS. With these resources Legacy was able to open with twice the ordinary number of teachers for a student–teacher ratio of 12:1, had state of the art resources, and was featured in the media as an example of the benefits of charter schools. On the other hand, Uplift Community School, a CPS public performance school begun by community activists and teachers under the aegis of Ren2010, received no additional funding from the RSF and continually struggles with inadequate resources. A 2010 study of school budgets by *Catalyst*, a Chicago journal that covers school reform, reports differential funding of charter schools vs. public schools (Karp, 2010), effectively devalorizing public schools, creating inequity in the system, and exposing the myth that Ren2010 promotes market "competition" that improves the system overall.

While the CCC seems ideologically committed to markets, Ren2010 is also pragmatic policy. In a worst case situation, failure to make adequate yearly progress on NCLB targets can trigger a state takeover of a school district. This, coupled with Chicago's persistently low graduation rates, could tarnish the city's bond ratings, affect the perceived quality of its workforce, and be a significant barrier in competition for investment. For the CCC, the specter of a state takeover was further justification for school choice and charter schools.[7] *Left Behind* (Commercial Club of Chicago, 2003), argues "NCLB has made the need for choice more transparent" to avert state action (p. 55). Closing schools and reopening them as new schools (primarily charters) restarts the schools' NCLB clock, buying the district time to meet federal benchmarks.

Neoliberals prefer governance by experts and elites (Harvey, 2005). The legitimation of corporate and financial actors to make crucial decisions about public education, without public accountability, is a neoliberal turn that goes beyond private operation of individual schools. It gives capital a direct role in decision making, in collaboration with the state, of institutions of social reproduction. The pivotal role of the RSF coupled with mayoral control of schools epitomizes the institutionalized fusion of corporate and state power in neoliberal governance. Ren2010 installs a body of powerful corporate and financial elites as direct actors in shaping public school policy and its implementation while the state anoints its agenda as public policy and the state's administrative apparatus ensures implementation. This direct intervention of corporate civic federations coupled with mayoral control of schools positions education to play a strategic part in the neoliberalization of the city.

Mayoral Control

Neoliberalism involves governance by appointed boards, "experts," and managers. Mayoral and other forms of state takeover of urban school systems typify the democratic deficits of neoliberal urban governance, allowing the state to fast track neoliberal initiatives without the "interference" of democratic deliberation. For example, the Louisiana governor's takeover of the New Orleans school district after Hurricane Katrina ensured its rapid restructuring. More typically, mayoral control (the mayor appoints the school board and school officials who carry out his or her mandates) is the tool used by the state to usher in neoliberal urban education restructuring. Mayors appoint "CEOs" who are managers not educators (e.g., New York's Joel Klein, a corporate lawyer; Chicago's Paul Vallas, city budget director; Washington, DC's Michelle Rhee, head of New Teacher Project; Chicago's Arne Duncan, Vallas's Deputy Chief of Staff). Mayor-controlled districts contract out schools and educational services to outside operators and providers and look to corporate principal and teacher preparation outfits such as New Leaders for New Schools, Teach for America, New Teacher Project, and the Broad Foundation (Wong, Shen, Anagnostopoulos, & Rutledge, 2007). They leverage public–private partnerships like the RSF and use their authority to force concessions from school employee unions. Notably, there have been no teachers' strikes in mayoral control systems (Wong, 2009). Mayoral control allowed Mayor Daley, to impose Chicago's high stakes accountability and the current policy of markets, choice, and privatization. In sum, mayoral takeover enables entrepreneurial, market-driven, efficiency-oriented, "performance-based" "public management" that characterizes the neoliberal state (Clark & Newman, 1997).

Replacing elected school boards with mayoral control is now a U.S. Department of Education priority. As of 2009, school districts of New York, Chicago, Boston, Cleveland, Washington, DC, Providence, New Haven, and Harrisburg were under the leadership of their mayors, and Baltimore and Philadelphia schools are jointly run by the mayor and governor of the state (Wong, 2009). Recently, mayors and mayoral candidates in Milwaukee, Dallas, Houston, Memphis, Seattle, and St. Paul expressed interest in direct control of their school districts (Wong). In his keynote address to the U.S. Conference of Mayor's National Forum on Education, March 31, 2009, sponsored by the Gates Foundation, U.S. Secretary of Education, Arne Duncan, said, "I fundamentally believe mayors should be in control of their school systems.... At the end of my tenure, if only seven mayors are in control, I think I will have failed" (2009a).

This imperative is backed up by the preference for mayoral control for states to receive "Race to the Top" federal economic stimulus funds for education. Secretary of Education Duncan began pressing this move soon after being appointed U.S. Secretary of Education. In Detroit, he told the news media that the Department of Education was prepared to give Detroit funds to improve its schools but only if the city took radical action led by mayoral takeover (Duncan, 2009b). Citing the need for "bold change" to improve economic competitiveness and narrow achievement gaps, Milwaukee's mayor and the state governor, in a joint statement, called for mayoral control of Milwaukee public schools. They noted that mayoral control is essential to receive federal economic stimulus funds and even other federal funding (Barret/Doyle deposition, 2009). As I write this in the summer of 2010, the push by Detroit's mayor and corporate civic organization is intensely contested. A broad-based teacher–community coalition defeated Milwaukee's attempt. In these and other cities, mayoral control is tied to a package of reforms that includes closing schools, turning schools over to outside operators, union "flexibility," expanding charter schools, and teacher merit pay tied to student test scores.

Chicago is a national model of mayoral control. Decision making virtually by mayoral decree has been fundamental to push through Ren2010. Underlying this strategy is the tight relationship between the mayor and the city's corporate and financial power structure. At the 2008 RSF symposium described above, CPS Director of New Schools explained that Chicago's political stability makes possible:

> a cyclical RFP process that creates certainty in market.... In Chicago we live in an oddly secure environment, in terms of leaders. Mayor Daley is [unchallenged]. Arne Duncan has been CEO for seven years and is appointed by the mayor. We have an appointed [school] Board. They know what they're supposed to do, support Ren2010 and make an entry into the monopoly.
>
> (Field notes, May 5, 2008)

This summarizes how the mayor's direct authority over public education facilitates the power of this governing alliance to push through its agenda in a school district that is 91% students of color and 85% low-income. Harvey (2005) points out that for neoliberals, "Democracy is viewed as a luxury, only possible under conditions of relative affluence coupled with a strong middle-class presence to guarantee political stability" (pp. 66–67). Thus the neoliberal state resorts to various forms of coercion to implement its agenda (Gill, 2003; Wacquant, 2001). Mayoral takeover is a case of the use of the coercive power of the state to enforce a neoliberal program. This is coupled with the institutionalized hollowing out of democracy through performative "public participation."

The Performance of Democracy

"Democracy in Chicago Public Schools: An Act in One Scene"

The scene: 125 S. Clark Street, Chicago Public Schools central office.

The act: It's 6 a.m. on a Wednesday and people are beginning to line up in the lobby to sign in to speak at the monthly school board meeting held during daytime work hours. Sign-in begins at 8 a.m. but you have to be early because only the first 30 to 35 will get to speak. Only one person can speak on an issue so fudging the topic is necessary—"school safety" aka Ren2010 school closings, "local school issue" aka Ren2010 school closings, "Wilson school" aka Ren2010 school closings. At 8 a.m. CPS employees generally move supporters of the CEO and his policies to the front of the line for the "good news" portion. After signing in we go through the metal detectors to the 5th floor where the Board meets. At least a third (for contentious meetings it might be more) of the seats are roped off for CPS staff who fill up seats every month, providing a supportive backdrop for the TV cameras and limiting the number of public seats. Once the remaining seats are filled, the rest of the public is sent to an overflow room on the 13th floor to watch the meeting on TV. Around 10 a.m. the meeting begins. If our number does come up we get exactly 2 minutes to speak to a seven person Board of corporate CEOs, bankers, and developers appointed by the mayor who are ensconced on a dais distant from the audience and who rarely say anything. Around 11:30 to 12:00 the Board goes into closed door session where all the decisions are made—that is if they were not already made elsewhere. We can return midafternoon to hear their edicts. When the Board announces school closings they don't begin testimony until around noon, perhaps hoping to exhaust the patience of the parents, grandparents, students, and teachers in opposition. On those days you might be there all day.

Apple (2006) reminds us that for neoliberals, democracy is equated with the freedom to consume in the market, and the ideal of the citizen is the consumer: "Rather than democracy being a political concept, it is transformed into a wholly economic concept" through voucher and choice plans in education (p. 39). Chicago illustrates this transformation of democracy. Schools are closed, phased out, and "turned around" with no real community participation (Brown, Gutstein, & Lipman, 2009; Lipman & Haines, 2007). The democratic deficits of the process are revealing: The CEO announces the list of schools to be closed and the Board votes 3 to 4 weeks later. Public "hearings," held with just a few weeks notice, are conducted by paid hearing officers, sometimes during work hours when most parents, students, and community members cannot attend, and the hearings are often not in the community. Each speaker has just 2 minutes. These are not dialogues. Board members rarely show up, and there is no opportunity for parents, students, teachers, or community members to question officials. In a demonstration that the decisions are purely "technical," the school district's case for closing schools is presented by its lawyer and demographer, with no official who actually makes the decisions present. Further, principals and teachers claim CPS's evidence for closing their school is not available to them or the community without filing a Freedom of Information Act request (principals and teachers, personal communication, February 2009). The farce of these "public participation" events was illuminated when Board members admitted at the February 2009 Board meeting they had not read the transcripts of any of the public hearings (Field notes, Board meeting February 25, 2009).

It is no wonder that in the many community gatherings I have attended, a consistent refrain is that working class communities of color have had no say in decisions that deeply affect them. The decisions have already been made.[8] That is not to say that public mobilizations have had no effect. Community outrage and bad publicity forced Board members to selectively attend the 2010 hearings, as observers, and the CPS CEO agreed to announce proposed closings earlier in the year. In 2009 the State legislature approved a School Facilities Task Force with community participation to oversee CPS's school closings and openings—the result of alliances between community organizations and progressive elected officials.

Ren2010 also undermines elected Local School Councils (LSCs) comprised mainly of parents and community members. Although the effectiveness and level of community participation in LSCs has been uneven, and has been eroded by school accountability, they nevertheless open up a space for parents and community members to make democratic decisions about local schools (Bryk et al., 1998; Fung, 2004; Katz, 1992; Katz, Fine, & Simon, 1997). On the other hand, charter schools are run by private charter school boards, and Ren2010 contract and performance schools have Transition Advisory Councils (TACs), appointed by CPS administrators (CPS Policy Manual, Sec. 302.7, p. 3). While LSCs make important school level decisions,[9] TACs are purely advisory and members are not required to live in the school community.[10] By eliminating LSCs in charter, contract, and turnaround schools, Ren2010 limits their number and sets a precedent to strip parent–community participation of any real power.

The significance of LSCs lies in their democratic potential. By eliminating local governing councils, Ren2010 enforces the neoliberal preference for governance by experts and elites as a politically stabilizing environment for the intervention of the market (Harvey, 2005). In a highly centralized, corporate-dominated city and mayoral regime, they are one of very few forms of elected grassroots democracy and dialogue. In a school system that is 92% students of color and 86% low income, they are a space where working class communities of color might organize to contend for power. LSC members, particularly African Americans and Latino/as, have taken a leading role in the resistance to Ren2010. In August 2008, 300 local school council members and supporters convened a summit to push for legislation to strengthen local school councils as part of the campaign for quality neighborhood public schools.

Thus, the contest over school governance is essentially about competence to participate in public life. In this sense, when they are at their best, LSCs play an important pedagogical role. They develop collective community capacities to engage in democratic debate and decision making about policies affecting them (cf. Gandin & Apple, 2003). LSCs "asserted the capacity of ordinary citizens to reach intelligent decisions about educational policy" (Katz, 1992, p. 62) by redistributing power to parents and community representatives. In practice, the road was rocky as parents grappled with curriculum and school organization, school budgets, arcane bureaucratic regulations, and effective decision-making processes.[11] Yet over time, some LSCs became authentic forms of community decision making (Katz, Fine, & Simon, 1997), and their leaders are significant community actors. Bypassing the community and eliminating LSCs is therefore about redefining civic competence as resting solely in the hands of elites.

The Imperative of Market-Driven "Change": A Discourse of Containment

Neoliberal urbanism is legitimated by globalized discourses of "change," "rebirth," "regeneration," "renaissance" of schools, housing, neighborhoods, and downtowns. In this discourse there are two alternatives: dynamic market-driven restructuring or the status quo (e.g., Lupton & Tunstall, 2008). As Ren2010 rolled out, Chicago's School Board president characterized opposed parents and community members as people "who don't want change." Admonishing them from the Board dais that "life is not a dress rehearsal," he scolded critics of Ren2010 (parent activists and LSC chairs) to "stop criticizing" and "be part of your community" (Field notes, August 24, 2004). At another Board meeting, an elected official chided critics for being "afraid of every little tiny little change" (Field notes, September 22, 2004). The willingness to make tough choices and enact radical change is the legitimating logic for privatization. Elevating this to the national stage, Duncan called for "radical new thinking ... ideas that are controversial and hard and tough...the political courage to challenge the status quo" (Duncan, 2009b).

By speaking to real problems and presenting neoliberal policies as the only alternative, "change" becomes a "discourse of containment" (Popen, 2002), stifling debate and claiming sole authority to speak in the interest of schoolchildren. As Ball (1990) reminds us, discourses are "about what can be said, and thought, but also about who can speak, when, where and with what authority" (p. 17). Lupton and Tunstall (2009) note that Bruce Katz, Brookings Institute Fellow and architect of HOPE VI market-driven housing "regeneration," who has been influential in transferring this policy to Britain, argues that neighborhood transformation "requires a dynamic, market-driven notion of neighborhood change, rather than any 'community control' vision dedicated to maintaining the status quo" (quoted in Lupton & Tunstall, p.112). Invoking the epistemic authority of the neoliberal version of reality as the only alternative denies that disinvested communities are "thirsty for change" (community resident) that will improve housing, schools, job prospects, and living conditions—for them in their communities.

The "change/regeneration" discourse is deeply racialized. It dismisses all aspects of existing communities of color as uniformly bad, denying the actual complexity of neighborhoods which are "realigned to being merely a matter of their being 'behind' in the historical queue" (Massey cited in Lupton & Tunstall, p. 112). The charge that community residents of color are simply "against change" denies their histories of struggle and privileged knowledge about their communities. This was summed up by an African American community leader speaking to the Board of Education:

> This process would not be happening in Lincoln Park [a wealthy White area of the city]. There has to be some humility from this body. To say we're against change is insulting. The issues we are bringing up are factual because we're experiencing it. The people sitting around here don't have to deal with these issues.... We've raised these kids. We understand them. We have their respect.
>
> (Field notes, August 24, 2004)

Yet, if neoliberals have succeeded in appropriating the discourse of change, in part this is because the power to act as a consumer has resonance in the face of entrenched failures of the welfare state model and administration of public education, particularly in cities (Pedroni, 2007). There *is* an urgent need to transform public institutions, starting with a thoroughgoing critique of the racism, inequity, bureaucratic intransigence, reproduction of social inequality, reactionary ideologies, disrespect, and toxic culture that pervades many public schools and school districts that purport to serve working class and low-income children of color. This critique was long made by progressive critics of public education (e.g., Anyon, 1980; Apple, 2004; Irvine, 1991; Kozol, 1992). The resonance of the neoliberal discourse speaks to the failure of progressives to frame a counter discourse and vision of a more inclusive, democratic, robust "public" that brings to the fore perspectives, interests, and visions of marginalized groups: women, people of color, immigrants, sexually marginalized people, and so on (Fraser, 1997). I return to this in the concluding chapter.

Developing Places, Dispossessing People: School Policy, Gentrification, and Racial Displacement

> When a family sees the neighbourhood around it changing dramatically, when their friends are leaving the neighbourhood, when the stores they patronise are liquidating and new stores for other clientele are taking their places, and when changes in public facilities, in transportation patterns, and in support services all clearly are making the area less and less liveable,

then the pressure of displacement already is severe. Its actuality is only a matter of time. Families living under these circumstances may move as soon as they can, rather than wait for the inevitable; nonetheless they are displaced.

(Marcuse quoted in Slater, 2009, p. 17)

As Marcuse notes above, closing community institutions makes a community less livable and increases pressures for displacement. Schools are community anchors in the face of gentrification, loss of affordable housing, lack of jobs and public services, and overall disinvestment. Policies that destabilize schools and displace children or their teachers undermine this important role, particularly at a time when the effects of the economic crisis are further destabilizing working class and low-income students and families. Simultaneous with the launch of Ren2010, CPS closed 8 out of 23 Child–Parent Centers in mostly African American low-income neighborhoods. The centers were nationally recognized as the "gold standard" of early childhood programs with well-documented long-term benefits recommended for national replication (Stanfield, 2002). In Chicago and other cities (Cucciara, 2008; Gulson, 2005, 2007), policies to close schools and replace them with schools targeted to the middle class are integral to both production and consumption of gentrification. Closing schools pushes existing residents out of neighborhoods primed for gentrification. The new schools that replace them, like new police stations and libraries, are key to attracting new investment, and once redevelopment is underway, they are part of place marketing the area to a new class of home buyers.

Ren2010 illustrates the connection between education policy, displacement, and gentrification. In July 2004, the African American Midsouth area was the initial target of Ren2010. CPS's proposal to close 20 of the area's 22 schools quickly became a hotbed of contention (Dell'Angela & Washburn, 2004). A CPS meeting in the community, called on a few days notice under pressure from community activists, drew hundreds of parents, teachers, students, and community residents who lined up at the microphone for 4 hours to voice near unanimous opposition to a blueprint for closing their schools and eliminating LSCs. A major theme was that the Plan was designed to further gentrify their community (Field notes, July 15, 2004). At the time the Midsouth was experiencing some of the most intense gentrification in the city, as reflected in two indicators: rate of increase in housing prices and rate of house sales (Lipman & Haines, 2007).[12] Confronted with demonstrations, angry community meetings, an overnight camp-out at the Board of Education, and a citywide coalition of parents, unions, and school reform groups, the Board withdrew the Midsouth Plan in December 2004.

The Midsouth exemplifies the bigger picture. New development is built on the debris of disinvestment, deindustrialization, and decline of public housing in the urban core over the past 25 years. Through the 1980s into the 1990s, as stable working class families became low-income and unemployed, parts of the Midsouth had one of the highest concentrations of poverty in the country (M. Bennett, 2006; Venkatesh, Celimli, Miller, Murphy, & Turner, 2004). Massive high-rise public housing projects gradually became concrete warehouses for African Americans who were largely excluded from the city's restructured economy (Demissie, 2006), abandoned by urban and federal social programs, disinvested of public infrastructure, racially segregated, and pathologized by corporate media, conservative think tanks, and academic scholarship (D. Wilson, 2006). The Chicago Housing Authority (CHA) failed to maintain the buildings to the point where they were uninhabitable, justifying their demolition (Popkin, Cunningham, & Woodley, 2003). As high-rise public housing developments were demolished under the CHA Plan for Transformation (January 6, 2000), the land where they stood in the Midsouth—near to Lake Michigan, the north–south subway line, expressway, University of Chicago, and Illinois Institute of Technology—became an enormously valuable commodity. For example, Michaels Development Company (whose development projects are partially financed with public HOPE VI money in cities across the country) has a $600 million investment in Legends South (Michaels), a new mixed-income complex of over 2,300 houses and apartments on a 2-mile stretch of land where the Robert Taylor Homes public housing complex stood. Michaels is just one of the investors in the project where less than 20% of the units are for public housing residents.[13]

A similar pattern of school closings linked to gentrification is apparent in the African American community of Englewood where several schools were closed for "failure" under Ren2010 at the time 550 new homes were being built in an area that had seen almost no new home construction for decades (Olivio, 2004). The same is true of North Lawndale, another Ren2010 site, described in the real estate sections of a local newspaper as a "hot" area, where Royal Imperial Group was building a 1,200 unit residential development in 2005 as schools were being closed (Almaca, 2005). Residents contend the new schools are not designed for them. At a church meeting, a long-time Englewood resident said, "We're being pushed out of the city under the guise of school reform" (Field notes, February 2005). As public housing projects and disinvested apartment buildings are torn down and new condominiums and luxury town houses rise up, the city and the real estate developers wipe clean any traces of the community that lived there. Closing "failing" schools and reopening them as new schools is part of "rebranding" the area and making it more "responsive to the investment criteria of real estate capital" (Weber, 2003, p. 619). In this sense school policy is part of what Neil Smith (2002) calls "the class conquest of the city" by the upper middle class.

The Midsouth and other Black and Latino/a areas are now valuable real estate. Their redevelopment is facilitated by their construction in the White cultural imagination as spaces of danger and lawlessness. A population that has become disposable in the restructured labor force and "dangerous" in the city's global city image of middle-class stability, sanitized cultural diversity, and upscale living must be removed or contained (C. Parenti, 1999; N. Smith, 1996). Ren2010 facilitates dispossession and dispersal of low-income African Americans while a new University-affiliated charter school network rounds out the appeal of the new Midsouth to African American professionals who comprise much of the initial wave of middle-class home buyers (Smith & Stovall, 2008). As cities compete in the global economy for markets and investment, their competitive advantage rests on their ability to market themselves as unique and authentic (Harvey, 2001). Thus, developers appropriate the Midsouth's history as a nucleus of African American intellectual cultural life and brand it a racial heritage site (Boyd, 2000) to sell real estate in multimillion-dollar housing complexes with names like *Legends South* and *Jazz on the Boulevard.*

Closing schools for "low enrollment" is another instance of the intersection of education policy and real estate development. Underutilization of school buildings is not simply a result of "natural" demographic shifts. Declining school enrollments in specific places are socially produced in the nexus of capital accumulation, White advantages, and the cultural politics of race and class. They have political and economic histories, as do dismantling of public housing and loss of small businesses in disinvested neighborhoods. As low-income working class families are pushed or priced out of neighborhoods by developers gentrifying the area, shrinking the stock of affordable housing, their schools lose enrollment. Loss of affordable housing is the result of capital accumulation strategies facilitated by city policies that support gentrification and displacement, such as the CHA Plan for Transformation, Tax Increment Financing zones, and other subsidies for developers. School staff in schools slated to be closed or phased out in Chicago also report that school district policies—changes in school boundaries and cutting back bus transportation for students—contribute to lower enrollment (personal communications, February 2008, February 2009). Underutilization then is both a product of housing and school policies that support displacement and a rationale for school closings and "revitalization," powerfully illustrating the dynamic intertwining of housing and school policies in neoliberal urban restructuring.

In 2008 and 2009, the most bitterly fought phaseouts of underenrolled schools with predominantly Latino/a and African American low-income students were in gentrifying areas with very high concentrations of half-million and million dollar homes that had been sold between 2002 and 2006 (Fleming et al 2009; Greenlee et al., 2008). Our investigation found that CPS enrollment data undercalculated the actual utilization of these school buildings while even more severely underenrolled schools in affluent areas were not targeted for phaseout (Fleming et al., 2009; Greenlee et al., 2008). One school in a gentrifying area with a student population that was mainly Latino/a and low-income was replaced by a highly selective, prestigious public magnet school branded to appeal to affluent Whites. Another school with a similar student population was phased out to make way for a new K–12 Renaissance 2010 "international"-themed school lobbied for by parents in the nearby Gold Coast, one of the wealthiest areas of Chicago. The new public school required a $2,500 parent "donation" for each incoming kindergarten child (*Substance News*, May 26, 2009), while CPS eliminated the school's old boundaries, excluding children from the neighborhood. Despite neighborhood parents' pleas to affluent parents to find an alternate space or share the building, Gold Coast parents insisted they needed the school building for *their* children's "exciting" new school (Field notes, community hearing, February 19, 2009).

This expropriation of working class public schools is justified by what George Lipsitz calls a racialized social warrant for competitive consumerism and private expropriation and the racialization of space. A social warrant is a "collectively sanctioned understanding of obligations and entitlements." It authorizes new ways of knowing and being and transforms what is permitted and forbidden (Lipsitz, 2006a). A deeply rooted "social warrant of competitive consumer citizenship encourages well off communities to hoard their advantages, to seek to have their tax base used to fund only themselves and their interests, and to displace the costs of remedying complex social problems onto less powerful and less wealthy populations" (Lipsitz, 2006b, p. 455). It justifies the entitlement of affluent and White parents to the assets of working class and low-income people of color.

Underenrolling schools, turning them over private operators, setting them up for failure exemplify the neoliberal state's divestment in social reproduction (N. Smith, 2002). But Chicago, Philadelphia, New Orleans, and other cities reveal this is *selective divestment* linked to selective devalorization and revalorization of urban space. Ren2010 expands the menu of selective, high-status public schools in gentrified/gentrifying areas while turnaround schools and charters are mostly in low-income communities of color.

The Corporate Turnaround Strategy: Chickens Coming Home to Roost

On February 9, 2009, two buses bringing parents, students, teachers, administrators, and community members arrived at CPS Headquarters from Oliver Wendell Holmes Elementary School in Englewood to attend the CPS public hearing on the proposed plan to turn around the Holmes school. Under the plan, Holmes would be turned over to the Academy for Urban School Leadership (AUSL), a private nonprofit corporation founded by venture capitalist Martin Koldyke. As they lined up to register to speak, Holmes 8th graders nervously rehearsed their speeches in which they would advocate that their school remain open with its existing teachers, administrators, counselors, support staff, custodians, kitchen personnel, security guards, clerical staff, and paraprofessionals—all of whom will be terminated if the Board approves the CPS turnaround plan.... *For the next two hours*, the children, and their mothers and grandmothers, along with their teachers and neighborhood residents, poured out their hearts to the hearing officer as they argued and pleaded to save Holmes...[one student] prophesized, "It will seem like substitutes are present all year round. They say turning Holmes school around will help students. I think [the] opposite."

(Fleming et al., 2009, p. 33)

In response to the disruption of closing schools and community resistance, in 2006 CPS added "turnaround" schools to Ren2010. Students remain but all staff (teachers, administrators, lunch room workers, etc.) are dismissed, and the school is turned over to an outside operator who hires a new administration and staff. Through the end of the 2010 school year, 14 Chicago public schools were handed over to "turnaround specialists." Turnaround schools generally receive a temporary large infusion of funds from CPS (and the Gates Foundation) for additional staff including national board certified teachers, intensive professional development and planning, and new program implementation (Fleming et al., 2009). Schools also get a physical makeover—new lockers, playing fields, gardens, and building renovations are typical. In public hearings and informal conversations, parents and teachers have asked why their school had not been offered these improvements rather than turning them over to private operators. This issue is of particular concern in African American communities with a history of disinvestment and inequitable resources because of the 42 schools CPS said were eligible for turnaround at the end of the 2008–2009 school year due to "'academic failure,'" their student populations were 97.7% African American in a school district that is 46.5% African American (*Substance News* cited in Fleming et al., 2009, p. 11).

Turnarounds are part of the national strategy to introduce private operators into public education, with Secretary of Education Duncan calling for 5,000 schools to be closed and "turned around" nationally (Duncan, 2009c). Duncan praises AUSL, the main turnaround operator in Chicago, as a national exemplar, but other operators are also getting into the potentially lucrative market. Chicago International Charter Schools, the largest charter school operator in the city, partnered with the San Francisco-based New Schools Venture Fund, to form a new nonprofit subsidiary called Chicago Rise to run turnarounds, and the national charter school operator, Victory Schools, got into the act in 2002, with six schools in Philadelphia (Myers, 2008). Yet, the "success" of these turn around operations, even on narrow measures of test scores, is not established (Fleming et al., 2009),[14] particularly in relation to destabilizing effects of replacing all familiar and trusted adults in the school building.

This point was tragically driven home when over one million people around the world watched on YouTube the horrific beating death of Derrion Albert, a student at Fenger High School in Chicago, in a school fight in September 2009. What many do not know was that Fenger was "turned around" in fall 2009. The story epitomizes the nexus of African American dispossession in which this policy is complicit. In 2000, students living in the Altgeld Gardens public housing complex on Chicago's far South Side were displaced when their neighborhood high school, G. W. Carver, was turned into a selective enrollment military school. Carver students were transferred to Fenger, almost 5 miles away in an entirely different neighborhood, and to other high schools even further from the Gardens. This added to the instability caused by decades of disinvestment and deindustrialization of the area, exacerbated by the current economic crisis. Tensions between Gardens and Fenger neighborhood students are longstanding. When CPS announced plans to make Fenger a turnaround school, parents and students warned it would cause further disruption and heighten the potential for violence. But CPS went ahead and all but 9 of the school's 100 teachers as well as all other adults in the building were fired. The school opened in fall 2009 with a new principal and staff who did not know the students or the community and lacked the moral authority to defuse conflicts and mentor students. From the beginning they struggled with student tensions. The fight that resulted in a student death was an outgrowth of the tensions.

This tragedy exposes interconnected effects of neoliberal education, housing, and urban development policies and racism. The violence at Fenger was part of the spike in violence as CPS closed schools in African American communities and transferred students to schools in other neighborhoods.[15] The volatility of school closings exacerbated destabilizing effects of dismantling public housing, abandoning the economies and infrastructure of Black working class communities, and discourses of racial pathology which legitimate the condemnation of whole communities to joblessness, poverty, policing, and incarceration.

This situation exemplifies the crisis of social reproduction as the state divests itself of responsibility for housing, education, and social welfare (N. Smith, 2002). The ensuing social failure of the market (its inability to provide housing and education, break-up of community, loss of social connections between adults and children in schools, and violence) requires intensified regulation and containment (Wacquant, 2001). The state's immediate response to the violence at Fenger was to blanket the area with police and make arrests the moment a fight broke out. Simultaneously, the state's therapeutic strategy reached further into the market for solutions—a $5.1 million contract to a Pennsylvania-based company to mentor 200 youth identified as at risk of violence, based on a computer program prediction.

Conclusion

Urban school policy instantiates the democratic deficits that typify urban governance. Under mayoral control, decisions are made by unelected corporate bodies (such as the RSF) and rubber stamped by appointed, corporate-dominated boards, while democratically elected bodies are supplanted by appointed advisory boards. Education reforms that blur the distinction between public and private establish the indirect political power of nonstate actors who "perform political functions under no effective political control" (Boaventura de Sousa Santos quoted in Dale & Robertson, 2004, p. 153). Chicago's Ren2010 and the restructuring of New Orleans Schools exemplify the state–capital alliance to remake public education to remake the city—materially and ideologically. As unelected public–private partnerships push through privatization of public schools, their moves insinuate into the fabric of daily life a market ethos of citizen as consumer and individuation of social activity. Education policy becomes an "agent of the *remercantilisation* [emphasis original] of interactions among the people" (Santos interviewed in Dale & Robertson, 2004, p. 154).

In Chicago and New Orleans, education policy is integrally linked to public and private investment decisions and race. Accountability, school closings, and privatization are interwoven in a policy nexus that lubricates real estate profits through devaloration and revaloration of the built environment and displacement of working class communities of color. Turning over public schools to private operators exemplifies the neoliberal state's divestment in social reproduction (N. Smith, 2002). But Chicago (along with Philadelphia, New Orleans, and other cities) reveals that this is *selective divestment* linked to selective disinvestment and reinvestment in urban space (Lipman, 2004). Through Ren2010, CPS expands its menu of selective, high-status public schools in gentrified/gentrifying areas while turnaround schools and charters are mostly in low-income communities of color. The exception is a prestigious network of charter schools associated with a local university in a gentrifying area. Thus education policy is both responsive to and constitutive of spatial restructuring for capital accumulation and racial exclusion.

But because education policies affect not only teachers and students but school employees and whole communities, they cut across geography and racial and ethnic differences. They have implications for union jobs, wages and benefits, local democracy, housing, and neighborhood vitality. Education is thus positioned at the center of potential alliances across diverse communities and social sectors. In this way, education might become a focus of democratic social struggles.

Neoliberalism is fraught with fissures and contradictions, and in Chicago grassroots opposition and contradictions of the policy itself have forced the powerful forces behind Ren2010 to continually revise and relegitimate it. As Williams (1978) reminds us, hegemony has to be continually re-created, defended, and modified. But the rather small victories of the grassroots movements have their own contradictions and limits. Yet years of grassroots resistance and accumulating evidence of failure of neoliberal policies have begun to jell in a counternarrative and a counterhegemonic program for educational improvement just as the dominant agenda has gone national. But the challenge is cultural as well as political. Antidemocratic policies take root in a culture of possessive individualism and White supremacy that makes them seem natural and inevitable, and contesting them involves actively challenging this culture.

> Policies implemented at the highest levels of government depend on the ideological legitimation they receive from cultural practices, stories, images, and ideas deeply rooted in the quotidian activities of life in the United States. Rethinking American culture and the role it plays in sustaining inequality and injustice requires us to identify this cultural system, to name it, trace its origins and evolution, assess, evaluate, and explain the work it does, and to identify the already existing alternative cultural forms that might lead our society in another direction. The hostile privatism, speculative instrumentalism, and countersubversive carceralism that characterized the Bush Administration's responses to the war in Iraq and to Hurricane Katrina have deep roots in contemporary American culture. It is time for us to name this culture and the social warrant that it produces, to recognize its rootedness in segregation and in the racialization of space, to acknowledge its deep consequences for our collective existence, and to change it.
>
> (Lipsitz, 2006b, p. 453)

In the next chapter I take up these issues again in a discussion of the strategy to develop mixed-income schools in mixed-income communities.

4

RACIAL POLITICS OF MIXED-INCOME SCHOOLS AND HOUSING

Moralizing Poverty, Building the Neoliberal City

[B]eing poor is a state of mind, not a condition.

(Alphonso Jackson, Secretary, U.S. Department
of Housing and Urban Development, May 20, 2004)

Every child in the United States—whether rich or poor, white or black,
Latino or Asian—should have access to the good education that is best
guaranteed by the presence of a majority middle-class student.

(Kahlenberg, 2001, p. 1)

There is a powerful consensus among policy makers and academics that the only
way to seriously reduce poverty in urban areas is to disperse low-income people
and move them to mixed-income communities. Imbroscio (2008) calls this the
"deconcentration consensus." The underlying assumption is that intractable
poverty is the result of social isolation and the "pathologies" it breeds: Mixing
low-income people with the middle class will supposedly give them access to
the middle-class values, social networks, behavioral norms, and resources they
are lacking. This theory underpins federal policy to dismantle public housing
units, disperse residents, and replace them with mixed-income developments.
The spatial-determination-of-poverty argument is part of a discursive strategy
to depoliticize displacement. This discourse also circulates internationally, with
mixed-income development projects in Australia and Britain. Nevertheless,
critical scholars challenge both the evidence and assumptions for its claims (e.g.,
Bennett, 1998; Bennett & Reed, 1999; Imbroscio, 2008; Lees, 2008; Lupton &
Turnstall, 2008; J. Smith, 2000).

In several U.S. cities, deconcentration and mixed-income housing are linked to the relocation of low-income students of color from majority low-income schools, to newly created mixed-income schools (Lipman, 2008a; Raffel, Denson, Varady, & Sweeney, 2003). The assumptions parallel the deconcentration thesis: mixing low-income students with middle-class students will improve their academic experiences and outcomes by exposing them to the putative positive influence of middle-class language, values, and achievement ethic as well as give them access to better teachers and school resources (Kahlenberg, 2001). The mixed- income strategy invokes the democratic goals of the common school and racial desegregation (Kahlenberg, 2001). It also calls upon New Urbanist planning for livable and communitarian cities designed to encourage social mixing and integrated housing, work, and recreation in a people-centered urban environment. Consider the optimistic image painted by Marysue Barrett, President of Chicago's Metropolitan Planning Council: "Picture a mix of incomes and housing types, nearby stores for groceries and movie rentals and decent streets, parks and schools" (2002).

Thus, mixed-income policies are framed as an egalitarian and democratic solution to intractable poverty and inequitable and failing urban schools (Lupton & Turnstall, 2008). Indeed, few would argue against the need to address intertwined effects of inequitable urban schools and lack of quality affordable housing. However, in this chapter, I take a critical look at the popular notion that mixed-income schools in newly constructed mixed-income communities are generative of educational equality and social justice. I maintain that although the mixed-income strategy is framed in class terms, the subtext is race. Students and families to be displaced, relocated, and reformed are mostly African American, and the discourses of social pathology attached to them are rooted in historical metaphors of White supremacy.

I suggest that mixed-income strategies can best be understood in relation to the construction of neoliberal social and economic arrangements and the politics of race. Specifically, they contribute to an urban agenda which has at its nexus capital accumulation and racial containment and exclusion through gentrification, dedemocratization and privatization of public institutions, and displacement of low-income working class people of color. My analysis addresses three interrelated issues: (a) the ideological basis and intellectual origins of mixed-income proposals, (b) the relation to neoliberal urban economic restructuring and African American dispossession, (c) implications for educational, racial, and economic justice. To illustrate this argument, I turn to Chicago, where mixed-income school and housing policies are interwoven, discursively and practically.[1]

I am not arguing against racially and economically diverse communities. Such communities represent the democratic potential of a diverse society. Quality affordable housing for everyone and culturally and socially empowering high quality education are, in my view, basic human rights and fully feasible in the United States given its overabundance of national wealth. Vibrant, racially and socially diverse communities and schools, coupled with economic redistributive policies and full parity of political participation would go a long way toward economic, cultural, and political democracy (Fraser, 2007). However, this is a far cry from a set of neoliberal policies that evoke these sorts of goals but concretely do little to eradicate poverty or improve educational opportunity and instead demonize, displace, and disperse low-income people, treating them as objects, rather than subjects, of public policy.

I argued in the previous chapter that Chicago's Renaissance 2010 (Ren2010) is strategically linked to the neoliberal development of the city and the exclusion of working class and low-income people of color. Four years before the launch of Ren2010, Chicago kicked off the Plan for Transformation (PFT) to demolish or renovate 38,000 units of public housing, demolishing 22,000, replacing 9,000, and ending with 25,000 units of public housing. Most of the demolitions—51 high-rise buildings, including all the remaining "family" units of three, four, or five bedrooms—are completed, but little replacement housing has been built (J. Smith, 2009b). Many of the new developments are designed to be mixed-income with no more than one-third public housing residents (Bennett, Smith, & Wright, 2006). Some experts estimate that less than 20% of former residents will finally return to the new developments (Venkatesh et al, 2004; Wilen & Nayak, 2006).

As described in chapter 2, the PFT is Chicago's implementation of the federal 1992 Housing Opportunities for People Everywhere Act (HOPE VI).[2] HOPE VI devolved federal responsibility for public housing to municipal authorities and replaced government housing provision with privatized management of public units. The federal government essentially moved from being a provider of housing to an agent of the housing market (J. Smith, 2006). The driving theory behind HOPE VI is that the concentration of very low-income people in dense public housing units has been a major contributor to "pathological" behaviors and the inability of poor people to rise out of poverty. The Act calls for revitalizing or demolishing "distressed" units and relocating public housing residents in scattered site housing, giving them vouchers in the private housing market, and financing new mixed-income developments as public–private partnerships. These partnerships draw on public tax dollars to subsidize developers. HOPE VI also requires public housing residents to work toward self-sufficiency and promotes home ownership. Significantly, the 1995 elimination of one-to-one replacement, meant residents could be displaced without guarantee of return to new or rehabbed units. As a whole, by demolishing public housing and opening up whole tracts of valuable land to development and by subsidizing large-scale private mixed-income development projects, the federal government provided a huge windfall to the housing industry and financial investors.

Under Renaissance 2010, CPS proposes to create mixed-income schools in the new mixed-income developments. The goal of the Midsouth Plan in 2004 (the first step in Ren2010) was to "reinvent the area's 25 schools and make them a magnet for the return of middle-class families" (Olszewski & Sadovi, 2003, p. 1). The MacArthur Foundation, which provided $50 million to support the Midsouth redevelopment, including loan guarantees for investors, underscored the role of schools in mixed-income developments: "The city has made a commitment to improving the local schools, without which the success of the new mixed-income communities would be at great risk." However, some scholars question whether class integration is actually the goal (M. Bennett, 2006; L. Bennett & Reed, 1999; L. Bennett, Smith, & Wright, 2006), or whether it simply masks (and facilitates) gentrification and displacement of public housing residents.

Although cast as a positive strategy for urban decay and the achievement of social stability, present-day gentrification is driven by finance capital at multiple scales. Viewed through the lens of neoliberal urbanism, the PFT is part of a capital accumulation strategy that merges local, national, and transnational capital in concert with city government and is a means for the (White) middle and upper middle classes to claim cultural control of the city (e.g., Fainstein & Judd, 2001; Hackworth, 2007; N. Smith, 1996). The class and race nature of this process is, as Neil Smith points out, hidden in the language of "regeneration." A global city driven by neoliberal economic and social policies simply has no room for public housing as devised in the 1950s and 1960s (M. Bennett, 2006) or for low-income African Americans who are, from the standpoint of capital, largely superfluous in the new economy and "threatening" in the White cultural imagination. Indeed, public housing and education policies are critical components of Chicago's bid to be a first-tier global city and to restructure its economy on neoliberal lines.

Hope VI and Mixed-Income Schools

Mixed-income schools are closely linked to HOPE VI developments in a number of cities. Varady, Raffel, Sweeney, and Denson (2005), who have extensively studied HOPE VI, propose that "income mixing in the classroom could improve the educational performance of low-income children" (p. 150) in the same way that HOPE VI mixed-income communities may increase the "social mobility" of low-income people (see also Raffel et al., 2003; Varady & Raffel, 1995). HOPE VI policy documents and academic advocates also contend that mixed-income schools play an important role in creating and sustaining mixed-income communities, for example, the Urban Land Use forum in Chicago, 2001 (Myerson, 2001). The strategy is national. Philadelphia is "rebranding" inner city schools to appeal to the middle class as part of a project to revitalize/gentrify the center city (Cucchiara, 2008). In Denver,

Colorado, mixed-income schools in gentrifying areas are part of the city's education reform strategy (Gottlieb, 2002). In the following sections, I look more closely at the evidence for these policies and their implications.

Evidence for Mixed-Income Schools

Richard Kahlenberg (2001), Century Foundation Fellow and leading proponent of mixed-income schools, asserts a good education "… is best guaranteed by the presence of a majority middle-class student body" (p. 1) to whom he attributes a range of behavioral and attitudinal virtues. Kahlenberg proposes large scale reform of public schools to create mixed-income schools with a majority of middle-class students and "ability grouping" for "faster" students. Kahlenberg's evidence for this proposal rests on the correlation between academic achievement and social class. He argues that the strength of this correlation, and the failure of other remedies, leave no other option than "economic integration" as a solution to improve academic achievement, educational attainment, and life chances of low-income students. To reach this goal, he proposes a controlled choice plan to create mixed-income schools with no more than 40% low-income students to ensure that the majority middle-class students will set the school culture and establish the work ethic and behavior standards necessary to transform and discipline low-income students of color. This formula parallels the quota of public housing residents required by law in mixed-income developments.

Kahlenberg cites a wide range of studies as well as proposals from think tanks[3] to support the correlation between family and school SES and educational success, but his argument relies particularly on the influential Coleman Report (Coleman et al., 1966), which found, in part, that educational achievement was more highly correlated with student characteristics than school resources. Drawing on Coleman, he argues that increased funding to low-income schools will have little effect. (For a summary of problems in the Coleman Report's methodology, distortions of its findings, and influence of conservative economists on this argument see Biddle & Berliner, 2002.) Kahlenberg also cites studies that show that low-income students are more likely to demonstrate poor academic achievement in high- than low-poverty schools and that low-income students and students of color who move to suburbs are more likely to show increases in academic achievement than students who remain in low-income urban areas (see Kahlenberg, chap. 3 for his sources). He also extrapolates from research on peer influence to argue for the positive impact of middle-class students on their low-income classmates. Finally, he concludes that the solution is to mix low-income students with middle-class students in carefully configured mixed-income schools.

Research generally supports a correlation between social class and educational experiences and outcomes (see Knapp & Woolverton, 2004; Sirin, 2005 for a review), but the evidence for benefits of moving low-income students to low-poverty schools and to suburbs is actually mixed. Studies show a strong correlation between family SES and the school and classroom environment the student has access to (Reynolds & Walberg, 1992), school quality (e.g., teacher quality, instructional resources, teacher–student ratio) (Wenglinsky, 1998), and the relationship between school personnel and parents (Watkins, 1997). The specific correlation between poverty and low-academic performance, school completion, and other education indicators is also well-documented (Anyon, 2005), as is the relationship between race/ethnicity and educational outcomes (Darling-Hammond, 2004). However, these correlations are moderated by various factors such as school location, race, and school level (Sirin, 2005). Some research found positive effects of moving low-income students to suburbs under the Chicago *Gatreaux* housing desegregation program (Rubinowitz & Rosenbaum, 2002). However, results from the national Moving to Opportunity program appear to show no significant increase in test scores at any age for students who were assigned housing vouchers to move from public housing to lower poverty neighborhoods (Sanbonmatsu, Kling, Duncan, & Brooks-Gunn, 2006).

Although there may be student social class composition effects on educational outcomes, the reasons are unclear. First, how do we interpret the benefits of middle-class schools for low-income students? Are they due to mixing with middle-class children, as Kahlenberg claims? Or are they the effects of better quality instruction and resources, such as significantly higher per pupil expenditures, more highly qualified teachers, better resources, lower student–teacher ratios, richer curricula, and higher academic expectations (Darling-Hammond, 2004)? For example, summarizing research on social class, community context, and schooling, Knapp and Woolverton (2004) note that "there is a reasonable possibility that classmates' social status could influence low-SES classmates' performance in various ways, even indirectly—for example through favorable resource conditions for teachers' work" (p. 663). If the benefits accrue from a confluence of advantages amassed by middle-class schools because of their political influence and wealth, then would low-income students do as well if they had similar advantages and conditions in their own schools? Indeed, this is the conclusion of those who argue for equalizing school funding (Biddle & Berliner, 2002). Yet, because of the dramatic inequities in school funding in the United States, there are few instances in which the rich resources showered on schools in economically advantaged communities have been available to low-income schools. (Among U.S. school districts, annual funding per pupil ranges from less than $4,000 to more than $15,000, Biddle & Berliner, 2002.) The assumption that the presence of middle-class parents will benefit low-income students is also questionable in light of evidence showing middle-class families deploy their material and cultural resources to secure educational advantages for *their* children (André-Bechely, 2005; McGrath & Kuriloff, 1999), particularly in the context of school choice (Ball, 2003; Butler with Robson, 2003; Fuller with Orfield, 1996; Gewirtz, Ball, & Bowe, 1995). There is also evidence that middle-class parents seek to insulate their children from lower-achieving students and lower-income students of color through school tracking and special programs (Oakes, Wells, Jones, & Datnow, 1997; Sieber, 1982).

Second, even more problematic, the contention that lower-income students will benefit from proximity to middle-class students evokes cultural deficit theories that situate educational outcomes in the characteristics of students rather than the constellation of structural, cultural, and pedagogical factors that perpetuate race and class inequalities in educational experiences and outcomes (Darling-Hammond, 2004; Knapp & Woolverton, 2004). Evidence of the persistence of these factors (e.g., tracking, teacher attitudes and expectations, Eurocentric curricula) in interracial, mixed-income schools indicates that they continue to produce disparities between White students and students of color in academic achievement, assignment to academic tracks, and punishment, despite strong proschool attitudes among students of color (Ferguson, 2001 Lipman, 1998; Minority Student Achievement Network, http://msan.wceruw. org/). In particular, mixed-income proposals deflect attention from the centrality of racial subordination and marginalization in the production of educational inequality, although race and putative deficiencies of low-income children and families of color are quite clearly the subtext of proposals for "economic integration" (Henderson, 2001; Ladson-Billings, 2005; Orfield, 2001). Qualitative research in racially desegregated mixed-income schools reveals ways in which structural and ideological forces combine to resegregate low-income children in low-track classes (Lipman, 1998) and ways in which middle-class parents successfully use their political and cultural capital to resist detracking efforts (Oakes et al., 1997) or to secure more creative and challenging classes for their children (McGrath & Kuriloff, 1999; Sieber, 1982). Explicit and informal stratifying mechanisms become a vehicle for middle-class parents to ensure class reproduction and insulation of their children from working class students of color. Yet, academic tracking is built into Kahlenberg's proposal.

Third, mixed-income discourse obscures the reality of racial subordination and marginalization at the heart of school and housing inequalities. Mixed-income proposals are an instantiation of the color-blind discourse that has permeated public policy over the past two decades (Bonilla-Silva, 2003; Brown et al., 2003). This discourse denies that racial discrimination and oppression are relevant in social and economic outcomes, thus undermining many of the gains made by the civil rights movements of the 1960s and 1970s; for example, school desegregation, affirmative action, and bilingual education. Yet, race and the supposed cultural deficiencies of low-income children and families of color, are the subtext. Kahlenberg, Raffel, Varady, and other mixed-income proponents cite no advantages to middle-class students of mixing with low-income students (of color) who seem, in their analysis, to possess a litany of deficiencies. Kahlenberg (2001) argues, "Money does matter to educational achievement, but research—and common sense—tells us that the people who make up a school, the students, parents, and teachers matter more" (p. 3). He claims middle-class students have greater motivation, better language skills, more positive attitudes about school, and better behavior, and middle-class parents are more involved and effective advocates for their children.

Frankly, this is a profoundly racist argument that flies in the face of 30 plus years of research on culture, language, race, ethnicity, and schooling in this country (e.g., Banks & Banks, 2001, 2004). It also negates the historical struggle for excellence by African American educators and parents in the face of grossly inequitable resources, White supremacy, and intimidation (e.g., Anderson, 1988; Siddle Walker, 1996). Recall that until the 1960s nearly every African American intellectual and political and cultural leader was educated in African American schools and universities. Moreover, there are examples of schools today in which, even with inadequate resources, low-income students of color not only perform well academically but develop tools of critical analysis and critical consciousness when they have the opportunity for intellectually rigorous curricula and high academic expectations, teaching that values and employs their cultural knowledge, and critical pedagogical approaches (e.g., Andrade & Morrell, 2008; Christensen, 2000; Gutstein, 2006b; Ladson-Billings, 1995; Lee, 2008). In none of these examples were the students mixed with middle-class students.

Formal and Informal Selection Mechanisms

Whether low-income students of color would actually be enrolled in substantial numbers in new mixed-income schools is also questionable. Both formal policy and informal social and cultural mechanisms exclude and marginalize low-income students. The Chicago example illustrates this point (also see Cucchiarra, 2008, on Philadelphia). Despite claims that dispossessed students will be included in the new schools, closely read, Ren2010 policy (Chicago Public Schools, 2004a, 2007) says students should have the right of return "to the fullest extent possible" and contains stipulations that are potentially exclusionary. Unlike regular CPS schools, which must admit all neighborhood students, many Ren2010 schools accept applications citywide, limit enrollment, use selection mechanisms including lotteries, do not reserve seats for displaced students, may not offer the same program or grades as the closed school, set admission deadlines, and have a complex admissions process, a factor that disadvantages displaced (or in transition) low-income families who have less certainty about their housing. Students from the Cabrini Green housing development were initially guaranteed 10% of the slots in a new state-of-the-art selective magnet school in the gentrified area, but they were excluded after the first year of operation on grounds that they could not keep up with their academically selected classmates. In the Midsouth, Martin Luther King, the neighborhood high school, was revamped as a selective enrollment magnet school. Patillo (2007) describes the hurdles one must navigate to apply: "It begins in November or December with an application that can only be obtained from a school counselor and which requires a letter from the counselor, test scores, attendance records, and additional student information. Students who qualify must then sit for a separate test. It is more like applying to college or graduate school than to high school" (p. 175).

More informal selection mechanisms also advantage middle-class school "consumers" who deploy their cultural capital and social connections to secure places for their children under school choice plans (e.g., André-Bechely, 2005; Ball, 2003; Whitty, Power, & Halpen, 1998). A Chicago example is an elementary school which served the Henry Horner public housing development on the city's West Side. The school was closed in 2004 and reopened as a public Montessori magnet school requiring an application process. As of fall 2006, only four students living in the Horner development, which is now in the middle of a gentrified area, attended the new school, although it was supposed to provide them with school choice. The parents explained to the *Chicago Catalyst* magazine that the school was not publicized to them, and they had no idea what kind of school it was (Finkel, 2006). In fact, by 2007, most students displaced by Ren2010 had been relocated to schools academically and demographically similar to those they left, with 84% attending schools with below the average district test scores and 44% in schools on probation (*Catalyst Chicago*, 2007). Research on HOPE VI developments elsewhere also indicates that original residents' children did not necessarily benefit from the new schools because of displacement; they also noted a lack of interclass, interracial "mixing" (Raffel et al., 2003; Varady et al., 2005).

It is unlikely that the majority of displaced students in gentrifying areas in Chicago will have access to mixed-income schools or be able to live in the area. Concerns about permanent displacement have been a central theme in the many community meetings, public hearings, press conferences, and rallies opposing Ren2010. Community members opposed to Ren2010 do not believe the new schools are being created for them (see also, Nyden, Edlynn, & Davis, 2006). A fact sheet produced by the Kenwood Oakland Local School Council Alliance states:

> Over 90% of the students who attend Mid-South schools are from low-income, African-American families. The Mid-South plan says that the schools will serve 1/3 middle-income, 1/3 moderate-income and 1/3 low-income students. What happens to the other 2/3 low-income students? DISPLACEMENT."

> (Midsouth Fact Sheet, 2004 [emphasis original])

Although most of the Ren2010 "mixed-income" schools have a lower percentage of low-income students than the schools surrounding them, the demographics are not dramatically different. However, as gentrification pushes these families out of the neighborhood, it is likely that school demographics will change also. In areas where gentrification is most advanced or in some schools with middle-class appeal (e.g., Montessori schools), new schools have significantly lower percentages of low-income students than those they replaced. Despite claims of the efficacy of mixed-income schools for low-income students, a primary goal is to attract middle-class parents and homeowners (Varady & Raffel, 1995). Arne Duncan, CEO of CPS remarked, "For far too long, middle-class families have gone private or Catholic or fled to the suburbs. We're starting to reverse that trend" (quoted in Duffrin, 2006, p. 11). In the Midsouth area, most remaining low-income students are attending neighborhood schools that are overwhelmingly low-income. Two schools that were closed have been replaced by new Ren2010 schools which have much lower low-income enrollments. In short, the discourse of opportunity in new mixed-income schools obscures the reality of displacement and racial containment.

In sum, the argument supporting mixed-income schools is problematic on several grounds. First, the contention of Kahlenberg and others that mixed-income schools will benefit low-income students because of proximity to middle-class students conflates correlation and causality. The correlation of educational experiences and outcomes with social class points to inequitable resources and advantages of middle-class students and schools. Second, it is fundamentally a cultural deficit model of working class students of color. Third, it ignores persistent disparities in academic achievement between working class students of color and White middle-class students in mixed-income schools due to structural and cultural inequalities in the school and marginalization. Fourth, the reality in Chicago is that closing schools and opening "mixed-income" schools is contributing to displacement while few low-income students of color have access to schools marketed to the middle class.

Evidence for Mixed-Income Housing

> As we got into this fight I began to see what they [CHA and city officials] [insertion original] were proposing for my people. They were proposing for my people to be evicted and become homeless … that is why I am in this fight; because I have been at the homeless shelters and I have seen people waiting to get in.
>
> (Carol Steele, public housing tenant leader,
> quoted in Wright, 2006, p.160)

Research on HOPE VI mixed-income developments suggests a similar discrepancy between claims and results. While HOPE VI has transformed some public housing units into more attractive buildings and communities and improved living conditions for a some public housing residents, there is substantial evidence that many original public housing residents have not benefited. Serious problems include inadequate relocation support for residents, continued racial segregation, lack of meaningful resident participation in relocation and in new developments, insufficient affordable options in the housing market, and exclusion of public housing families from mixed-income developments (Popkin et al., 2004; Venkatesh et al., 2004). Pitcoff (1999) notes, "A close look at the national numbers reveals that HOPE VI developments usually create fewer units than they tear down, and many of the new units aren't within financial reach of families being displaced" (p. 6). For example, Atlanta's HOPE VI facilitated downtown development by dislodging African American public housing residents from the downtown area, opening it up for development, and simultaneously diminishing the stock of low-income housing (Keating, 2000).

Maximizing returns on investments is driving this process. It reflects a shift in emphasis of government priorities—from providing for people's basic needs to a profit-driven agenda. In the 1990s, private developers interested in investing in public housing redevelopment exerted pressure to change the HOPE VI formula from one-to-one replacement to a limit of one-third public housing residents. They claimed a larger percentage would jeopardize its attraction to market rate buyers (L. Bennett, Hudspeth, & Wright, 2006). Renée Glover, CEO of the Atlanta Housing Authority (2005) said, "The long-term success of mixed-income communities must be driven by the same market factors that drive the success of every other real estate development" (p. 4), with competition to attract market rate renters the priority and keeping public housing residents below 40% a principle. Mixed-income developments in Chicago follow the formula one-third public housing, one-third affordable, and one-third market rate units. (To qualify for "affordable" rates one's household income cannot exceed 80 to 120% of metropolitan area median income, $75,000 a year.) Some scholars question whether mixed-income is actually the goal (see M. Bennett, 2006; L. Bennett & Reed, 1999; L. Bennett, Smith, & Wright, 2006). For example, in the ABLA public housing redevelopment, CHA forced out public housing residents at the very time the area was becoming mixed-income (L. Bennett et al., 2006).

As with schools, evidence from HOPE VI challenges the underlying rationale that middle-class residents will deploy their social capital to connect low-income residents to job markets and resources, intervene to promote safety and social harmony, and bring resources to the community. Bennett, Hudspeth, and Wright (2006) could identify only a "smattering of evidence" that mixed-income communities improve the life chances of low-income people. The assumption of New Urbanists that proximity will lead to social connections is also questionable. Varady et al.'s (2005) study of HOPE VI mixed-income developments indicates little social interaction across class. In the most extensive study of mixed-income housing, comparing seven mixed-income developments, there were low or very low levels of neighboring and few market-rate tenants attended building activities (J. Smith, 2002). In the Orchard Park development, adjoining Cabrini Green public housing in Chicago, developers erected a fence to separate market rate from public housing (see also Joseph, 2008). Although race is a key factor there, there are similar issues when the first wave of gentrifiers is Black and the discourse of mixed-income is intertwined with "racial uplift." Although Black gentrifiers on Chicago's South Side believed they were contributing to the upgrading of everyone in the community by bringing in middle- and upper-income people, Boyd's (2005) research shows that Black gentrification as a strategy for racial uplift misses the differential opportunities for low- and middle-income African Americans to live in and participate in the new communities. Boyd argues the discourse of racial uplift intersects with mixed-income discourses to create "the illusion that gentrification strategies are implemented both in the interests of, and with the approval of the poor black residents it displaces" (p. 286).

These discourses negate the rootedness of community in mutuality and common struggles. Community networks take a long time to build and are constructed from common experiences. For example, in mixed-income non-English speaking immigrant communities, people tend to rely on each other and support each other out of necessity and common understanding, across class. As community organizers explain, it is presumptuous to assume that new higher income residents would build community in a neighborhood where they have no ties, or that the long time residents who are desperately trying to hold onto the community they have built over generations would welcome or want their "help" (S. Gutstein, personal communication, June 8, 2010).

In Chicago, developing evidence suggests that overall the PFT has generated displacement and racial containment, not mixed-income living. Demolition has far out-paced replacement construction, and CHA officials admit they do not have funding to replace all public housing units (Sharon Gilliam, CEO of CHA, Gatreaux at 40 Forum, Field notes, March 3, 2006). In the first 6 years of the PFT (up to September 2005), CHA had constructed or rehabilitated only 766 public housing units in mixed-income communities (Wilen & Nayak, 2006, p. 219). From 2000 to 2008, only 1,126 of the 7,186 demolished family units had been replaced (Grotto, Cohen, & Olkon, 2008). Most plans call for just one-third of replacement housing to be designated for public housing residents (J. Smith, 2002). Michaels Development Corporation has a $593 million investment in Legends South, a HOPE VI development complex of over 2,300 houses and apartments on a 2-mile stretch of land where Robert Taylor Homes public housing stood. Based on Venkatesh et al.'s (2004) estimate of 2,700 residents before displacement, over 2,200 will not have housing in Legends because of the influx of new residents who will be given priority over the previous residents of Robert Taylor. Overall, researchers and public housing advocates estimate that under the CHA's screening criteria only 12 to 15% of displaced families will be allowed to return to mixed-income developments built on the site of former public housing (Wilen & Nayak). Janet Smith (2006) concludes, "We can expect poverty to go down in some of these new mixed-income communities but not necessarily because poor people have escaped poverty—rather because poor people have been moved out and been replaced by higher income families" (p. 277).

Nor has HOPE VI "deconcentrated" poverty. The PFT displaced many of the African American tenants to low-income racially isolated areas or out of the city altogether, or they became homeless (Venkatesh et al., 2004). The affordable rental market in Chicago is extremely tight, due to gentrification, condo conversions, an inflated real estate market, and now foreclosures. The city is increasingly defined by gated communities, condominiums, and townhouse developments for the middle and upper middle classes and lack of good affordable rental housing (Affordable Housing, 2006). There is also an aversion on the part of landlords to rent to public housing residents or those with housing vouchers, forcing these tenants into specific, racially segregated areas of the city (Bennett, Hudspeth, & Wright, 2006). An official report on CHA relocation in 2003 stated, "vertical ghettos from which the families are being removed are being replaced with horizontal ghettos, located in well-defined, highly segregated neighborhoods on the west and south sides of Chicago" (Bennett, Smith, & Wright, 2006, p. 307). Looking at 11 census tracts on the near West Side in Chicago with booming market rate residential development, Bennett, Hudspeth, and Wright (2006) found 80% of new public housing to be built will be concentrated in two census tracts and a "narrow slice" of an adjoining third (p. 211). The majority of the Chicago Housing Authority's 35,000 Housing Choice Voucher households reside in predominately African American, poverty concentrated communities in Chicago, and more are now concentrated in predominantly African American communities with poverty rates above the city's average than 10 years ago ("Are We Home Yet?" 2009).

"Root Shock"

> People, too, need roots. Human communities, like the tree, cannot produce their "crown" without the massive network of connections that move nourishment from the earth to the entire organism of the group. The evil of urban renewal is that people were stripped of their roots, and forced, without aid, to struggle through the period of shock to replant themselves as best they might.
>
> (Fullilove, 2005, p. 191)

As HOPE VI reached the end of its first decade, critics argued that the policy had made things worse for many public housing residents. Far fewer units had been built than were lost under the policy, and few residents had returned to their communities refashioned as mixed- income. Residents suffered the trauma of dislocation, some numerous times (Popkin, 2006). This is just the latest iteration of urban displacement. Mindy Fullilove (2005) describes the trauma of displacement as "root shock"—"the traumatic stress of the loss of [one's] lifeworld" (p. 20). Her research documents the loss of community and psychic pain of displacement experienced by people uprooted by urban renewal and gentrification in the 1960s.

In our interviews and observations, "root shock" captures the experience of students relocated to schools outside their immediate neighborhoods and in some cases to as many as four schools in 3 years, as part of HOPE VI and Ren2010. Parents reported they were given little notice before their school was closed and some siblings were sent to different schools. A parent described her experience:

> Children were separated, because my boys were separated…. My younger son [age 4] was sent all the way to [school]…. But they were getting out at the same time, which was hard on me, you know, because my older son [age 7] couldn't get out on time to come get [younger son]. So [my younger son] he's over here being let out amongst the crowd … it was very frustrating that whole year.
>
> (Lipman, Person, & KOCO, 2007, p. 42)

Multiple studies show that student mobility negatively affects children's academic achievement, emotional health, and general well-being (e.g., Kerbow, 1996; Kerbow, Azcoitia, & Buell, 2003; Minneapolis Family Housing Fund, 1998; Rumberger & Larson, 1998; Wood, Halton, Scarla, Newacheck, & Nessim, 1993). In interviews with parents and teachers in Chicago schools that received transfer students due to Ren2010, we heard about the anxiety experienced by dislocated students:

> A lot of the children can't even explain themselves, you can see the nervousness in them (teacher interview).
>
> (Lipman, Person, & KOCO, 2007, p. 30)

> And then another factor which is a factor in education is most students are comfortable when they leave one grade to go to another grade and they know you … versus transferring to [a new school] and this has been happening with transfer students … versus going into a school and you don't even know the teachers, you don't know anybody…so, you've got to make all these new adjustments … whereas, when a student has been at [home school] since Kindergarten, it's like going home (teacher interview).
>
> (Lipman, Person, & KOCO, 2007, p. 30)

Urban schools in the United States are often pathologized in the media and in scholarship, but they are far more complex spaces in which community and caring prevail although there are also uncaring teachers and inadequate resources (e.g., Ladson-Billings, 1994). What may appear to outsiders as "deprived," "run-down," even pathological communities and "bad" schools, have far more complex meanings for those who live there.

> One of the changes you feel the most I think the greatest impact is that there's no longer this sense of community atmosphere. You know, you've got students that are from all over the place. So you no longer have a sense of community. You know when ___ was a COMMUNITY school [emphasis original], the parents knew the other parents. You began to meet the parents because you have the siblings, cousins, or what have you. You know, it becomes uh, uh … almost like a family-orientated learning environment. And so there's a greater connection to the child…. (teacher interview).

> (Lipman, Person, & KOCO, 2007, p. 24)

In 2008, CPS proposed to close 10 schools alleged to be underenrolled[4] as part of ongoing Ren2010 school closings. The schools served low-income African American and Latino/a students in areas of the city that were gentrified or were in the process of being gentrified. An example is Abbott Elementary School, located in Wentworth Gardens Public Housing Development. Wentworth is one of a few CHA complexes where residents won the full right of return to rehabbed buildings. It is also in an area where median house prices rose 30 to 70% from 2002 to 2004 (Greenley et al., 2008). CPS proposed to close Abbott, the community's only elementary school since the housing complex was built, and bus the children, all African Americans, almost 2 miles to a school in a neighborhood with a history of racial hostility against Blacks. The safety issues and lack of a neighborhood school that was the center of the community would discourage families from returning in fall 2008 when the remaining building rehab was to be completed. As one parent said, this would accomplish "what CHA couldn't do"—drive out the public housing residents (Abbott parent, personal communication, January, 2008).

The meanings of existing community and the traumatic experiences of displacement are not to be found in planners' seemingly benevolent designs to engineer mixed-income development. The racially coded discourse of cultural and moral deficiency underlying this social engineering obscures the reality of displacement and disregards the value of social and cultural connections, particularly in communities experiencing race and class oppression. Greenbaum (2006) makes this point in relation to displacement of low-income working class African Americans in post-Katrina New Orleans. "People need to be connected to those who they know and trust. The sorrow that has spilled out in stories of [New Orleans] evacuees who find themselves cut off from the neighbors and places that were destroyed reflects that social truth" (p. 111). The "choice" to uproot oneself is reserved for the economically and racially privileged. It is qualitatively different from forced removal from one's school and community. Genuine "choice" should also mean ensuring "the right to stay put" (Imbroscio, 2008, p. 120) and the up-grading of one's own community.

Moralizing Poverty and Educational "Failure" and Pathologizing People of Color

At the core of the deconcentration/mixed-income policy agenda is a nexus of racialized, neoliberal academic discourses and ideologies that substitute cultural explanations of poverty for structural causes, pathologize people of color, and promote individual responsibility and market solutions. In this section, I look more closely at the central premise of HOPE VI: that high concentrations of very low-income public housing residents produce social pathologies (violence, drug abuse, gangs, unemployment, low academic achievement) which are at the root of poverty (Popkin, 2006). Deconcentrating poverty therefore will lead to improvements in behavior and workforce participation and integrate public housing residents into "mainstream" society (Popkin et al., 2004). On the assumption that middle-class homeowners will provide the role models and social capital low-income people need to work themselves out of poverty (Brophy & Smith, 1997; Popkin et al., 2004), HOPE VI aims to transform residents as much as transform housing (Zhang & Weisman, 2006). In the words of the U.S. Department of Housing and Urban Development, "[T]he intentional mixing of incomes and working status of residents [will] promote the economic and social interaction of low-income families within the broader community, thereby providing greater opportunity for the upward mobility of such families" (quoted in Bennett, Smith, & Wright, 2006, p. 20). The political clout of middle-class residents is also expected to bring better services, including schools, to the area (Popkin et al., 2004).

Nowhere in this narrative do we see the dignity, resilience, and analyses of public housing residents themselves or the record of intellectual, cultural, and political leadership of people who grew up in public housing and public schools (Williams, 2004). We do not hear about the persistent struggles of African American and Latino/a families for quality public education and housing. Not a word about pathbreaking, nationally recognized long term organizations of public housing residents, such as People for Community Recovery in Altgeld Gardens in Chicago fighting environmental racism on a shoestring. These are the resources and leadership for sustainable, community-driven transformation.

The assumptions of mixed-income planners are also contested in housing policy literature (e.g., L. Bennett, 1998; L. Bennett & Reed, 1999; Imbroscio, 2008; Schwartz & Tajbakhsh, 1997). Janet Smith (2000) argues that devolution of federal housing administration to local authorities and mixed-income policies do not take into account the economic and social forces that have historically shaped where poor people live; that is, race and class practices of exclusion and market forces that work against affordable and mixed-income housing. Instead, HOPE VI puts responsibility exclusively on public housing residents to transform in order to make the program work.

The common sense of mixed-income solutions braids recycled culture of poverty theories (Brophy & Smith, 1997) with a new set of racialized neoliberal and New Urbanist claims on the city. Michael Katz (1989) outlines a long history of moralizing poverty in the United States in which notions of the "undeserving poor" ... "represent the enduring attempt to classify poor people by merit" (p. 9). The concentration-of-poverty-breeds-pathology argument recalls this tradition in its most racialized form, echoing Oscar Lewis's (1966) influential thesis on the intergenerational transmission of the "culture of poverty" and Daniel Patrick Moynihan's claim that the "dysfunctional" Black family was at the root of a "tangle of pathologies" that locked African Americans into poverty (M. Katz, 1989). Although temporarily discredited in public policy discourse in the 1970s (though very much present in cultural deficit theories in education), the "culture of poverty" was revived with sociologist William Julius Wilson's (1987) influential theory of the underclass, and misreadings of that theory. Wilson argued that structural changes in the economy and the exodus of middle-class African Americans from inner city communities bred an underclass culture which is a principal barrier to African American labor force participation.

Bruce Katz, of the Brookings Institute and others (see Massey & Denton, 1993) picked up the concentration of poverty argument to support HOPE VI while, importantly, overlooking Wilson's argument for economic redistribution. Katz cites public housing as "the most egregious example of how spatial concentration of poverty leads to welfare dependency, sexual promiscuity, and crime" (quoted in L. Bennett, Hudspeth, & Wright, 2006, p.194). This narrative is pervasive in HOPE VI literature. For example, Rene Glover, CEO of the Atlanta Housing Authority, states, "A three- to five-year investment period must be made in the human development of families relocated from areas of concentrated poverty to assure their successful mainstreaming into society" (Glover, 2005, p. 3). This civilizing discourse is joined to the architectural determinism of the New Urbanist School of city planners who claim the architecture of high-rise public housing shapes the destiny of poor people. As urban sociologist Janet Abu-Lughod (2005) points out, "The awful conditions in the projects were redefined as a 'new pathology' caused by the high-rise architecture itself" (p. 299). Interestingly, while this discourse circulated to explain demolition of high-rise public housing, upscale high-rise residential buildings are sprouting up throughout the downtown area.

The conflation of race, concentration of poverty, and social pathology is prevalent in popular accounts of the benefits of gentrification in African

American areas such as Chicago's Kenwood-Oakland (the Midsouth), where *Chicago Tribune* reporters tell us, "It's focus is shifting from cleaning out bad elements to bringing in good ones" (Grossman & Leroux, 2006, p. 12). Boyd describes the potency of this discourse to redefine the race and class topography of the city:

> The discursive frameworks that individuals and organizations use to understand gentrification are more than rhetorical texts to be deconstructed; they are also reflections of political economic arrangement that have consequences for the quality of urban life. By providing evaluative criteria with which to consider and judge gentrification, they not only influence public debate on the subject; they also buttress the concrete distribution of material resources that supports uneven neighborhood change.
>
> (Boyd, 2005, p. 268)

In the United States, there is a long history of locating educational problems in the "deficient" cultures, languages, and family structures of immigrants, the working class, and people of color: the Americanization movement in the early 20th century, culture of poverty in the early 1960s, "compensatory" education in the 1960s and 1970s, and the Coleman Report in 1966, which found that differences in student background and socioeconomic status have a greater effect on educational outcomes than school resources and curriculum. The current influence of education entrepreneur Ruby Payne (1998/2005) has breathed new life into the conservative, racially coded theory of the relationship of a "culture of poverty" and educational "failure" (Ng & Rury, 2006).

Race is not mentioned, but culture is a proxy in a discourse about certain essentialized negative cultural traits, such as lack of effort, inappropriate values, problematic behaviors and that prevent people from succeeding (Bonilla-Silva, 2003). In the post-Civil Rights era's rearticulation of race to a discourse of culture, it makes "sense" that mixing low-income students (with "cultural deficits") with middle-class students would be a corrective to their "low educational performance." Refrains of this discourse run through justifications for closing schools under Ren2010. At a February 2005 press conference announcing the closing of Englewood High School, the CEO of CPS explained that the school would be closed because it exhibited a "culture of failure."

The representation of Black and Latino/a urban space as pathological is yoked to the supposedly regenerative and disciplining effects of the market. According to this racialized neoliberal logic, while public housing and public schools breed dysfunction and failure, private management and the market foster entrepreneurship, individual responsibility, choice, and discipline. For example, Terry Peterson, head of the Chicago Housing Authority, claimed that the PFT will not displace those who "want to work hard" and "share in the success" (Field notes, November 12, 2005). HOPE VI codifies the policing of these virtues. Under the 1998 Quality Housing and Work Reform Act, designed to promote "self sufficiency," public housing tenants in HOPE VI mixed-income developments must pass background and drug screening and housekeeping checks, must adhere to specific behavior rules, and meet work requirements (Wilen & Nayak, 2006).[5] Under the One Strike rule, tenants can be evicted if any family member commits a criminal offense on or off public housing property (Hackworth, 2007). In public meetings I attended, residents and social service workers reported that relocated public housing residents are afraid to voice complaints about their housing for fear housing officials will use HOPE VI rules to evict them (Field notes, November 12, 2005; December 5, 2005). No comparable rules and regulations are required for higher income residents living in the same housing complex. Far from its democratic rhetoric, these developments are reminiscent of a colonial system of containment and regulation of a subordinated population.

Rachel Weber (2002) points out that the neoliberal state has to grapple with two contradictory imperatives: creating conditions for capital accumulation and managing potential resistance. The democratic and inclusive discourse of "mixed-income communities" can be interpreted as a response to this contradiction. Mixed-income schools may serve a similar legitimating function, masking economic processes and policy decisions that reduce resources and withdraw support for struggling schools. Once devalued, the schools are labeled "failures," closed, reopened, and rebranded for a largely new clientele. In the eyes of teachers and administrators we interviewed in African American schools in the Midsouth, they were "set up for failure" (Lipman, Person, & KOCO, 2007). They recounted a history of shrinking resources, lack of support for teachers, and cuts in support staff over the past few years while they were simultaneously held to ever-rising benchmarks of Chicago's accountability system and No Child Left Behind. A teacher described the effect of overcrowding in special education classes: **"And you're actually expecting to teach a...child who has been labeled LD [learning disabled] with 16 other children with one teacher. You're lying to me because you don't expect that child to learn. You expect them to fail. You want that community rousted..."** (Lipman, Person, & KOCO, p. 35).

The "Third Leg": Mixed-Income Schools, Neoliberal Development, and Racial Exclusion

[N]obody down here was really taken into account when they were doing it [closing the school]. No one in this community was supposed to even know about it until it was time to slap it on us.

(Interview, school support staff, Lipman, Person, & KOCO, 2007, p. 39)

"[I]inequitable real estate development in cities is the knife-edge of neoliberal urbanism, reflecting a wider shift toward a more individualistic and market-driven political economy in cities. Gentrification, publicly funded projects for private benefit, and the demolition of affordable housing are part of this knife-edge ..." (Hackworth, 2007, p. 192). Closing schools in gentrifying areas and opening mixed-income schools of choice that appeal to new middle-class residents are also part of this "knife-edge." When Ren2010 was unveiled in 2004, the Chicago Metropolitan Planning Council made this connection explicit:

> Looking ahead, a number of issues should be addressed as Renaissance 2010 unfolds, including how to coordinate the development timelines of mixed-income communities with the openings and closings of schools nearby, how to establish ongoing communication mechanisms to report on the status and progress of Renaissance 2010 to all of the stakeholders involved in the process, and how to market these new schools to parents considering moving into the new mixed income communities.

Good schools and options within the public school system are important in the global competition to attract highly skilled professionals, to court investors to potential gentrification sites, and to subsequently market gentrified and gentrifying areas to new middle-class residents. Terry Mezany, CEO of Chicago Community Trust and member of the planning team for the Ren2010 Midsouth Plan, described the connection between schools and development: "It's a delicate balance to pull something like this off. You can't do it just with the housing and retail development. You have to get the third leg and that's the schools" (Olszewski & Sadovi, 2003, p. 1).

Ren2010 is concentrated primarily in low-income African American and Latino/a areas of the city that are in various stages of gentrification. To close schools is to further undermine these communities by creating additional instability in an already unstable housing environment. A community resident said, "When you destroy a community's school, you destroy a community" (Field notes, February 17, 2005). The importance of schools as a point of connection is reflected in our interviews with teachers who reported that some displaced families continued to send their children to their home schools, even though they had to travel long distances (Lipman, Person, & KOCO, 2007).

Before communities can be gentrified, they have to be devalued, prepared for redevelopment, and reimagined as places of value; to do so it is necessary to construct a reality of "easily discardable people and social life" (D. Wilson, Wouters, & Gremmenos, 2004, p. 1181). Race is at the center of this process. Gentrification of African American communities is facilitated by an urban mythology "that has identified Blacks with disorder and danger in the city" (Haymes, 1995, p. x). Similarly, closing schools in African American communities is facilitated by their construction in the media and public policy as dysfunctional and violent.[6] These portrayals mask the nexus of racialized public policy and investment decisions that produced deindustrialization, disinvestment, unemployment, and degradation of public health, the built environment, and education in communities of color over the past 50 years. The predicament of urban schools cannot be understood outside this history. And closing schools to reopen them as mixed-income schools branded to appeal to the middle class and Whites (even when initial gentrifiers are African American) is located in this social process.

This sort of social engineering, in which people are objects to be manipulated according to a plan devised elsewhere, destroys not only the material places in which people live and work but also what Fullilove (2005) calls, a human ecosystem, "a web of connections—a way of being" (p. 4). Space is not simply a container, but a social process whose meaning is constituted by those who live and work there. It is both "the 'perceived space' of material spatial practices and the 'conceived space' of symbolic representations and epistemologies" (Soja, 1999, p. 74). Mixed-income communities/schools that are contrived by the state in partnership with capital are part of a racialized project to eliminate Black urban space, symbolically and materially (Haymes, 1995).

Plans for "transformation" and "renaissance" negate the history of Black urban public spaces as central to a culture and politics of resistance (Haymes, 1995, p. 10) and African American schools as centers of community (Siddle Walker, 1996). When people are uprooted and relocated to contrived mixed-income communities/schools not of their own making, what is at stake is issues of identity, place, solidarity, political resistance, and material survival (Haymes). The arrogant attitude of policy makers who presume to know what is best for these communities is illustrated by Alexander Polikoff, senior staff counsel of Business and Professional People for the Public Interest (BPPI), a policy group supporting mixed-income development in Chicago:

> For me the case made by William Julius Wilson is entirely persuasive … [ellipsis original] Wilson speaks of the "social pathologies" of ghetto communities … so persuaded am I of the life-blighting consequences of Wilson's concentrated poverty circumstances, that I do not view even homelessness as clearly a greater evil.
>
> (quoted in Wright, 2006, pp.159–160)

This attitude reflects disregard for the knowledge and experiences of African American and Latino/a students, parents, and committed educators. Their exclusion from decisions that deeply affect them is a prominent theme in the rallies, press conferences, town hall meetings, and forums on Ren2010. In our interviews (Lipman, Person, & KOCO, 2007), a consistent criticism was that the school community was not consulted. Not only is this deeply disrespectful, but, by disregarding the community, school authorities failed to take advantage of the knowledge and experience of those who live there and work with the students. Some teachers and families reported that they were not even informed in advance that their school was to be closed. A parent said,

We were not informed [even] a month ahead of time. It was like a couple of weeks. And we were not informed by word of mouth. We had a flier. Basically, it was like this. Read this. Take it home and read it. And I mean, it's like, it's closing and there's nothing we can do about it. No voting, no taking a stand or nothing. This is law.

(Lipman, Person, & KOCO, 2007, p. 39)

This is another instantiation of neoliberals' aversion to democracy and their preference for top-down decision by fiat to streamline policy making without "interference" from a democratic polity as well as to squelch potential resistance (Gill, 2003; Harvey, 2005; Wacquant, 2001, 2008). In contrast, when people in the Midsouth inadvertently found out in advance about the Midsouth Plan to close 20 of 22 schools in their area, they were able to organize an effective coalition to stop it. This parallels the experience of public housing residents systematically locked out of fundamental decisions about the PFT. As Bennett, Hudspeth, and Wright (2006) write in their study of the transformation of public housing in Chicago: "From the standpoint of the city and CHA, effective dialogue with public housing residents appears to be consultation in which the residents, at the outset and throughout the process, agree to premises advanced by city and public housing agency officials" (p. 202). CHA resident organizations had to pry their way in with demonstrations, noisy public hearings, persistent organizing, lawsuits, and even the intervention of the United Nations Special Rapporteur on Adequate Housing (Wright, 2006). This was also repeated in other HOPE VI cities (e.g., see Pitcoff, 1999).

Thus, public housing residents and parents and low-income communities of color are "objectified," "acted upon by progressive policy action," and "treated" through programs to promote better housekeeping, work motivation, and social behaviors in schools (Bennett, Smith, Wright, 2006, p.10). It is not an exaggeration to claim that people who have faced dislocation, containment, and moral "rectification" since 1619, through slavery, the Black codes, segregation, red lining, and urban renewal are again displaced, contained, and socially engineered through neoliberal housing and education policy (see Wacquant, 2001, 2008). Uprooting African Americans from "homeplaces," in the service of capital accumulation (investment in real estate development) and race and class appropriation, is justified by a racialized social warrant for private expropriation of Black urban space (Haymes, 1995; Lipsitz, 2006b). It continues a long history of assumed entitlement of the affluent and Whites to the material and cultural assets of people of color.

Conclusion

Mixed-income schools and communities are not inherently wrong. Racially and economically diverse and democratic cities and neighborhoods could be a step toward a more egalitarian society. Connecting unemployed people and low-income families to new educational opportunities and jobs is essential if we are to reduce poverty. And upgrading the deplorable stock of affordable housing and reinvesting in communities that have been profoundly disinvested for the past 30 years is an urgent task. That youth and their families need excellent health care and schools, good housing, rich opportunities for leisure and recreation, safe neighborhoods, and inexpensive and easily accessible transportation is obvious. And people should have the right to live where they choose, regardless of race or social class or any marginalized identity.

But current neoliberal proposals for mixed-income schools/housing are distant from these goals. The contrived mixed-income schools/housing developments being created or promoted in Chicago and elsewhere are a far cry from organic and egalitarian communities. Nor are they an outgrowth of greater racial tolerance or reduced poverty or equalization of resources. In a number of ways they codify and institutionalize social separation and stigma through separate sets of rules and surveillance, through educational tracking and special educational programs, and formal and informal selection mechanisms. Despite good intentions by some local housing and education advocates, mixed-income schools and housing under HOPE VI legitimate private redevelopment of the land on which public housing and working class neighborhoods stood. They disperse and thus dilute the political power of low-income working class African Americans in particular. They serve to attract middle-class property tax payers and consumers of gentrification while legitimating the displacement of those who formerly lived there on the premise of bettering them. They shift millions in tax dollars to developers, open new arenas for capital accumulation, and fuel speculative financialization of the urban economy. The centrality of real estate development and gentrification to capital accumulation and the politics of racial exclusion and containment are rationalized by pathologizing Black and Latino/a urban spaces and denying the humanity of people ejected from their homes, schools, and communities.

In sum, mixed-income discourses and policies negate four important points: (a) The roots of unemployment, violence, failure of schools, material deterioration of communities, and intensification of poverty and racism are in the power structures of society. As Susan Smith (1993) points out in reference to a similar set of discourses in England, the racialization of culture in the social construction of racial segregation "portrays urban deprivation as a moral problem, so deflecting attention away from the power structures creating and sustaining the inequalities dividing 'Black' and 'White' Britain" (p. 136). (b) Improved architecture does not resolve ideological and social conditions. The aesthetics of new urban residential developments can't make people of different classes mix and express solidarity nor can they help low-income people get a good job or education or improve their standard of living. (c) The assumption that values of middle-class people are necessary for low-income people of color (specifically African Americans and Latinas/os) is a colonial model. In the U.S. context, this deeply racist ideology negates particularly the historical role of Black urban communities as spaces not only of intellectual and cultural production but also bases of political and cultural resistance in the face of racist terror and discrimination (Haymes, 1995). It also negates African Americans' historical struggles for education and examples of excellent African American schools despite inequitable resources and persistent discrimination. (d) Plans to relocate and resocialize low-income people of color without their participation or self-determination are not only unworkable, and clearly racist, but they further the dedemocratization of society. The state's superficial performance of soliciting community input coupled with its appointed advisory boards, as in HOPE VI and Renaissance 2010, reflect the democratic deficits of neoliberalism.

Mixed-income deconcentration strategies discursively shift the terrain of public policy from economic redistribution to behavior modification. These strategies gain traction, in part, because they are grounded in deeply held ideologies that moralize the poor and pathologize people of color, reframing structural problems as moral and behavioral. This framing obligates the state to do nothing about the root causes of poverty, racism, substandard and scarce affordable housing, and crumbling oppressive schools. Nor does it require critical examination of the structures and ideologies that perpetuate poverty and educational inequity and marginalize low-income students of color. Moving students into mixed-income schools is a strategy that leaves unquestioned the curricula, pedagogies, and school structures, cultures, and practices *within* schools that have been shown to produce unequal opportunities to learn and that reproduce broader social inequalities. Similarly, HOPE VI mixed-income strategies do not account for the economic and social forces that have historically shaped where poor people live; that is, race and class exclusion and market forces that obstruct affordable and mixed-income housing (J. Smith, 2000).

Challenging racialized neoliberal explanations of poverty and educational outcomes is an important step toward reframing education "failure." Darling-Hammond (2004) proposes a shift from presumed student deficits to policies that guarantee every student the right to equitable education.[7] This shift was embraced by the *Civil Rights Framework for Providing All Students an Opportunity to Learn*, released by seven national civil rights organizations in July 2010. Ladson-Billings (2005) also argues that we need a paradigm shift from the "achievement gap," which focuses on students, to the "education debt" owed to African Americans and other people of color and which can only be rectified by collectively addressing its full spectrum of historical, economic, sociopolitical, and moral components. The same can be said for the housing debt owed African Americans, Latino/as, Native peoples, and other people of color and working class people in general. Counter to claims that nobody knows how to fix "poor" schools (Kahlenberg, 2001) and that public housing is a failed experiment (The Final Report of the National Commission on Severely Distressed Public Housing, 1992), significant redistributive remedies have never been tried. There has been no substantive effort to equalize school resources or transform structural and cultural aspects of schools that reproduce inequality and marginalization. The same is true for providing quality housing and other basic human needs and eliminating poverty, although these remedies are well within the scope of U.S. resources. The anemic Keynesian welfare state policies are no model for what is needed.

The kernel of an alternative to the neoliberal strategy is concretely present in the voices of public housing residents, displaced families, and parents who insist on full participation in decisions which affect them, recognition of their knowledge and community wisdom, and a just distribution of resources. Discourses of deficiency and pathology are contested on the ground. An African American community leader challenged: "CPS should be held accountable for decades of unequal education in communities of color rather than making parents and students the scapegoat" (Field notes, January 14, 2008). A teacher, who testified at a public hearing, one of hundreds of parents, students, and teachers present to oppose their school being "phased out," said, "Let us become a model of responsible and thoughtful urban change. Low-income is not synonymous with low-achievement. That myth must be phased out" (Field notes, May 15, 2008).

The discourse of mixed-income and choice (through housing vouchers and school choice) reframes the reality of disinvestment, displacement, subsidies to developers, racial exclusion, and surveillance as *opportunity* for low-income people. As I have discussed in previous chapters, these policies gain credibility with some low-income people themselves in the face of the failures and exclusions of bureaucratic, professionalized, racialized state welfare policies that made public housing and schools untenable for many working class people of color. Yet, in reality, low-income families in the areas experiencing mixed-income development have little real choice. While some have benefited, the majority will not be admitted to new developments, and they must negotiate an extremely tight private housing market. While some children attend better schools, many are transferred from one school to the next with few good schools available, and have no guarantee of a place in new mixed-income schools. Although CHA carries on a concerted good news campaign to tout the opportunities of mixed-income developments for public housing residents, media accounts have also revealed some of the contradictions and exclusions. The benefits accrue to some individuals, not the collective of public housing tenants and other low-income people who have a right to decent housing and schools, regardless of their housekeeping practices, number of children, success in the housing lottery, income, or ability to navigate the system.

At nearly every community meeting I have attended, there has been a strong sentiment that, as one African American resident put it, "Ultimately the purpose is to get us all out of the community" (Field notes, July 15, 2004). Still, community perspectives are mixed. Given the uninhabitable state of many U.S. high-rise public housing complexes, the chance to move somewhere else is a relief, although it carries the cost of leaving friends, support networks, and roots, and the uncertainty of not knowing if one can return. This deep contradiction is captured by the documentary, *Voices of Cabrini* (Bezalel & Ferrara, n.d.), that voices perspectives of those who resist and those who welcome the demolition of Chicago's Cabrini Green high rise public housing. (At its peak, Cabrini was home to 20,000 residents in 28 high and low rises on 70 acres of land. In the early 2000s, the area's real estate prices skyrocketed and CPS built a new premier magnet high school.) And given the persistent failure of some schools to educate low-income African American children, parents are desperate for change. In the absence of alternatives, wading into the system of mixed-income schools, choice, and charters at least allows for some individual agency for those able to exercise it. Absent in these "choices" is "the right to stay put" in regenerated communities and schools, by and for the people who live there.

I delve into these contradictions in chapter 6, but first I examine a key actor in the neoliberal education policy complex, corporate venture philanthropy.

5

VENTURE PHILANTHROPY

From Government to Governance

With Cristen Jenkins

An account of the political economy of urban education is incomplete without examining the role of corporate philanthropy. In the past 15 years, philanthropy has leveraged market-driven, managerial education reform agendas in the United States and beyond. Its influence is the product of a new brand of aggressive entrepreneurialism in corporate foundations that finds fertile soil in the neoliberalization of public institutions and government. This new, entrepreneurial "venture philanthropy" has also reshaped social struggles and practices of community-based nonprofit organizations (Incite! 2007). City government reliance on public–private partnerships, the centrality of cities to capital accumulation, and the race and class inequalities that threaten urban social stability put cities at the center of foundation strategies. As we will show, these strategies are a vehicle for multilayered influence over education policy by a small number of venture capitalists.

This chapter explores the role of venture philanthropy in the neoliberal restructuring of urban education and its intervention in the terrain of urban social struggle. By funding a web of educational research, initiatives, and policy priorities, corporate foundations shape hegemonic neoliberal ideologies and policies about schooling (Hassel & Way, 2005; Kumashiro, 2008; Roelofs, 2007). Saltman (2009) summarizes: "Venture philanthropy treats schooling as a private consumable service and promotes business remedies, reforms, and assumptions with regard to public schooling" (p. 53). Strategically, foundations focus funding on leading edge neoliberal experiments in urban school districts and leverage them to shape the national education agenda. In Chicago, the Gates Foundation has invested millions of dollars in a web of initiatives to support school choice, turnaround models, high school restructuring, and performance-based pay for teachers. These high profile projects have become central planks of a national education agenda. They promote the ideology of the market and entrepreneurship and serve capital accumulation by promoting market solutions and focusing education on workforce preparation to serve economic competitiveness.

In this chapter, Cristen Jenkins and I argue that venture philanthropy in education contributes to neoliberal urban restructuring. The interweaving of philanthropic organizations and city government is part of the shift to managerial governance and public–private partnerships. Venture philanthropists have become part of the "shadow state" (Wolch, 1990), playing key roles in setting urban policy and performing government functions with no public accountability. We look at the role of venture philanthropy in promoting market reforms, co-opting democratic projects, and stabilizing neoliberal urban education policy by attempting to undermine, or steer, oppositional social movements. However, this picture is complicated by ways in which community and education activists may tactically use funding for progressive projects, exemplifying the fluidity and contested nature of hegemony and possibilities for agency.

This is not to deny that there are progressive program officers and directors of some large philanthropies and small progressive foundations that promote a grassroots, participatory agenda to defend and transform public education. The field of philanthropy is itself contested. But this is not our focus here. Instead we focus on the role of corporate venture philanthropy in the neoliberalization of urban education and its role in the neoliberalization of urban governance.

We begin by describing the shift in philanthropic strategies in the neoliberal context. We go on to analyze venture philanthropy's role in urban education nationally and implications for the political economy and racial politics of the city. Then we briefly describe four Gates Foundation projects in Chicago— small schools, Academy of Urban School Leadership (AUSL), youth organizing, and parent organizing. Our analysis draws on public archival data, data produced by community organizations, interviews with community activists and education reformers, and observations of numerous community forums, coalition meetings, public events, and press conferences.

Bringing Venture Capitalism to Urban Policy

> Sometimes, to promote innovation, we need to take calculated risks on promising ideas. Some of these risks will pay off; others won't.
>
> (Bill and Melinda Gates Foundation Overview, August 31, 2009a)

Corporate philanthropy has historically played a significant role in shaping U.S. education to serve capital accumulation, social control, and White supremacy. Following the Civil War, foundations launched by "robber barons" used their newly acquired wealth to shape a colonial Black education system in the

South that was central to the development of racially stratified labor markets in the United States (Anderson, 1988; Watkins, 2001). At the turn of the 20th century, corporate foundations supported eugenics and sterilization and intelligence testing for control and order in the liberal corporate state (Karier, 1972; Selden, 1999; Winfield, 2007). Progressive Era industrialists, bankers, and land speculators (such as steel magnate Andrew Carnegie; Leland Stanford, governor of California who made his fortune speculating on land for railroad construction; Johns Hopkins, who owned the Baltimore & Ohio Railroad; and John Rockefeller, head of Standard Oil) spearheaded the development of major U.S. universities. Their expressed purpose was to strategically use higher education and the social sciences to steer social policy in the interest of developing capitalism and social control (Guilhot, 2007; Karier, 1972). During the 1960s and 1970s, foundations primarily funded school-based projects, provided "seed money" to initiate educational programs, and supplemented state funding (Jehl & Payzant, 1992). The relative fiscal stability of schools during the Keynesian period minimized foundation influence.

However, in the 1980s, in reaction to declining U.S. economic dominance and falling rates of profit, corporate foundation-funded think tanks "manufactured" an education crisis, shifting educational discourse to economic competitiveness and efficiency (Berliner & Biddle, 1997), and corporate philanthropy shifted to comprehensive education reform. The latest iteration is an outgrowth of the neoliberal turn to venture capitalism. It is their entrepreneurial strategies that distinguish venture philanthropists. They seek to shape social agendas through strategic investments in cutting-edge projects and institutional experiments. As scholars and activists we have seen this role first hand in the operations of the Bill and Melinda Gates Foundation in Chicago. Gates steered the small schools movement away from its initial educationally progressive direction. The Academy for Urban School Leadership (AUSL), a major recipient of Gates funding, is the principal organization contracted by the School Board to take over neighborhood schools. AUSL has emerged as a national model for urban school takeover operators. Gates also funds parent and youth organizing efforts with complex implications, as we describe below.

The policies venture philanthropists promote open up new outlets for capital accumulation. By the late 1990s business publications were describing education as a potential $600 billion investment opportunity (Saltman, 2005, p. 4). Today, charter schools are big business. In May 2010, JPMorgan Chase, a global financial services company, announced a $325 million investment in charter school expansion (JP Morgan, 2010). Venture philanthropy projects may also serve particular business sectors, as with Bill Gates, founder of Microsoft, promoting investment in science, engineering, technology, and math education. But like the robber barons that preceded them, their broader goal is to shift policy in the interest of capitalist growth as a whole by promoting neoliberalization of the public sphere and gearing education to global competition. Through their focus on urban education, they also help shape urban policy.

The influence of venture philanthropy should be understood in the context of the vast fortunes amassed through neoliberalization of the global economy in the 1980s and 1990s. Like primitive accumulation of capital through colonialism, and like the fortunes amassed by the robber barons and industrialists of the 19th century, the unprecedented concentration of wealth generated through neoliberal "accumulation by dispossession" (Harvey, 2003), positioned a few billionaire capitalists to influence policy through the largess of their foundations. Simultaneously, cuts in federal funding to cities provided an opportunity. As discussed in chapter 2, city governments turned to privatization of public services along with real estate and tourism as key sources of revenue (Hackworth, 2007), and they partnered with corporate actors, including foundations, to help fund urban agendas. Corporate philanthropies were ideally positioned to leverage their enormous wealth to strategically shape the direction of social policy in areas such as health, education, and the environment. Entrepreneurs Bill Gates and Sam Walton and investor George Soros are iconic of this new breed of philanthropy.

Venture philanthropy is constitutive of the neoliberal shift from government to "governance," importing private sector management processes and discourses into the state. The "managerial state" deploys business practices and metrics (cost benefit analysis, outputs, performance indicators) to restructure public institutions for efficiency and effectiveness (Clarke & Newman, 1997; Rizvi & Lingard, 2009). In the culture of the "new public management" it is "normal" for the state to draw on the management skills of the private sector to run public institutions; for example, CEOs leading urban school districts. And the state joins up with corporate groups, such as Philadelphia's Center City District and the Commercial Club of Chicago, in public–private partnerships to make key decisions about urban policy and institutions. Corporate foundations both promote and utilize this environment to influence public policy.

We argue, as have others (K. Mitchell, 2001; Wolch, 1990), that corporate philanthropy plays a key role in the shift from government to governance through the growth of the "shadow state." Wolch describes the "shadow state" as an assemblage of voluntary organizations that operate in the interstices between the state and society. In the neoliberal context, these nonstate organizations take over provision of social services, thus absolving the state of responsibility for social welfare functions, yet they have no accountability to the public. We would add corporate philanthropy and for-profit service providers to voluntary organizations. Corporate philanthropists leverage local projects and experiments, that they fund to shape policy, and that are then supported and funded by the state or opened up to private providers, such as charter school operators.

Neoliberalism as a process is materialized through discourses and social practices on the ground (in chapter 6, I describe the role of parents and teachers) and through voluntary organizations and other nonstate actors (in this case, philanthropy). While philanthropic grants may be a relatively small part of city budgets and social sectors like education, their projects are often experiments in neoliberalization which help reshape common sense about the structures and purposes of social institutions. For example, we argue below that reliance on foundation grants has instilled a culture of entrepreneurship in public schools that is self-reproducing. As K. Mitchell (2001) points out, neoliberalism is "economically and socially entrenched in the minds of citizens and the capillaries of society to the point where, even with a change of government, the practices and ideology remain" (p. 166). Like voluntary organizations that have taken over provision of services from the state, venture philanthropy insinuates neoliberal practices and discourses into the microworkings of social institutions and the life of the city by establishing the legitimacy of corporate actors to promote public initiatives and thus take over state functions.

The New Lords of Urban Education

We are going to approach philanthropy with the same lack of reverence we gave to the traditional methods of the retail business when we started out there.

(Sam Walton, founder of Walmart and the Walton Family Foundation; waltonfamilyfoundation.org)

In the first decade of the 21st century, traditional donors such as the Carnegie and Rockefeller Foundations began scaling back grants to K-12 education. Meanwhile, venture philanthropists that included the Bill and Melinda Gates Foundation and the Walton Family Foundation emerged as leading education donors (Foundation Center, 2006). The new donors come from entrepreneurial backgrounds and bring an agenda of market-driven reform, managerialism, and economic competitiveness. By emphasizing a narrative of failing schools, they set the stage for neoliberal interventions (Kovacs, 2007). Like venture capitalists, they seek out innovative projects and expect returns on their investments. Their market orientation is reflected in their language: "Grants become investments, programs are ventures, and measures of impact generally involve the ability to scale up an initiative" (Scott, 2009, p. 115). They aggressively seek out educational grantees (rather than waiting for grant applications) and use their access to media, public officials, and think tanks to advocate for educational policies and programs (Scott, 2009). They leverage their funding to promote scaling up particular models to school districts, states, and nationally. In this way, these foundations have become "central and active drivers of policy making, research, and advocacy" (Scott, p. 108), steering education reform toward school choice, charter schools, and private management in underfunded urban districts. Like venture capitalists, they take risks in the hope that they will pay off in pathbreaking innovations and monitor their investments by tracking measurable results (a requirement of the grants).

The Eli and Edythe Broad Foundation, a key venture philanthropy, says on its Web site, "We don't simply write checks to charities." Broad strategically seeks out cutting edge projects with the expectation their investments will bring returns—in this case reshaping urban school leadership in line with business management principles and expansion of charter schools. Broad has provided nearly $400 million to urban areas to support school leadership training, school efficiency measures, and competition. They aim to redefine educational leadership in large urban districts by recruiting and training superintendents and principals from corporate and military ranks, shifting administrator training from universities to private business-oriented operations, and placing candidates in "medical style" residencies in urban school districts or charter management organizations (Saltman, 2009). Broad also runs a superintendent preparation academy, specifically to recruit noneducators, thus institutionalizing and propagating the business management–CEO model that has redefined the "superintendent" and even the principalship in Chicago, New York, and other large urban school districts (Anderson, 2010). Broad also supports charter schools, including a $50 million loan pool for charter school facility financing (Saltman, 2009).

Over the last few decades, a group of conservative foundations has used its wealth to bolster "limited government," free market economies, and private enterprise. Demarrais (2006) argues that while many "liberal" or "centrist" foundations (these include Gates) fund projects or targeted initiatives, conservatives provide long-term support to institutions and think tanks to shape public policy discourse and ideology. For example, the Children's Scholarship Fund, American Enterprise Institute, Heritage Foundation, and Cato Institute are among the groups that receive large grants to advance school privatization. Demarrais points to the "four sisters," Olin, Bradley, Scaife, and Smith Richardson Foundations, as illustrative. Their foci include right-wing think tanks to build conservative ideology in the university and conservative media outlets, policy institutes, and lobbying organizations to help shape public discourse and debates. Conservative foundation funding of the Milwaukee voucher movement (Pedroni, 2007), for example, has had a significant impact on the school choice movement. The conservatives' overlapping grantees create an interconnected web of organizations which leverage the conservative agenda into public policies. Some of their initiatives, particularly school choice, intersect with the neoliberal agenda (Apple, 2006). As of 2007, the Walton Family Foundation, established by ideological conservative Sam Walton who built the retail giant Wal-Mart, provided more funding for school choice than any other foundation (Cohen, 2007). Its target is urban districts.

Promoting an Entrepreneurial "Grants Culture"

The increased role of philanthropy in education has reframed how access to resources is accomplished, especially in urban schools. An entrepreneurial "grants culture" permeates all levels of the school system, from district headquarters to the classroom. Schools need additional resources to address social needs due to the economic and social hardships generated by investment, tax, labor, and social welfare policies over the past 30 years (Anyon, 2005). To meet these needs, teachers, administrators, parents, even students, routinely write grants for education projects, classroom books, professional development, technology, and student activities. This feeds a culture of entrepreneurism that is part of renorming and revaluing education (Ball, 2004) and changing teacher professionalism (Gewirtz, Mahony, Hextall, & Cribb, 2009). This grants culture absolves the state of responsibility to provide basic education services, shifts responsibility to teachers and schools, and covers over the social crises produced by neoliberal policies. It has become "unthinkable" that schools could operate without private funds.

This cultural shift both positions venture philanthropies as the normative leaders of the new educational entrepreneurship and it legitimates their role in shaping education agendas. An indication of this is a recent study showing that policy makers ranked billionaire Bill Gates as the most influential individual in education policy, ahead of then-U.S. Secretary of Education, Margaret Spellings (Swanson & Barlage cited in Scott, 2009). Grant Makers for Education (2008) also found that leading foundations look to Gates for leadership in educational philanthropy. Paradoxically, the corporate sector responsible for deindustrialization and cutting wages while receiving tax breaks that starved cities of revenue is now repositioned as beneficent donor, if not savior. The global billionaires who accumulated unfathomable wealth at the expense of most of the world's people are now our benefactors and leaders.

As with nonprofit organizations, reliance on corporate philanthropy contains a built-in agenda-shaping process. The foundations announce agendas and grant applicants and recipients reframe classroom practice and educational goals to fit them. For example, a major funder in Chicago provided a competitive grant to high schools to develop small learning communities. Teachers who had established a social justice academy within a neighborhood high school saw the grant as an opportunity to expand by framing the academy as a small learning community. But attached to the funding was a set of potentially compromising rubrics, requirements, outcomes, and frameworks. This is not to say that people on the ground cannot subvert these agendas in practice, but they do set a direction.

Setting and Resetting Education Agendas

Our high schools are obsolete. By obsolete, I don't just mean that they are broken, flawed and underfunded—although I can't argue with any of those descriptions.... Until we design high schools to meet the needs of the 21st century, we will keep limiting—even ruining—the lives of millions of Americans every year. Frankly, I am terrified for our workforce of tomorrow.

(Gates, 2005)

The Bill and Melinda Gates Foundation demonstrates the range of influence of venture philanthropy on urban education. The stated goal of the Gates Foundation, launched in 2000, is to bring innovations in health and education to the global community. In 2006, Warren Buffet announced a pledge to the Foundation of 10 million shares of Berkshire Hathaway, Inc. "B" stock worth more than $31 billion at the time. In 2008, the Gates Foundation had over $38 billion in assets available for charitable giving (Foundation Center, 2010). As of October 2008, they had distributed $17.3 billion in total grant commitments (gatesfoundation.org). The U.S. Program, which primarily focuses on public education, paid $483 million to grantees in 2007 alone. Gates funds tax exempt organizations that are independently identified by Gates staff.

When Bill Gates announced in 2005 that U.S. high schools are "obsolete," he set the stage for a huge investment in high school restructuring. By 2007, the foundation had invested more than $1.7 billion to restructure high schools, funding projects in more than 1,800 schools in 47 states and the District of Columbia (Gates Foundation, 2007). Gates sought out and engaged hundreds of partners in dozens of cities, mostly new school developers who work with charter management organizations (CMOs), to solidify school designs and replicate their models through a larger network of schools. By 2006, Gates had invested more than $128 million in CMOs to support 365 high schools across the country (Gates Foundation, 2006). In all, Gates invested nearly $4 billion to transform high school education and support college-readiness (gatesfoundation.org) using business strategies, practices, assessments, and goals. Gates explains the underlying objective is to retool the workforce for economic competitiveness, "This goal matters to all of us because much of the future growth in the workforce will come from precisely those groups of students that we have historically failed to ensure receive a strong education" (Gates Foundation, 2009b).

The foundation also promotes charter schools and teacher merit pay. These interventions undermine union protections and teacher collaboration. For example, Gates recently invested $90 million in Memphis City Schools and $40 million in Pittsburgh Public Schools to support teacher evaluation systems linked to student's academic achievement and $60 million to five public charter networks in California to implement new market strategies to recruit, evaluate, retain, and reward teachers. These productivity-driven teacher evaluation systems are incorporated in the federal Race to the Top education grants. Seizing the economic crisis as an opportunity to further market-based reforms,

Gates told the National Conference of State Legislators in July 2009, "Difficult times can spark great reforms" (gatesfoundation.org). He encouraged them to use stimulus funds to leverage standards, data systems, and competitive teacher evaluations. In November 2009, the foundation provided collateral to help secure $300 million in tax-exempt bonds to expand public charter schools in Houston (gatesfoundation.org). The foundation also provides large grants to charter school networks, including Green Dot, Aspire, IDEA, and EdVision to create new schools and design data systems to measure achievement.

Intensively funding neoliberal reforms in specific cities exemplifies the venture philanthropy strategy of leveraging local projects to shape broad policy agendas and discourses with implications beyond education. By introducing market-oriented, productivity evaluation for teachers, corporate philanthropy helps create a new common sense generalized to other public sector workers. Support for public advocacy and community organizing is a key part of this strategy (Grantmakers for Education, 2008). In Chicago alone, Gates has invested over $2 million toward strategic communications and grassroots advocacy initiatives. The Foundation has also contracted consulting agencies, such as Public Interest Projects, Inc., to strengthen their connection to national and local education organizing (gatesfoundation.org).

Gates's shifting emphases reflect venture philanthropy's insistence on measurable results (quick returns on investments). In the Foundation's early years, it supported high school restructuring. But when it concluded that schools "did not take radical steps to change their culture" (Gates, 2009a, p. 11), Gates pulled the plug on a project that involved thousands of teachers, students, and principals and moved on to charter schools. This arrogant instrumental brandishing of enormous resources to shift and shape schooling in urban school districts with a vast majority of low-income students of color parallels the role of private think tanks in shaping the destruction of public housing, displacing hundreds of thousands of low-income people of color (discussed in chapters 3 and 4). Like the robber barons and land speculators a century ago who formed foundations to determine the "appropriate" education for African Americans in the South and working class immigrants in the North, these new lords of urban education use their vast accumulation of wealth to influence what kind of education urban students should have and how teachers' work should be regulated.

Neoliberal Urbanism and Philanthropy

The education ventures driven by agenda-setting corporate philanthropy are constitutive of the entrepreneurial city and its attendant race and class inequalities and marginalities. Venture philanthropy plays a role in neoliberal urban restructuring, materially and ideologically. Its aggressive, highly publicized participation in public–private partnerships legitimates the role of corporate actors to shape urban policy and is an instantiation of decision making by publicly unaccountable nonstate actors that is central to neoliberal governance.

Laced with managerial approaches to the reform of public institutions and the logic of "investments" and "returns," venture philanthropies inject corporate strategies and discourses into urban policy. For example, Gates funded Mass Insight, a Boston based consulting group, to produce *The Turnaround Challenge*, a report promoting corporate turnaround strategies nationally.[1] The School Turnaround Strategy Group at Mass Insight, which has a contract with the Colorado Department of Education to help develop school reforms, provides "expert" knowledge to counter public opposition to closing neighborhood public schools in Denver (Meyer, 2009). In 2005, Chicago's Mayor Daley announced Gates's $11.2 million grant to Chicago for high school reform ("Daley Seeks," 2005). The grant also funded the Boston Consulting Group, a transnational strategic management consulting firm, to develop "a comprehensive strategy for managing a portfolio of high performing high schools." And it included $786,000 for New Leaders for New Schools, a business management oriented principal development organization. In 2005, Gates awarded over $2 million for the expansion of two charter school networks in Chicago ("Daley Seeks," 2005).

When corporate foundations enable the shift from public provision of services to the market in one urban sector, such as education, they contribute to the neoliberal restructuring of cities in broad terms. The $11.2 million Gates investment in Chicago education included $6 million to the University of Chicago's Center for Urban School Improvement to open charter schools and develop a network of high schools on the South Side. In previous chapters I discussed the relationship of closing neighborhood schools to gentrification of that area. Gates's funding facilitates replacing public schools with university-affiliated charter schools that, regardless of good intentions of those involved, are part of rebranding the area for middle and upper middle class homebuyers. In this sense, Gates parallels the role of the Chicago-based MacArthur Foundation in the plan to redesign the Midsouth area by guaranteeing initial investments in mixed-income developments to replace public housing.

Nowhere is the role of corporate philanthropy in restructuring the city more dramatically illustrated than in post-Hurricane Katrina New Orleans where foundations swooped in to push to the forefront longstanding proposals to privatize public schools and public housing. Instead of rebuilding the public school system, $17.5 million from the Broad, Gates, Walton, and other venture philanthropies supported the creation of charter schools, alternative business-oriented administrator preparation programs, and Teach for America alternate teacher certification (Saltman, 2009). This targeted funding assisted the city's corporate-led redevelopment commission to gut the public school system.

In New Orleans, as in Chicago, this move was integral to displacement of low-income people of color and their exclusion from the "new" New

Orleans (Buras et al., 2010). Foundations helped create an elite charter school network for more affluent and privileged residents assuring their presence in a Whiter, more affluent New Orleans. At the same time, the state's refusal to rebuild public schools in working class African American areas was tied to refusing to rebuild homes and neighborhoods. Closing schools was coupled with tearing down public housing and closing public hospitals—all of which ensured that low-income African Americans would not return to the city while it opened up what had become prime real estate (Saltman, 2009). In short, venture philanthropy-funded education projects linked to disinvestment and reinvestment in urban space are another lever in the racialized neoliberal restructuring of the city.

Detroit is shaping up to be a similar story. The city's mayor, with the initiative of several foundations, launched a plan to, as residents say, "clearcut" low-income neighborhoods, relocate residents to "opportunity zones," and destroy the sustainable communities they are attempting to build. According to Sharon "Shea" Howell, Detroit activist and professor at Oakland University:

> What we're facing now is the major philanthropic organizations who have absolutely no public accountability are pouring money behind both the demolition efforts and to target some neighborhoods they will develop and other neighborhoods that they will let fall. So our philanthropic organizations, without public accountability or any public discussion, are reshaping the face of the city on a vision they have not even bothered to share with the citizens.
>
> (Howell, 2010)

This plan is linked to closing 44 neighborhood schools and opening up a market of charter and specialty schools. Foundations are funding new school start-ups and establishing an accountability system to evaluate schools for closing or opening. Nate Walker, Detroit teacher, has said: "So that is totally taken out of the realm of the public sphere where parents and community members decide on a type of education that is necessary for the city, and foundations and folks who are not necessarily considering those voices are deciding what is good education" (Walker, 2010).

Venture Philanthropy Agenda-Setting in Chicago

The Gates Foundation agenda finds fertile ground in Chicago, an urban school district in the forefront of neoliberal education reform, with Renaissance 2010 cast as the national model. In this section we briefly discuss four Gates projects in Chicago which illustrate the intervention of philanthropy in the terrain of urban struggle: small schools, school turnarounds, youth organizing, and parent organizing.

Small Schools

> I asked what the proposal process was. He [Gates representative] whipped out a pad and jotted some things down, on the pad. I got somebody to type it up and gave it back to him and that was the proposal ... the rest was all downhill after that.
>
> (Interview, Small Schools leader, March 18, 2009)

In 1991, a group of university faculty and public school teachers started the Small Schools Workshop in Chicago. The goal was to support the development of several small high schools and teacher-initiated charter schools. According to founders, the small schools movement was grounded in the histories and theories of the Civil Rights Movement, Deweyian progressive education, teacher professional communities, and personalized learning environments (Klonsky & Klonsky, 2008). The movement was inspired by the Coalition of Essential Schools which emphasized curricular depth, and particularly by Central Park East High School, a small experimental school in New York where all students were known well, teachers worked collaboratively, and the curriculum pivoted on "essential questions" (Meier, 1996). In the early 1990s, these projects invigorated the national conversation on education reform, spoke to problems of large bureaucratic urban high schools, and inspired small schools as a way to carve out space for progressive pedagogical practice. The idea was to develop these exemplars to influence the system as a whole. "The small schools movement was not just about small, but the idea of restructuring, rethinking traditional schooling in a more emancipatory way for teachers. It was hoped that would lead to bigger changes in the system" (Interview, Small Schools leader, March 18, 2009).

The Small Schools Workshop, funded mostly by local foundations, seemed to involve compromise from the outset, with participation of the Commercial Club's Leadership for Quality Education and other business-oriented groups, African American civic organizations, school reform groups, and the teachers' union. This was reflected in the Workshop's agreement that new small schools would not be required to have elected Local School Councils (LSCs). Since all Ren2010 schools are by definition small schools, this set conditions for Renaissance 2010 to later eliminate LSCs. Still, in the early days, small schools adhered to much of their initial democratic agenda, although the Workshop was always contested territory (Interview, Small Schools leader, March 18, 2009).

However, what began as a largely teacher initiated project in the late 1980s and early 1990s was picked up by major national foundations. "By 1995, the muscle philanthropists had begun to exert a profound influence on the small-schools movement" (Klonsky & Klonsky, 2008, p.129). Gates staff visited the Workshop in 1999, toured some small schools, and immediately expressed interest in funding the project at $20 million over 5 years. Local funders insisted that Gates coordinate with them and with the mayor's agenda, and the

Small Schools Workshop lost control of the overall direction. "It dawned on me that what Gates funding was about was they wanted to hire me/us to manage their $20 million initiative in Chicago.... This wasn't an empowerment thing. It was a way to bring the money in and the big power guys would hire us to implement their program" (Interview, Small Schools leader, March 18, 2009).

Gates's vision was quite different from that of the Workshop. For Gates, breaking up big schools was a technical solution without the teacher autonomy, democracy, and social justice that motivated many in the small schools movement. Under Gates the discourse of small schools shifted to business metaphors, accountability metrics, and a corporate franchise model to replicate a prototype to be imposed on teachers and communities (see Gates, 2008). In 2001 Gates invested nearly $1.5 billion in the small learning communities initiative (Klonsky & Klonsky, 2008, p. 31). The foundation used its enormous financial resources to reroute the small schools movement in Chicago to its goals and then used Chicago to leverage this agenda nationally (Klonsky & Klonsky, 2008). According to a leader of the Small Schools Workshop, Gates staffers would visit a school district, see a small school they liked, and mandate its replication many times over. Hassel and Way reported in 2005 that Gates accounted for 95% of small schools funding nationally. Predictably, replication did not work because each school's conditions were different and there was no substantive teacher–community support. When urban high schools with intractable problems tied to larger structural and historical factors failed to budge on measures of achievement and college readiness, the foundation became disenchanted with the small schools strategy. Already in 2004 the foundation's representative, Tom Vander Ark, announced a shift from the small schools strategy to simply closing failing schools (Klonsky & Klonsky, 2008, p.134) and replacing them with charter schools.

In the end, the Gates Foundation killed small schools and moved on. "Their funding was the beginning of the downfall of the small schools movement. Then they got tired of it" (Interview, Small Schools leader, March 18, 2009). After Gates entered the picture, all small schools funding in Chicago was pooled, so there were no alternative sources of funding for teachers who wanted to continue to initiate small schools on the original model. Today, Renaissance 2010 uses the argument that small schools are better as a rationale to close schools and replace them with new charter, contract, and CPS small schools without Local School Councils, and in the case of charters, without unionized teachers. In this way, Gates funding transformed a grassroots progressive education experiment into a vehicle to privatize schools and undermine democracy and teachers' rights.

Academy for Urban School Leadership

In Chicago, Gates funds the Academy for Urban School Leadership (AUSL). Founded in 2001 by venture capitalist Martin Koldyke, AUSL is a nonprofit teacher preparation and education management organization that partners with CPS to turn around "failing" schools, typically in high-poverty areas. From 2005 to 2010, AUSL took over 16 public schools and has a goal to run 50 elementary schools and an unspecified number of high schools by 2018, creating a "district within a district" (www.ausl-chicago.org). The U.S. Department of Education under Obama/Duncan made turnarounds a key education reform strategy and named AUSL a national model. In a turnaround, all adults are fired and AUSL hires an entirely new staff. The stated goal is to "dramatically change the culture and expectations." Typically, a significant number of new teachers are recent graduates of AUSL's teacher training program. Thus the turnaround schools provide a guaranteed pipeline for its program.

AUSL is CPS's go-to player for Ren2010. When spikes in violence occurred due to student mobility resulting from Ren2010 school closings, there was much public outcry and negative publicity. CPS responded by diversifying its strategy to include phasing out and consolidating schools and turning them over to new management without moving students. CPS claimed turnarounds were not disruptive to students who remain in the building while adults are terminated and replaced. (This claim was challenged in September 2009 by the beating death of student Derrion Albert at Fenger High School, a non-AUSL turnaround school discussed in chapter 3.)

By funding AUSL at over $10 million, Gates helped create showcase schools that legitimate turning public schools over to outside operators. While AUSL claims of "success" in transforming what were "the worst" schools in the city is disputed (Fleming et al., 2009), it is the case that Gates and other funders provide an initial infusion of resources into the underresourced schools they take over. The new schools are able to hire National Board Certified teachers and additional staff (up to three teachers per classroom), and provide $500,000 to $750,000 in additional funds for staff, professional development, planning, and new program implementation (Fleming et al., 2009). The AUSL turnarounds I have visited got a building makeover, new playing fields, and science labs, contradicting the idea that it is the competitive market that produces reforms.

Thus the CPS-AUSL-Gates partnership creates a hyperresourced model against which disinvested public neighborhood schools are compared. However, the Director of CPS Office of School Turnarounds said in April 2008 that CPS could only sustain its additional investment in AUSL turnarounds "for three to five years" (Myers, 2008). And because venture philanthropies require quick results, they may withdraw when results do not match expectations, just as Gates did with high school reform and small schools. Far from the competitive market touted by Ren2010 and corporate philanthropies, AUSL represents a high-level top-down manipulation of school funding and interventions by corporate actors to generate school "improvement." Inadvertently, it demonstrates the need for more resources for public schools in low-income communities of color.

Parent Organizing

> There are about 200 mostly African American and Latino/a parents and
> some teachers, students, and community members from across the city
> at the Parent Summit. A leader of one of the sponsoring organizations
> tells the audience, "If you are trying to renovate a house, you don't stand
> outside of it throwing bricks. You go inside and find out what needs to
> be done." After several community organizations present their education
> projects, a representative from the Commercial Club of Chicago rallies
> the crowd, exclaiming, "I want to get involved with you! The issues we
> face are dramatic!" She directs participants to an information packet which
> outlines how charter schools outperform neighborhood schools. The
> summit ends with a call to rally in Springfield [the state capital] to support
> charter school expansion and to oppose a moratorium on school closings.
>
> (Field notes, March 26, 2009)

Gates funds local parent organizations with the goal of taking parent organizing
"to scale." In October 2006, Gates gave $1,550,000 to Public Interest Projects,
Inc. based in New York City, to "strengthen education organizing to be a
powerful school improvement tool, both nationally and locally" (Gates, 2009a,
p. 4). A key example is a Chicago parent organizing coalition jump-started
in 2007 when the Gates Foundation contacted the director of a community
organization and offered to expand support for his projects. Gates staffers
steered him to the West Side (personal communication, 2008) where CPS had
closed several schools and turned them over to AUSL, a move that generated
a storm of community opposition. The coalition's purpose was to build parent
support for the turnarounds and counter parent and student opposition.

Gates committed $225,000 to the coalition in its first year to develop and
distribute a survey to nearly 1,400 parents across the city and nearby suburbs,
produce a report based on the findings, and release it at a citywide education
organizing summit. The purported goal of the survey was to assess parents'
knowledge about CPS policies and practices and their perceptions of the
quality of their children's education. The report, organized around a theme of
education crisis, found that "parents did not have an accurate understanding
of current education problems—but once they learned of these issues, parents
wanted to enter the education debate" (Field notes, Parent Summit, March 26,
2009).

Although the survey indicated parents are generally optimistic about their
child's education, the coalition augmented these findings with data indicating
that CPS is largely failing its students. The coalition also conducted focus groups
across the city in which parents were asked to respond to data in an "education
crisis" handout which reported dismal graduation and college readiness
rates. These concerns could have been mobilized as part of a movement for
change in public schools, but instead the crisis discourse set up an agenda to

support new schools, including charters and turnarounds. Summit speakers repetitively returned to the notion that the system was failing its students and that expanding school choice was the best option. Organizers also distributed literature advocating charter school expansion and a flyer urging those present to lobby against a bill in the state legislature that would put a moratorium on school closings and provide legislative and community oversight for the CPS school closing process. This was a bill the grassroots coalition against Ren2010 championed and which was about to come to a vote in the state legislature.

Chicago has a rich history of parent organizing for education reform. In the 1960s African American parents, students, and teachers mobilized a massive school boycott to protest racial segregation, overcrowding of schools in Black communities, and the lack of African American administrators (Danns, 2002). In the 1970s, Latino/a parents and students mobilized for equitable facilities and bilingual education and against the high Latino/a dropout rate (Kyle & Kantowicz, 1992). The 1988 School Reform arose from grassroots mobilization for meaningful parent and community participation and led to Local School Councils (Shipps, 2006). In 2001, a group of Latino/a residents and parents staged a hunger strike to demand a new high school on the Southwest side.

Gates is tapping into this history to bolster its agenda. In fact, summit speakers invoked the hunger strike. However, the hunger strike was a bottom-up movement, based on democratic, homegrown, public solutions to inequality. In contrast, the Gates-funded summit presented its findings to parents and then advocated for top-down market-based reforms, including expansion of charter schools and support for AUSL. Four of the five groups highlighted at the summit are funded by Gates, and the Commercial Club of Chicago is the parent organization's unlikely ally. Paradoxically, the AUSL schools Gates supports will not have LSCs, stripping them of parents' right to control the school budget, hire and fire principals, and shape school practices.

The Renaissance Schools Fund (RSF), initiated by the Commercial Club with contributions from Gates and other corporate philanthropies and corporations and CPS's partner in Ren2010, also identified parent organizing as a strategic lever to catalyze a market in public education (Field notes, May 2008). To this end, the RSF invested $1,115,650 to foster demand for new schools at the neighborhood level (Renaissance Schools Fund, 2008), including funding Parents for School Choice and their annual New Schools Expo (www. parentsforschoolchoice.org). A workshop at the May 2008 RSF symposium, "Free to Choose, Free to Succeed: The New Market of Public Education," focused on the strategic role of parent organizing to garner support for education markets. In fact, the head of the Illinois Network of Charter Schools previewed a 9-month training program in community organizing for parents (Field notes).

People are conscious social actors, maneuvering within conditions not of their own making, and there is resonance in policies like turnarounds that promise solutions for struggling schools (Apple, 1996). However, in this case, the impetus for community organizations to coalesce and mobilize around charters and turnarounds seems to come primarily from corporate funders. While parents genuinely hope to get some immediate relief, the venture philanthropy agenda aims to disarticulate these concerns from traditional struggles for equitable public education, as in the coalitions opposing Ren20210, and rearticulate them to the market agenda, strengthening the hegemony of corporate interests in education (Incite, 2007). Yet as I argue in the next chapter, parent support for charter schools or turnarounds should not be construed as ideological alignment with neoliberal agendas; the field of contention and exercise of agency are more complex (see Pedroni, 2007).

Student/Youth organizing

> The presentation is in an airy auditorium with an atrium. It is packed with community organizers, dressed up for the occasion, youth, familiar faces of education activists, media, CPS personnel, a sprinkling of university faculty, and a representative of the Gates Foundation. People are seated at round tables, 8 to a table, 22 tables, with others in chairs along the walls. After a video about the youth participatory action research project and orchestrated voices of a diverse group of high school students from across the city, a student speaker summarizes: "These are just some of the voices around high dropout rates and low college enrollment from our study.... We united around divisions of race, class, and sexuality. We need each other's support.
>
> (Forum on youth participatory action research project on causes of high school dropout, November 2008)

Youth have historically played a critical role in progressive and revolutionary social movements. However, youth organizing coalesced as a "field" in the 1990s, in part due to the rise of foundation-funded nonprofit organizations. Through these organizations, corporate philanthropy has been able to influence the direction of youth organizing (Incite!, 2007). In 2007, Gates provided $1,600,000 to support a youth action research project to address the high school dropout problem in Chicago (Gates Foundation, 2007). A collaborative of students came together from seven community-based organizations and 12 high schools serving primarily low-income students of color and immigrant students. The stated purpose was to use participatory action research to insert the voices of students into high school reform.

With Gates funding, the students conducted surveys and interviews and observed successful schools in other states to understand youth perspectives on high dropout rates. Their analysis of the data led to a series of recommendations to CPS to improve students' achievement and connection to school. They presented their findings at a forum of community organizations and educational leaders which was cosponsored by CPS. Arne Duncan, CEO of CPS, pledged that CPS would partner with the student coalition on a pilot-project basis to implement some of the recommendations. CPS chose to focus on student and teacher interventions. Other student recommendations, including exploring alternatives to CPS's punitive zero-tolerance policies and increasing access to higher education for undocumented students, were not adopted by CPS (Youth Project report [pseudonym], 2008). Thus while potentially productive, the pilot projects do not address structural inequalities or policies that exclude students' access to education.

Several speakers framed the partnership between the students and CPS as mutually advantageous. A scholar of community organizing celebrated the project as a new paradigm of organizing for school reform. This new paradigm moves away from the traditional approach of "banging on the doors from the outside" to school leaders and community "sitting at the table together to make recommendations" (Field notes). While positive results may be achieved, from the standpoint of building up organization and consciousness for long-term fundamental change, this partnership approach is problematic. Situated in the neoliberal governance paradigm, it negates profoundly unequal power relations, as well as material and ideological constraints that undermine parity of participation of low-income students of color (Fraser & Naples, 2004). And it misses the reality that school officials are corporate managers driven by a nexus of corporate-financial agendas.

However, on the ground, some community organizations express a clear understanding of these realities but believe their tactical involvement can support youth organizing. While Gates may have an agenda of cooptation and diversion of grassroots organizing into toothless partnerships and roundtable conversations, youth have also used this opportunity to bridge divisions of race, ethnicity, gender, sexual orientation, and neighborhood to build new solidarities. This is not trivial in a city divided by racial misunderstanding, turf, and insularity. They have also learned research skills for critical investigations into the conditions of their lives (Cammarota & Fine, 2008). The cross-city collaboration has opened up spaces for critical dialogue, social inquiry, leadership development, and a sense of agency. An adult mentor closed out the event stating that the project is an "opportunity to show we can change our conditions"; it gives youth a "sense of hope" as they see their role in society. "There is wisdom in communities and things to learn from our youth." Speaking to CPS, he called for access to social justice curriculum and knowledge of how institutions work. This community leader said, "Young people are a vital part of the community. But community voice is not often considered in school reform. Particularly African American and Latino communities are thought of as a problem to be dealt with instead of engaged...." (Interview, March 23, 2009).

The direction of the youth project, once unleashed, cannot necessarily be controlled. Through collective inquiry, youth have opportunities to disrupt dominant discourses and reframe educational debates. When a media person at the forum tried to differentiate the youth participants from other youth whom she claimed needed training in values and did not want to be engaged in school, one of the student researchers countered with data, "This is not what we've seen from our interviews. Students do want to be involved and do want to be challenged" (Field notes). While corporate foundations have their own agendas for youth organizing, cooptation to these agendas is not determined. People also exercise agency at the grassroots and may employ sophisticated tactics to use the very foundations that seek to use them. It is contested territory.

Conclusion

Venture philanthropy is at the cutting edge of neoliberal education policy. For Gates, Broad, Walton, and other corporate foundations, the overarching goal is to restructure U.S. education to serve economic competitiveness. They see market based reforms such as charter schools, mayoral takeovers, turnarounds, and business managers running schools as a means to achieve that goal. This agenda also opens up new opportunities for capital accumulation as public education is privatized and contracted out to private operators.

The influence of venture philanthropies rests on their vast wealth and entrepreneurial strategies. They can fund cutting edge initiatives and deploy their economic and political resources to leverage and publicize their projects and agendas. They have influence with policy makers at the top, as reflected in Bill Gates's address to the National Governors Association in 2005, his keynote at the 2010 national conference of the American Federation of Teachers, and the central role of Gates staffers in the Obama Department of Education (personal communication of several national school reform leaders, April 2010). The groundwork for philanthropic influence was laid by disinvestment in urban public schools, cuts in federal funding to cities (Peck & Tickell, 2002), and local neoliberal education reforms (Lipman, 2004; Lipman & Haines, 2007). As public–private partnerships flourished, the way was opened for billionaire funders to play a pivotal role in public policy. They deploy their economic and political resources to initiate experiments, take them to scale, and leverage them and their influence with the media and public officials to shape education agendas.

We also want to emphasize the role of corporate philanthropy, as part of the shadow state, in urban governance. Philanthropy, along with public–private partnerships, corporate "experts," and unelected bodies, and nonprofit and private service providers, plays a key role in setting urban policy and performing government functions without public scrutiny. Venture philanthropists are self-appointed political actors, who, by dint of their superwealth, operate in the space between the state and society to engineer public policy, without public discussion or control. In reshaping urban education they also help reshape the city, affecting the lives of millions of primarily low-income working class people of color. The education policies they instigate determine who has access to public goods, particularly public schools. They dictate governance processes, such as mayoral takeover of school districts. Their role in closing public schools is integrally related to restructuring urban space. And their insistence on performance based pay for teachers further undermines urban public sector unions, a strategic force, if mobilized, against development for capital accumulation and racial containment.

Our data suggest these corporate funders also seek to pull the potential of grassroots education organizing into their orbit. They strategically direct funding to tap into local innovations (such as small schools) and use grassroots mobilizations to promote their agenda. Gates's support for both parent and youth organizing in Chicago can be read as an attempt to penetrate and divert social movements. This strategy has a long lineage in the United States (see Incite! 2007). We are reminded of the role of foundations in steering social movements of the 1960s in more conservative directions (A. Smith, 2007), particularly the Ford Foundation's role in shifting Black Power organizations from revolutionary politics to Black capitalism (Allen, 1969). On the other hand, people on the ground also have agency. Community organizing is highly contested.

The influence of corporate philanthropy is an extreme case of the conquest of the public by the private and another aspect of the neoliberal erosion of democracy. It is a profound irony (and outrage) that some of the most powerful transnational capitalists in the world who accumulated an unfathomable store of wealth through the freewheeling deregulated capitalism of the past 25 years have chosen to steer the educational experiences and futures of millions of working class youth of color whose immiseration is bound up in the exploitative relations that produced enormous transfers of wealth upward. As Ruth Gilmore (2007, p.46) reminds us, they do this with "twice stolen wealth... a) profit b) sheltered from taxes." This is a deeply racialized project which arrogantly seeks to use the very tools of resistance of oppressed people to further its agenda.

6

CHOICE AND EMPOWERMENT

The Cultural Politics of Charter Schools

The New Schools Expo, held at Williams School Multiplex and sponsored by CPS, Parents for School Choice, Illinois Network of Charter Schools, and the Commercial Club of Chicago's Renaissance Schools Fund. The expo to market charter schools to prospective students and their parents was, according to the *Chicago Defender* (African American newspaper), attended by over 700 parents and students. The school parking lot is jammed with school buses which provided free transportation from South and West Side African American communities. Tracy Hayes, Communications Director of the Renaissance Schools Fund told the *Chicago Defender*: "We are very pleased with this event and plan to make it an annual affair." The public face of the event is Parents for School Choice, an organization of mainly African American parents which is funded by the Commercial Club and the Gates Foundation. Registration tables are staffed primarily by African American women wearing red T-shirts emblazoned with the slogans: "My Choice: Great Schools" and "Our Children's Education in OUR Hands."

The registration packet contains two glossy Ren2010 brochures. The school gym is filled with booths set up by all the charter school operators and Ren2010 public schools in the city, displaying brochures, photos of their schools, and application forms. The gym is packed with mainly African American, but some Latino/a and White parents and students.

(Field notes, February 9, 2008)

This chapter examines the cultural politics of charter schools and how neoliberal policy is materialized through the actions of teachers, parents, and marginalized communities. Charter schools are a form of public–private partnership that opens up public education to the market by "shaving off" aspects of the education system to private providers (Robertson & Dale, 2003). As Roger Dale (1989–1990) points out, "before education can be brought into the marketplace and made subject to consumer choice; a range of possible alternatives has to be created" (p. 9). In the United States charter schools perform this function. Charter schools are publicly funded but run by private operators. And although some state laws require charters to be run by nonprofit entities, they may contract with for-profit educational management organizations (EMOs) to run the schools (Ford, 2005). Charter schools also are nonunion (except for recent unionization efforts in a few cities), and many hire inexperienced or uncertified teachers who are paid significantly less than unionized public school teachers. Authority is invested in private boards, and in Chicago, they do not have democratically elected Local School Councils, the school governance bodies with a majority parents and community residents. Yet, charter schools have support beyond corporate board rooms and neoliberal politicians.

The origins and meanings of charter schools are complicated, located in neoliberal ideology and the logic of capital but also in aspirations of communities for educational and cultural self-determination and teachers' desire for greater professional autonomy (Pedroni, 2007; Rofes & Stulberg, 2005; Stulberg, 2008; Wells, Slayton, & Scott, 2002). While corporate-style operators dominate the market, there are also charter schools initiated and operated by community organizations or groups of teachers seeking an alternative to dominant public school practices. They attract progressive teachers and recruit students of color, and some educators and communities of color have taken advantage of the greater flexibility offered by charter schools to develop culturally relevant, community-centered education, in the tradition of Black independent schools (Stulberg, 2008), such as the Betty Shabazz International Charter School in Chicago (http://www.bsics.net/). The emergence of these schools is a powerful indication of the desire of communities and progressive educators to take education into their own hands. It is also an indictment of the persistent failure of public schools to provide equitable, meaningful education in these communities. In this sense, charter schools represent an urgent call for action, particularly in urban school districts.

However, the explosive growth of the charter school movement in the first decade of the 21st century can be traced to neoliberal and neoconservative agendas, particularly rollback of "big government" and rollout of "local control," deregulation, and privatization. These agendas in education began with Reagan in the 1980s and evolved through the next three presidencies culminating in the present Obama administration's Department of Education. Whatever its progressive origins, the charter school strategy has been exploited and rearticulated to the interests of education entrepreneurs, venture philanthropists, investors, and corporate-style charter school chains. Charter schools have become the central vehicle to open up public education to the market, weaken teachers' unions, and eliminate whatever democratic control of public education there is. As noted in chapter 5, charters are a focus of Gates, Walton, and other venture philanthropies. As I summarize below, from the standpoint of equity, the results are problematic. Although charter schools promise flexibility, they also tend to reinforce inequality, and the capacity for grassroots charter initiatives to sustain themselves and compete in the corporate charter school market environment may be limited (Wells, Scott, Lopez, & Holme, 2005).

> New Schools Expo Workshop: "Your child, your choice—new schools from a parent's perspective." A panel of parents and students talk about their negative experiences in public schools and the benefits of choice and charter schools. During the question and answer session, a parent in the audience appeals for support for her community's struggle to keep their neighbourhood school. (The community had fought since 1992 for a new building to replace their dilapidated school. Now that the new facility is almost completed, under the latest round of Ren2010 school closings, CPS plans to turn it into a selective enrollment magnet school to which most neighborhood children will be unlikely to gain admission.) "I want the choice to send my kids to the new [school]. The Board [of education] is taking that away with Ren2010 and turning it into a magnet school. We have a right to the school. That's our choice…. Since you all are for choice, I hope you will support us.
>
> (Field notes, February 9, 2008)

This vignette captures some of the complexity of the cultural politics of choice and charter schools. How do we understand the allegiance of African American working class parents, as represented by Parents for School Choice, to charter schools and choice? How do we understand parents supposedly on opposite sides of Chicago's policy of closing neighborhood schools and opening charters both talking about choice? Some might argue that Parents for School Choice is funded by the Renaissance Schools Fund and therefore not a "genuine" grassroots organization. But this hardly explains the 700 parents who attended the New Schools Expo in 2008 or the 4,000-plus who attended the 2009 and 2010 Expos, the African American parents who staffed registration tables and rallied at the expos, the waiting lists for charter schools in the city, and the progressive teachers who have opted to teach in charter schools. Something else is going on. Charter schools and choice appeal. Understanding their appeal is crucial to forging counterhegemonic alliances and a reinvigorated and expanded definition of public education (Apple, 1996; Pedroni, 2007).

In this chapter I aim to complicate the charter school debate by examining complexities and paradoxes of neoliberal policy and the politics of race. I ask: Why do charter schools resonate with some teachers and parents? Put another way, what is their "good sense," from a Gramscian perspective? How does the charter school movement illustrate ways in which hegemony is constructed and neoliberalism is materialized (Pedroni, 2007) on the ground through the actions of politically and economically marginalized parents and teachers? How might understanding the appeal of charter schools and moves of charter school teachers and parents help reframe public education in a more liberatory direction?

After providing a context of charter school expansion nationally and in Chicago, I focus first on teaching. I outline how neoliberal reforms affect the changing nature of teacher professionalism. I argue that teachers' experiences demonstrate that accountability systems undermine teaching as an ethical, socially just practice, and this pushes some teachers toward the market with its promise of greater flexibility and autonomy. Next, I examine ways charter schools "make sense" to parents in oppressed communities. Finally, I discuss the rearticulation of discourses of equity and self-determination to the market and individual choice and explore the implications for neoliberal urbanism and a counterhegemonic movement. My analysis in this chapter draws particularly on eight in-depth interviews with Latino/a and African American charter school parents and a director of a teacher education program associated with charter schools. These interviews (all names are pseudonyms) were conducted as part of a larger study. In addition I draw on field notes from charter school meetings (2006–2009); documents from Parents for School Choice, charter schools, and Chicago Public Schools; conversations with charter school teachers; and data from a qualitative study of high stakes accountability (Lipman, 2004).

In the face of the state's persistent disregard for the claims of working class and people of color, the market offers an alternative by speaking to real needs and aspirations even when their long term material interests may be opposed (Apple, 1996). A fundamental condition is that marginalized, oppressed, and exploited people act in conditions not of our own making. Oppressed people rally together to push for liberatory agendas in a time of strong, progressive social movements, as they did in many parts of the world in the 1960s and early 1970s, and may even forge a counterhegemonic social bloc to contest for a new social order. However, in periods when dominant forces effectively reshape common sense around their program (as has been the case with the rise of neoliberalism over the past 25 years) and there is no strong counteralliance with its own agenda, options are more limited. In this context, individuals may opt to "work the system" and organized oppressed groups may tactically ally themselves with elements of the dominant agenda in an effort to meet immediate needs (Pedroni, 2007). In this chapter, I examine this dynamic in relation to the politics of charter schools.

The Explosive Growth of the Charter School Market

In places where charter schools have been prevented by restrictive policies from pursuing this kind of high market share, the imperative is to overcome these barriers and create an environment where charter schools can thrive. The ongoing resistance to change by the defenders of the status quo, in the face of overwhelming evidence that change is needed, is worse than misguided: it is educational malpractice.

(U.S. Department of Education, Office of Innovation and Improvement, 2008, p. 16)

The explosive growth of privately managed but publicly funded charter schools has been the principal vehicle to privatize public education in the United States. In the 1998–1999 school year, 21 states reported one or more charter schools, with California having the most—144. In comparison, Illinois reported 12 (U.S. Department of Education, 2000). Fast forward to 2008, there were over 4,300 charter schools in 40 states and the District of Columbia, serving more than 1.2 million students—about 3% of all public school children (U.S. Department of Education, 2008). Charter school expansion is concentrated in urban areas. According to the U.S. Department of Education (2008), "In some cities, charter schools' 'market share' is even higher, exceeding 50 percent in New Orleans and 25 percent in Washington, DC. And charter schools have not yet filled the demand for quality school choice options; tens of thousands of families are on waiting lists to enroll in charters" (p. 1).

This rapid expansion was fueled by the failures of public education, its inequities and exclusions, and the diversion of the civil rights agenda into magnet and specialty schools for the privileged (mainly Whites) while public schools for the majority of urban students declined. The path was cleared by rollback and rollout neoliberal policies. Disinvestment in urban communities of color and high stakes education accountability were followed by an infusion of government funding and policies that supported charter schools and other education markets in, for example, supplemental education services (Burch, 2009). From 2000 to 2008, the U.S. Department of Education awarded $1.8 billion in start-up funds for charter schools and over $320 million for charter school facilities. The Department proposed that replicating successful charter schools should be a national priority, its language revealing the market logics behind the charter school drive: "As with any new venture, there is a risk of failure with brand new start-ups. Not all new or exciting charter models will succeed in improving student performance. In the long run, not all will become replication worth" (U.S. Department of Education, 2008, p. 7). In 2009, the Obama administration put additional teeth into the charter school push by making lifting the state cap on charter schools a competitive advantage in the national competition for economic stimulus funds targeted to education. As I write this in June 2010, states across the country have already passed legislation to lift their caps on charter schools.

Charter schools are moving full steam ahead even as authoritative national studies show they are more segregated by race and poverty than public schools, particularly in Western states that are havens for White resegregation (Frankenberg, Siegel-Hawley, & Wang, 2010), and in the aggregate, students in charter schools are not doing as well as those in regular public schools, with 17% of charter schools performing better than public schools, 37% significantly worse, and 46% showing no significant difference (Center for Research on Education Outcomes [CREDO], 2009). Brown and Gutstein (2009) found Chicago's charter high schools produce on balance no better academic achievement while they serve fewer English language learners, special needs, and low-income students and have less experienced teachers. Yet in January 2010 the New York City Panel for Educational Policy approved closing 19 public schools while Mayor Bloomberg was pressing state legislators to lift the charter school cap, instantiating a national trend. While some parents and teachers may find better schools through charters, research indicates that markets and choice trend toward greater race and class inequality (Ball, 2003; Whitty, Power, & Halpen, 1998). There are independent charters that might serve as models of the kinds of public schools we want, but corporate-style charter school chains and for-profit Education Management Organizations (EMOs) dominate. Charters and choice extend education stratification by creating a market in which the most savvy and effective consumers with the right mix of cultural and social capital and power and privilege will obtain the best results for their children (André-Bechely, 2005; Ball, 2003; Brantlinger, 2003).

The material and ideological conditions for charter school expansion were set by the unfulfilled aims of civil rights strategies (Bell, 2004) and high stakes accountability codified in the federal No Child Left Behind (NCLB) law (2002). NCLB established a system to sort, classify, and demarcate students, teachers, and schools and to identify and label "failing" public schools. This designation legitimates turning them over to the market, which is supposedly more effective. NCLB's sanctions also provide an incentive for districts to expand charter schools because replacing a public school with a new school allows the school district to avert sanctions for failing to meet annual NCLB benchmarks. Ideologically, the path to education markets was also paved by expanding selective enrollment schools (i.e., magnet and specialty schools). Expanding "options" within the public system instilled the notion that "choice schools" are superior to open-enrollment neighborhood public schools. Chicago was a prime example of this in the last decade (Lipman, 2004).

But there would be no audience for charter schools if public schools had been doing their job in the eyes of parents, students, and teachers. The charter school push is dialectically related to this country's historical disinvestment in communities of color and persistently second class, Eurocentric, and racist public education for working class students and students of color (Anyon, 1980, 2005; Irvine, 1991; Kozol, 1992; Woodson, 1933/1990). It is not surprising that Chicago's charter schools are concentrated on the predominantly African American West and South sides. While some have argued that "public school failure" is discursively produced by promoters of the market, and there is certainly merit to this argument, the reality that too few public schools actually *educate* working class and low-income students, especially students of color, needs no documentation, especially for those experiencing it. Indeed, racism and reproduction of social inequality through schooling has been a central theme of critical scholarship in education since the mid-1980s.

Charter Schools in Chicago

> The key to Renaissance 2010 is that it seeks reform of the entire public school system—through choice, competition and intensified focus on results. If Chicago can take competition "to scale," then all schools will be improved.
>
> (Eden Martin, President, Civic Committee,
> Commercial Club of Chicago, n.d.)

As I discussed in chapter 3, Ren2010's high-profile school closings and mandate for charter schools shifted the terrain to education markets in Chicago, but accountability without adequate resources laid the groundwork, presaging what is occurring nationally under NCLB (Lipman & Haines, 2007). At the Commercial Club sponsored "Renaissance Schools Fund Symposium: Creating a New Market of Public Education," in May 2008, the Fund's director said the goal was to reach a critical mass of 200 to 300 charter schools [this would be about half all Chicago public schools] at which point the Fund could set the whole Chicago Public Schools agenda (Field notes). The Symposium demonstrated Chicago's national leadership in closing public schools to open charter schools, with representatives of 14 big-city and smaller urban school systems in attendance. In one workshop, the head of the National Alliance for Public Charter Schools noted that Chicago is "leading the country," in its "unique" and "ambitious" process of soliciting proposals for charter schools and "reaching out to developers who can create multiple schools to scale" (Field notes). In 2009, the Illinois State Senate doubled the number of charter schools allowed state wide and allowed Chicago 45 new charter school operators (in addition to the 30 previously allowed). Some operators have multiple sites.

Closing public schools to open charter schools is, like housing policy, an explicit strategy of disinvestment in public goods to further marketization. In Chicago a variety of charter schools appeal to specific market niches: schools of entrepreneurship, vocational training, strict discipline, fine arts, culturally centered, single gender, university-affiliated, and so on. However, most are branches of "nonprofit" charter school chains[1] that franchise out individual schools to for-profit EMOs. For example, Noble Street Charter's Lloyd Bond branch in the Altgeld Gardens public housing project is run by EdisonLearning, a for-profit corporation owned by Liberty Partners, an international investment firm. Charter school operators receive public funds and make money by shaving costs. They do this by hiring less experienced teachers, requiring them to perform functions that would be done by support staff, bringing curriculum and staff development "to scale," charging parents fees (Lloyd Bond charged parents for chairs at the eighth grade graduation), skimping on resources, barring unions, and so on. Meanwhile they drain money from the public system as per pupil expenditures follow the students.[2]

Chicago's charter schools are concentrated in very low-income African American and Latino/a communities where public schools have been closed and which bear scars of years of public and private disinvestment and racism. As their students transfer to charters, neighborhood public schools lose additional funding. In some areas of Chicago, so many schools have been closed that charter schools are parents' only "choice." In a large stretch of the African American West Side there are now almost no general public high schools. In their place is a mushrooming crop of charter schools.

In the next section, I examine contradictions of teaching in neoliberal times, the pressures on teachers of high stakes testing and managerialism, and ways in which charter schools appeal to some teachers as an alternative. Then I explore the good sense in charter schools from parents' perspectives.

Teaching in the Face of Neoliberal Accountability

Susan Robertson (2007) notes that "neo-liberalism has transformed, in both predictable and unpredictable ways, *how* we think and *what we do* [emphasis original] as teachers and learners...." (p. 3). Centralized accountability and education markets have produced deep changes in teachers' work (e.g., Apple, 2006; Gewirtz et al., 2009; Hursh, 2007), including increased regulation and surveillance, narrowed curricula, competition through differentiated pay scales and performance-based pay, and the emergence of a new teacher *subject*—teacher as entrepreneur. This is part of a larger discursive shift from the Keynesian welfare state's formal commitment to equity and education for personal development and citizenship to postwelfarist (neoliberal) emphasis on economic productivity. It is a shift from teacher professionalism and relatively complex, socially situated notions of learning and teaching to postwelfarist emphases on instrumental efficiency, effectiveness, productivity, and measurable performance (Clarke & Newman, 1997). The effects of this shift transcend preoccupation with processes of measurement and comparison. They also change what is measured, and thus taught, as teaching is driven by the idea that the only things worth teaching are those that are measured or easily tested.

The social processes involved are also mechanisms for reforming teachers' subjectivities—changing "what it means to be a teacher" (Ball, 2003, p. 217). In the United States, in general, these shifts have undermined teaching as an ethical practice and teachers' agency and sense of professionalism, particularly in the lowest performing schools which face the harshest accountability sanctions and generally serve low-income students of color (Lipman, 2004). This amounts to a moral and political crisis in teaching as democratic and humanistic purposes of education are superseded by corporate economic goals, and one-size-fits-all standards and high stakes tests reverse equity gains of the 1960s and 1970s. While standards and accountability have improved test scores in some low-income schools of color, overall they have had little impact on academic disparities between White students and students of color (Hursh, 2007). For teachers, high stakes accountability as a mechanism of surveillance is taking a toll in increased stress, demoralization, and exit from the profession (Valli & Buese, 2007), what Ball (2003) calls "existential anxiety and dread," and the dissuasion of people who might have been good teachers from even entering the profession. This neoliberal transformation of teaching is a global trend (Compton & Weiner, 2008).

From 1998 to 2002, I studied the implications of Chicago's high stakes accountability for student learning and teachers' work (Lipman, 2004). I found that accountability pressures, centralized regulation of schools and teaching, standards, and sanctions for failure were applied differentially across the schools I studied based on their racial/ethnic and social class compositions and standing in the school district's hierarchy of high-performing to failing schools. Top-down accountability policies also had a differential influence on curriculum, definitions of student learning, and notions of what constituted teacher professionalism.

With neoliberal accountability, the state shifts responsibility for educational improvement to teachers and schools, but gives them less control over end goals, pedagogy, and conceptualization (Ball, 1990), stripping teachers of opportunities for professional and ethical judgment (Freire, 1998b). In the schools I studied, accountability introduced a "qualitatively different regime of control" of teaching (Gewirtz, 1997, p. 222), particularly for teachers in "low-performing" schools. The loss of control over pedagogical decisions increased for schools on, or threatened with, probation. Technical rationality and measurable results were substituted (to varying degrees) for teachers' complex professional judgments and for ethical and social purposes of education. Over time, the pedagogical culture of lower-performing schools was pervaded by practices and discourses of test preparation, including regular test practice, routinized and formulaic instruction, emphasis on discrete (tested) skills, substitution of test-prep materials for regular texts, and differential attention to students depending on their likelihood of passing high stakes tests.[3] While some inexperienced teachers found support in semiscripted curricula and instructional practices, more experienced and confident teachers found the routines simplistic and professionally demeaning (see also Anderson, 2010).

Top-down accountability has produced a racialized system of surveillance and control. A panoptic system of surveillance and an ensemble of everyday practices shape teacher as well as student identities, teaching them to discipline themselves. The separation of "good" and "bad" schools that is accomplished through the testing, sorting, and ordering processes of standardized tests, distribution of stanine scores, retention of students, and determination of probation lists, constructs categories of functionality and dysfunctionality, normalcy and deviance that label students, schools, neighborhoods, and their teachers. "Deficiency" is made visible, individual, easily measured, highly stigmatized, and punishable as test scores are published in the newspaper and teachers experience the public shaming of their school being put on probation. By shifting responsibility for school failure from the state to individual schools, students, teachers, and parents, the accountability regime nurtures a culture of self-blame and shifting blame onto others (Lipman, 2004; cf. Gewirtz, 1997). The accountability regime is also a discourse of containment, silencing teachers by excluding discussion of educational goals and processes and closing down spaces for debate (see Smyth, 2001). This was especially so in the schools I studied in low-income neighborhoods of color which were on probation and least in charge of their own destiny.

While all teachers are, to some degree, enmeshed in the policies and practices of accountability, accumulated race and class advantages translate into differential constraints which are enshrined in a system of punishments and rewards. While some schools are put on probation under strict centralized supervision, others in Chicago are rewarded for high achievement with greater autonomy from district oversight. There is a similar pattern in New York City where high achieving schools serving mainly middle class students were exempted from district mandated curricula. In this way, accountability reproduces and extends racialized and class disparities in schools where teachers work. These disparities are intensified by school closings whose effects loop back onto low scoring schools. The threat of one's school being closed for low test scores (and losing one's job) increases pressures to teach to the test and provokes even more monitoring of teaching.

These policies have engendered an ethical crisis in teaching. The "ethical retooling" of the public sector (Ball, 2003) emphasizes a narrow, instrumental notion of "excellence and effectiveness" and that which can be measured. It has changed how teachers think about teaching, what they do (Robertson, 2007), and what counts as effective teaching (Mahony & Hextall, 1998). In the discourse of accountability, teachers in my research (Lipman, 2004) who were "good" according to multidimensional and complicated ethical, cultural, and pedagogical criteria, including those constructed by families and communities, became less so. Teachers recognized for commitment to children and communities, determination to help students "read" and "write" the world, in Freire's (1994) terms, and valuing children's languages and home cultures were, and are, ultimately judged by a single, instrumental measure— their ability to raise scores on high stakes standardized tests. In the schools I studied, imposed pedagogical practices corrupted relations with students and ran counter to the intellectual and ethical purposes at the core of these teachers' professional identities.

As teaching was redefined by test scores and teachers were encouraged to differentially focus on students who could raise the school's scores, some talked about "a moral crisis." Mandates for technical and routinized teaching ultimately pushed out teachers who exemplified independent professional judgement (see Teachers Network, 2007 for national parallels), critical and culturally relevant pedagogies, and community-centeredness. Some left teaching altogether or fled to suburban schools. Others went to charter schools where they hoped to find the flexibility and relative autonomy squashed by accountability policies.

Since I did this research, CPS's new CEO (who formerly ran the Chicago Transit Authority) has ramped up neoliberal management practices and discourses. In CPS, all aspects of teaching, learning, and leadership are measured by and accountable to "performance standards" and assessed based on "performance management indicators" which are part of a "performance management matrix." Teachers are expected to spend hours filling in performance "matrices." The role of new "Chief Area Officers" (middle level management) is to monitor schools for results, and in turn, principals monitor teachers' performance on the indicators. This new form of surveillance intrudes into daily life in the classroom subjecting every aspect of teaching and social relations to mechanisms of managerial control. In some schools teaching is largely scripted with teachers expected to "be on the same page at the same time" (Teacher, personal communication, January 2010). School closings in 2010 were justified by their scores on performance matrices, a system of weighted indicators (not made public) that assessed a school's degree of "failure." This performance management is further driving out teachers, in some cases, toward community-based charter schools where they hope to retrieve the joy and moral purpose and space for professional judgment that constitutes the meaning of "teaching" (personal communications, CPS teachers).

Contradictions of Teaching in Neoliberal Times

My investigation suggests that teachers' experiences in charter schools reflect the contradictions and multiple meanings of the charter school movement itself (cf. Wells et al., 2005). Since charters are governed by private boards and have varied philosophies, budgets, pay scales, and administrative structures, conditions and teaching experiences vary. Yet, because they are not unionized, are not required to hire 100% certified teachers (in Chicago), and are subject to the vagaries of market forces, charter schools have generally introduced greater insecurity into the teaching profession. In 2004, a California for-profit EMO shut down a multisite charter school in midschool year, leaving 10,000 students without schools and hundreds of teachers without jobs. Because charter schools receive less public dollars than public schools and are mostly nonunion, "teaching" may include tasks typically performed by other school personnel (Johnson & Landman, 2000) and teachers are more easily fired. For example, teachers at a charter school chain in Chicago reported they had no breaks and were required to work extra hours and clean floors and classrooms with no additional pay. They were afraid to protest because they could be fired at will (personal communication, October 18, 2008).

Yet, some educators see charter schools' greater autonomy from state and local regulations as an opportunity for innovation that is increasingly closed off by centralized accountability measures. A director of an education program associated with a charter school network said:

And [the directors] were receiving conflicting messages and conflicting directives from CPS about curriculum and so on, and we felt that the only way that we would be able to move our work forward was to be able to create a model of, a place where the kind of literacy instruction that we were advocating could be modeled for people. And sort of looking at the options, it seemed like going for a charter was the situation that was going to give us the greatest degree of freedom. And that was basically the rationale for getting involved with charters.

(Interview, August 5, 2009)

A few charter schools also open up space for ethical and politically progressive education. The initial round of Chicago charter schools in the 1990s included several started by teachers frustrated with the constraints of high stakes accountability and intractability of their public high school. There are also a few Afro-centric, environmental, or arts-oriented schools and a few with a strong college focus that serve low-income students. As the space for ethical professional practice narrows in public schools, these schools may attract dedicated, progressive teachers. An example is a charter high school, in a low-income African American community, with a strong college preparatory focus, precollege experiences, and a high graduation and college matriculation rate. The social studies department developed a 4-year course of study that began with "Identity and Difference," moved on to "Revolution and Resistance" in the United States and globally, U.S. foreign policy (including "White man's burden" and "imperialism"), and ended with local government and political action. However, the school's direction is at the discretion of its (unelected) board. After operating for 10 years, a similar school took a corporate turn when the Board replaced the principal and began emphasizing preparation for the corporate sector.

It is a paradox of teaching in neoliberal times that one set of neoliberal initiatives (high stakes accountability) has begotten another (charter schools/education markets) which, although overall regressive, open up cracks for progressive agency. Some teachers working in social justice oriented charters also talk about a "moral dilemma." They know charter schools are part of the neoliberal restructuring of public education which undermines the public interest and produces educational inequities. They feel complicit in this process yet guard the space for teaching that they believe in and a context of ideological support and collaboration of like-minded colleagues. As one teacher put it, "I know charter schools are bad for public education, but I could never teach like this in CPS."

However, "professional autonomy" is articulated to the neoliberal discourse of individual freedom and entrepreneurship. This is quite different from teachers' agency within a system of reciprocal accountability and democratic decision making. Yet the discourse of individual freedom gains potency in the seeming absence of a viable alternative. Caught in the neoliberal mantra that there is no alternative to current policy, teachers face an ethical dilemma either way they turn.

In any case, the space for agency may be temporary, and the autonomy offered by school choice is highly individualized and may be less real than it appears (Ball, 1994). Charter school "visions" can be quite constraining, and quite a few enforce a highly rigid curriculum. Also, the state imposes accountability on charter schools even while offering them more flexibility, and in the face of recent reports revealing their mixed record, there are calls for more accountability.[4] Some charters have been closed for not meeting test score targets, and others are induced to select or exclude students (formally or informally) to ensure they meet targets. Long hours at relatively low pay and the pressure of additional responsibilities may explain the rapid turnover of teachers (Karp, 2010) bringing into question the long-term viability of these schools. At a January 10, 2009 hearing on school closings organized by a coalition of progressive teacher and community organizations in Chicago, a number of disaffected charter school teachers talked about their disillusionment as they learned their charter school organization was a top-down corporate operation and the school did not serve students with special needs or whose first language was not English.

Parent Perspectives

Rally at the New Schools Expo 2009, sponsored by the Renaissance Schools Fund and Parents for School Choice: An African American parent leader of Parents for School Choice leads off with chants of "My choice, my choice!" Behind her parents and students wave hand printed signs reading, "Children are our future." "Put money into our schools, not into more jails." She explains she became part of the "movement" in 2003. "It's good you are here empowering yourselves with information to select the right school…. Get with these operators, find out what they offer. Empower yourselves." "Our new President Barack Obama [cheers] gave a call to service. You are doing that by coming out and getting information on schools for your children."

The rally is closed out by a White priest, a well-known advocate for his Black congregation, who rouses the crowd: "Too often the quality of education in America has depended on the color of your skin, your address, your zip code.... Education is the new civil rights issue. We need to equal the playing field of education opportunity. We need radical new thinking—new opportunities, new alternatives, healthy competition. Sometimes closing schools is necessary. I pushed for closing a school in a neighborhood where kids can't read. We need to make education a priority, by any means necessary. We need to give parents a choice to decide what school they send their children to.

(Field notes, January 31, 2009)

The New Schools Expos are a gauge of the growth of charter school popularity as well as their embrace by corporate interests in Chicago. The first Expo was held in a Ren2010 school and attended by about 700. The 2009 and 2010 Expos were convened at the United Airlines Club at Soldier Field (where the Chicago Bears football team plays) and attended by over 4,000. There was *free* parking at Soldier Field (a rarity) and signs advertising the Expo were posted on the major highway along the lake. Interest in the Expo is not surprising given the disinvestment in many public schools in communities of color, persistent indicators of subpar education, and the unresponsiveness of school districts to the concerns of African American and Latino/a parents. The Parents for School Choice Web site points out, "Only 45% of Chicago Public School students graduate from high school, and only 3 of every 100 African-American and Latino males in Chicago Public Schools earn a college degree" (http://www.parentsforschoolchoice.org/). Concerns with school safety, lack of academic and social support for young Black men, lack of individual attention, and unresponsive administrators run through the group's materials. In a contrasting narrative, the glossy brochures displayed by charter, contract, and military schools at the Expo market their schools with promises of rigorous college prep curricula, the latest technology, and some claim graduation rates and college admissions of 90% or more.

These are precisely the issues that drove the parents we interviewed to charter schools. If we assume that people are not "social dupes," but are conscious social actors acting under the constraints of the situation they face, then alliances with hegemonic agendas may be a two-way street. In his study of African American parents' responses to the Milwaukee voucher plan, Tom Pedroni (2007) argues that parents and African American provoucher organizations make tactical decisions to support vouchers as a way around inequitable and recalcitrant public schools. However, their support for vouchers does not mean they side with conservative voucher advocates' ideologies and larger agendas. In fact, the parents largely remain supporters of public education, but can find no way to get what they need for their children in Milwaukee Public Schools. Pedroni's analysis complicates critiques of charter schools. It is also helpful in imagining a counterhegemonic agenda that speaks to the real concerns of parents, teachers, and students who are drawn to charter schools. In the following sections I explore charter school parents' perspectives.

"Drowning in a Sea"

The dilemma faced by students and parents with few options is illustrated by highly publicized Urban Prep Charter School. In 2007 CPS closed Englewood, a neighborhood high school, despite strong opposition from students and the community. Englewood was an anchor of a once-thriving Black working class community, but, like the community itself, one of the lowest income areas in Chicago, it had experienced decades of disinvestment and neglect. The building's condition was appalling, and despite some excellent teachers, only a small percentage of students were reading on grade level. Marquin Gibson, saw the charter school as his only option:

> I live on 73rd and Emerald. If I wouldn't have gone to Urban Prep, honestly my mom would've moved out to the suburbs, like the Homewood Flossmoor area and I would've had to attend one of the schools cause I really didn't have no options left so it was kind of my saviour, I guess you could say. I had took some selective enrollment tests for many other schools and mostly I didn't do really well on any of the tests and therefore we looked around. I didn't want to attend any of the neighborhood schools because they were so bad and because of their reputation. My mom didn't want me to go to any of those.
>
> (Potter, 2008)

Marquis's mom was echoed by the charter school parents we interviewed. They were desperate for change, or, in the language of school choice, looking for "options" to their neighborhood public schools. Ms. Williams, a charter school parent, said parents need "choices" because "they are drowning in the middle of the sea." If "someone rows up in a boat and offers them an oar" (charter school), they're going to take it "because it's better than nothing." Ms. King, a parent at another school in the same network was also searching for a way out:

> Well, actually, I heard about Morgan Charter School. I heard about Morgan. And that's when I would start—you know, because sometimes you feel like there's no way out when it's the neighborhood schools and you try to go other places and put your kids in better settings, but they won't—you know, you have to live in that area. You have to live in that

area. So it's like catch, you know, what can I do? What can I do with the CPS? So it was, I had even tried another school...

I'm glad I made the decision to send them and being really honest, I didn't know where I was to send them because it, I didn't have a lot of options, you know. Because if you wanted someone sharing with you, there's a good school here, it's a good school there, you know, how can I get you in? How can I get my son in if we're not in the neighborhood?

(Interview, August 27, 2009)

It should be noted that many of our interviews were with parents in a prestigious charter school network that I call CollegeBound (a pseudonym), that has access to intellectual and material resources most charter and public schools lack.

Ms. King and other parents we interviewed did not claim ideological allegiance to school markets or privatization. Their choice of a charter school was tactical, pragmatic, Ms. King made this explicit. She said divisive charter school debates don't take into account that parents feel like they "need better options" and "just want to do what's best for their child." The parents voiced a common litany of complaints and frustrations with neighborhood public schools: lack of individual attention to students' academic needs, lack of communication and responsiveness to parents, paucity of resources and programs, overly large class sizes, incompetent or uncaring teachers, too much focus on test prep and lack of experiential learning, low graduation rates, and especially for Latino/as we interviewed, lack of safety and discipline. What parents objected to and what they wanted is entirely possible within public education, as demonstrated by the school district's selective enrollment schools. In fact, most parents voiced support for public education in general, and African American parents spoke nostalgically of their own public school experiences. Nor were they wedded to charter schools. One parent found her daughter's charter school "too tight knit" and moved her to a college prep public school; another transferred her son to an alternative school. Ms. King took pains to situate her choice of a charter school within public education. "I don't feel like I should have to feel like I have to sacrifice for my children's education, you know, because I'm in support of public schools because this is still a public school as well. But people have a lot of misconceptions about charter schools."

Parents also wanted more. They rejected the minimalized education produced by high stakes testing and accountability. They aspired to more holistic development than is available to them in Chicago public schools. Ms. Watkins talked about wanting a multifaceted educational experience for her children. Despite the inequities and racism of public education in African American communities, she and other parents harked back to a more all-rounded education that preceded the stripped down test prep regime that dominates many urban public schools in working class and low-income communities of color today (Lipman, 2004). "And I also like that they have music, art. I mean, they have performing arts. They have Spanish, gym, recess. They have all the stuff that the neighborhood schools don't and so that's very important to me. I remember how important it was when we were younger." (Her experience may be different from the majority of charters which are corporate-style chains and lack the resources of CollegeBound.)

But there is more. These parents have an expanded vision of education. Some see the potential of charter schools to go beyond the stultifying, routinized, banking model of education that characterized too many schools, particularly in low-income communities of color, *before* the regime of high stakes testing took over. Ms. Carter's educational philosophy emphasizes creativity and engaging experiential learning.

Ms. Carter: It doesn't have to be new or modern, but it has to be engaging. It has to be bright. It has to be vivid. It has to be some sort of creativity there for me. Like science should come off the page of the book....

My son has done a lot of robotics. We have seen, been to local universities. We've visited the doctorate, the Microbiology Department. Some of the, we've seen some of the experiments with some of the Delta, some of the doctors who are doing studies. They have studies going on. We studied Katrina and New Orleans, studying how to prevent the Delta from sinking again. And we've seen science, saw a lot of the different things that they're working with [at CollegeBound]. So those things bring science off the page....

The law students, they actually did a trial of Goldilocks in a real courtroom, defendant, plaintiff, jury, judge. So those are the reasons why. (Laughs)

Interviewer: So that was something that you felt like they wouldn't be able to get at the neighborhood school?

Ms. Carter: No. No, they definitely wouldn't because who's backing them up? The rectangle book? (Laughs) With the painted face, you know, two-dimensional. No. (Interview, September 10, 2009)

Dr. Rosen, the director of an education program affiliated with a charter school network, is a long time advocate of public education. His educational vision is aligned with Ms. Carter's, but he is frustrated with public schools' resistance to change. Thoughtful, committed, troubled by the "collateral damage" charter schools may do to public education, nonetheless, his pessimism about the public school system has nudged him, pragmatically, toward the market.

I also think that too many of the neighborhood schools have failed kids for too long, and that parents deserve a better option than that. And if there was a magical way to make the neighborhood schools be a successful rival to charter schools, I would say there are a lot of virtues to neighborhood schools, but I don't see that happening. And therefore, and this is not the level of political economy that you operate on, but I think we have 1,200 kids in our schools now. And I know those 1,200 kids are getting a good education. And that's nothing to sneeze at.

(Interview, August 5, 2009)

Dr. Rosen is ideologically aligned with the public sphere, but concretely, reinvigorated public schools seem out of reach. The apparent efficacy of working in charter schools trumps ideology. Neoliberal solutions make practical sense given the recalcitrance of public institutions and the TINA thesis (there is no alternative). They offer a space for agency where no other seemingly exists.

Generalizing Selectivity and Choice

Neoliberal discourse rearticulates democracy to participation in the market. Rather than participating as part of a collective in public institutions, a parent is an "empowered" consumer. This shift is facilitated by already existing selectivity and markets in education. In reality, there is a long history of school choice in the United States—for a privileged few. One of the most pervasive "choice tactics" of the middle and upper middle classes is to buy homes in areas with the "best," most well-resourced schools (Varady & Raffel, 1995). And there are selective public schools, such as magnet and speciality schools, requiring certain cultural and intellectual capital (if not social connections) for admission; elite and not-so-elite private schools; and a parallel system of parochial schools serving working and middle class students who can afford the fees or win scholarships. Over the past decade, the pump was primed for school choice by expanding the tier of highly selective enrollment schools in urban school districts. Several selective enrollment schools in Chicago have become iconic for high quality education and emblematic of the benefits of choice and "options." The acceptance rate at the most selective is less than 5% of applicants *prequalified* to apply.[5] A principal of one magnet high school told parents the school received 12,000 qualified applications for 200 slots in 2009 (parent personal communication, March 17, 2009). This is what allows liberal Whites to sanctimoniously declare that they "support public schools," but it's not the same "public" to which the poor have access. It's a private public you buy by buying a house or by deploying your economic, cultural, and social capital (Tom Pedroni, personal communication, August 7, 2010).

In neoliberal discourse, the new market in charter schools democratizes selectivity. Arne Duncan, is quoted in a CPS Renaissance 2010 brochure: "We have never believed that one size fits all. We need to create different school models for the needs of different students—especially in the case of those students who are struggling." (Never mind that standardized test prep curriculum, evaluating schools by a standardized measure, and scripted and regimented teaching are the result of CPS's accountability policies.) In the choice discourse, everyone can have options rich people and "smart" kids have had. This has resonance given that African American and Latino/a parents have had much less opportunity to act as school choosers or consumers. An applicant to a charter school enters the realm of the privileged with the opportunity to select and be selected, to exercise agency vs. the great mass who are undifferentiated recipients of what the state doles out. Moreover, because every charter school markets its specialness, the charter school market seems to generalize what has always been reserved for an elite few—the choice to attend a school of distinction. There is a powerful good sense in this logic given the deeply stratified and inequitable system of public education in this country and the willingness of the wealthy and privileged to "choose" or opt out. The association of charter schools with private, magnet, and selective schools resonates in parent interviews.

Ms. King: It's almost like a private school but it's not.
Ms. Williams: So that, to me, felt like a more private, more personal type of environment because I went to a Catholic grammar school and it reminded me kind of that setting. So I like that.

Charter school purveyors and advocates trade on this discursive association with private and selective public schools. Their elaborate promotional brochures announce their schools are rigorous, college preparatory, replete with resources, and implicitly not like a regular public school. As Ms. Trautman, a critical charter school parent, explains, it is this connection with selective schools that makes charter schools seem special:

> Referring to her cousin: He's like, "I work in one of the charter schools." Somehow that means more than if he was just working in a public school. Like there's this prestige piece that comes along. You know, they've become like the new designer jean. And I don't want to make it seem like it's charter school/public schools or charter school/neighborhood schools because, like I said, they've become cousins of the magnet schools and the AMP schools,[6] and now it's like this other tier of prestige schools that you would apply to. So it's the same beast that created this competition to get into [selective magnet school], where I went in the '80s, the late '80s. It's that same beast.
>
> (Interview, November 11, 2009)

In fact, charter schools are a mixed bag, and Chicago is no exception, ranging from a charter chain focusing on basics and rigid discipline to an online learning school to a school based in exploratory learning that was started by teachers—all largely unproven. Yet in the parlance of school choice they are equal entrees on a menu of "great options" alongside the best magnet and specialty schools. The selection process itself enhances their value—independent of what actually goes on there. Ms. Trautman:

And then because it's a lottery and there are limited amounts of spots, it feels incentivised if your child gets in. Like you feel like you've won something and because all these other parents are trying to get this spot, this spot must mean something without even understanding—and I still don't even know like the questions to ask about curriculum and what questions to ask if you have a young African-American daughter as opposed to a young Latino boy.... Not knowing any of those things, but just looking at shiny, shiny brochures means something. It translates into resources. If they have money (chuckles) to build up an interactive Web site then I can only imagine what they'll be doing in the classroom.

(Interview, November 11, 2009)

Charter schools illustrate how markets erode solidarities through competition for scarce goods. As Ms. Trautman put it, "They want to be able to say that their kid attends a school that makes other people's eyes light up." Several parents we interviewed assumed that because charter schools have a selection process (albeit a lottery) they have a "better" group of students and parents, situating blame for school problems in parents who make bad choices or are not serious consumers. Ms. Carter:

It's (public school) just a much wilder environment so, I think, that's why I stuck with the charter schools. I chose Catholic school because people that pay tend to care more, which means you have more disciplined children because, number one, they have the right to refuse your child, to expel your child. So most people, to me, in my opinion, most parents that are paying tend to discipline their children better or they tend to care, have more control over their children.

(Interview, September 10, 2009)

Reproducing Inequality

I run into Ofelia on the street in her neighborhood. She was one of the most active Latino/a parents fighting to keep her neighborhood school, with a state of the art hearing impaired program, from being closed by CPS and turned over to a specialty school for a wealthy, mostly White nearby community. The parents lost that fight and with the school being phased out, Ofelia has been searching for a school for her hearing impaired daughter. She checked out a new charter school but "they didn't know what an IEP[7] was! 'Yes we have services,' but they couldn't explain them. And there is no transportation.... They say they take all kids but there are no services [for special education students]." She has visited four charter schools. One wants parents to pay $75 for each child to assure a place. She has three children and the fee is prohibitive, especially because she just lost her job as a teacher assistant at an early childhood center due to budget cuts.

Of course, selectivity has an inherent downside. Not everyone gets in. Research on school choice internationally demonstrates that it tends to reproduce inequalities as choice systems benefit middle class families who are more able to move their children around the system and have more flexibility to visit prospective schools, and those with the requisite social and cultural capital to work the system and present themselves as attractive consumers (Apple, 2006; Ball, 2003; Whitty, Power, & Halpen, 1998). This is largely because even formal selection mechanisms lend themselves to informal aspects of inclusion and exclusion. Parents of a student with special needs or whose first language is not English are counselled that the school is not a good fit, or the school does not provide necessary services, as in Ofelia's story above. (Chicago's charter high schools have a lower percentage of special education, low-income, and Limited English students compared to regular Chicago public high schools, Brown & Gutstein, 2009).

But social class does not tell the whole story of inclusion and exclusion. Intraclass differences are obscured by income data, masking the way the selection process itself is exclusionary. Dr. Rosen pinpoints this in the charter school with which he is affiliated.

> [M]y impression at [charter] was that a lot of the low income parents that we attracted were the same kind of parents that were attracted to parochial schools. They were families that didn't have resources, but they had aspirations. So when people accuse charter schools, and particularly our charter schools, of creaming kids I say it's not the case. Except for the fact, and I'm hardly the first person to say this, but there's a whole bottom layer of the class structure that's cut off. Because those are the folks who have an incredible amount of trouble working the system, and they can't follow through on the application process, they don't have access to the information in the first place. At least for [our] schools, and I can't say that this is the case for other charter schools, there is this tendency to draw parents who have certain kinds of aspirations for their kids.

> (Interview, August 5, 2009)

Our interview data illustrate his analysis. A mother we interviewed worked her way into a charter school by pestering the principal and demonstrating she would be an involved parent. At highly regarded Urban Prep, before students are admitted they must attend a 3-week summer immersion program which potentially eliminates many students who work during the summer or have family responsibilities. Moreover, competition for enrollment is city wide, advantaging children whose parents can provide transportation and excluding those who cannot do so. Lotteries, sibling preferences, and behavior/parent contracts all skew admissions and facilitate pushouts not permitted by public schools. For example, a charter school parent we interviewed in a Mexican community told us students with three very minor discipline infractions were expelled from her son's charter school. This could not happen in a Chicago public school.

Rearticulating Collective Movements to Individual Choice and Entrepreneurship

The neoliberal discourse of empowerment through choice permeates the policy advocacy of corporate foundations and school managers. The Renaissance Schools Fund Symposium in May 2008 was titled, "Free to Choose, Free to Succeed: The New Market of Public Education." Opening speaker, Arne Duncan, then CEO of CPS, called Renaissance 2010 a "social justice" program. Again and again, democracy, empowerment, and participation were defined as choice in the education market. In a workshop highlighting the partnership of the CPS Office of New Schools and the Renaissance Schools Fund, the head of New Schools said, "We are operating a portfolio of diverse schools. We believe in a pluralistic society." Choice itself implies quality. During a lunchtime panel, the Chair and CEO of Commonwealth Edison, Chicago's electric corporation, and coinitiator of a charter school explained, "Parents are more invested because they have chosen the school. Parents have power when choices are out there." The lead staff person for the Renaissance Schools Fund also explained that the RSF solicits feedback from the community in the selection of charter school operators. This "gives the community a voice … communities choose the product that works best for them." The CEO of a chain of charter schools echoed this theme: "Choice is parent power, even more powerful than LSCs." (I remind the reader that LSCs are democratically elected bodies with a majority of parents and city wide composed of a large representation of low-income people of color. LSCs have authority over school discretionary budgets, principal selection, and approval of school improvement plans and are the only democratic, community decision making bodies in CPS.) Although powerful corporate and political elites have shaped the discourse, it is materialized on the ground in the wake of the failure of public schools to serve working class and low-income communities.

> Urban Prep Charter Academy for Young Men, Englewood Campus Convocation, September 6, 2007. The gym is nearly filled with African American families attending the opening ceremony welcoming the new class. Moms, dads, grandparents, babies on laps occupy nearly every folding chair. The faculty wear convocation gowns and academic regalia, and a red carpet is laid down the center aisle. To the beat of African drums the students file in, young African American men dressed in identical khakis, white shirts, blue blazers, red ties. These are the "upper classmen." They are followed by the freshmen, minus jackets. This is the "jacketing ceremony" when new students are inducted into the school and make their opening commitment. From the dais, the Director of Institutional Advancement

says: "You have chosen UPCA. We have chosen you. You have chosen this path. We have chosen to support you." As he calls on them to stand up, the audience jumps to their feet in a standing ovation. As the ceremony proceeds through speeches interspersed with music (no African American freedom songs, all traditional "American" songs), the adult audience seems thoroughly engaged, clapping, cheering, nodding as the CEO and various Board members speak. A woman near me cries as her son walks on stage to get his UPCA jacket.

(Field notes)

This vignette captures the good sense of a policy that introduces charter schools into school districts bereft of decent schools for African American children and captures the rearticulation of liberatory struggles for education to the neoliberal agenda. Discursively, the school locates itself in the history of African American struggle for education as collective uplift (Perry, 2003). The convocation conveys powerfully that these young men are our future, that Urban Prep offers opportunities and hope other schools do not, and that it provides collective support while encouraging individual responsibility and agency. The school's CEO tells the freshmen, "You are not climbing by yourself. That's not what families do…. There are bad influences out there and you have to resist them…. We can choose a particular future." At the same time, the school's ethos is corporate. The program lauds corporate funders (a White woman executive of Sarah Lee, oddly out of place in this space, receives an award—the company is a major donor); the all-male mentors are mostly from the corporate world, a couple from academia; the dress is corporate; the Board is made up of African American corporate executives. Students are encouraged to strive for careers in business or as lawyers, and then give back to the community as future mentors. There are no mentors who are community organizers, activists, artists, teachers, or working class men in the community. Entrepreneurship and individual success replace social movements. This neoliberal rendition disarticulates the struggle for Black education from its emancipatory history and rearticulates it to individual advancement and middle class uplift of the poor, echoing the logic of the deconcentration thesis that justifies mixed-income schools and housing, as discussed in chapter 4.

Yet, in the absence of collective alternatives one does not have to look far for the good sense in this appeal to agency, community, brotherhood, family, academic rigor, college opportunity, and promise to "give back"—all generously supported by corporate backers, a cadre of successful board members and mentors, and directed by highly effective leaders who exude competence and valued cultural capital. It is hard to imagine *not* choosing Urban Prep over a disinvested neighborhood high school. Yet it is important to remember that this is a selective high school that most Englewood students do not attend.

The slogan of Parents for School Choice, "Our children's education in our hands," also rearticulates African American struggles for self-determination to choice in the education market. A central message of the New Schools Expos I attended was that if a parent cares about her or his child's education and wants to be "empowered," she will make the individual sacrifice to shop around for a great school and find a way to get her child there. The parent organization does not work collectively for quality education but advises parents how to become savvy consumers and individual advocates for their children, including how to locate one of the new private transportation companies that have sprung up as a cottage industry to serve parents who are sending their children to schools around the city. (There is no free public transportation to charter schools.) With success determined by one's ability to navigate the market, Expo workshops I attended were filled with questions about transportation, choosing a school, and the application process.

As a whole, the charter school parents we interviewed are a savvy and interventionist bunch, confirming research that indicates that education markets and choice favor those with the cultural and social capital and knowledge to work the system (e.g., Ball, 2003). But it says something else as well. As parents feel stymied by the recalcitrance of some unresponsive public schools, they find space to maneuver, to exercise some agency, in the charter market. Ms. King related a detailed story about constantly navigating schooling for each of her five children, including moving them in and out of charter schools to find the best fit. Ms. Williams relocated to a particular area specifically because of a nearby university charter school. She is very involved in the school and volunteers regularly. Ms. Torres had problems with her daughter's school's discipline policy and its overcrowded classrooms. So she started "scouting for other schools" and did "research on charter schools."

For Ms. Hernandez, a new charter school in her community gave her a way to exert some power over her children's education. Being a consumer afforded her agency denied to her by her unresponsive public school (see Pedroni, 2007). She was dissatisfied with the lack of discipline, extremely large class sizes, and bilingual education program at her neighborhood school. "I never liked Winters, but I didn't have another option. It was the only one they go to. Once they opened [charter] I very quickly decided to change schools." Winters' administrators tried to dissuade her, but she did research on school district regulations:

> I was going to enroll them and see for myself if it was a good school or not. They would then tell me that if [charter school] closed down that they would not readmit my kids to [neighborhood school]. I knew that it was not their decision, and that that was something the state would decide. I knew that if I wanted them back at Winters they would have to enroll them. I told them that I was the mom and I had the choice to enroll them at whatever school I wanted.

Yet, the aggregate result of redefining democracy as consumer choice is to further atomize and disempower people, like the child who was expelled from a charter school for three minor discipline infractions.

Conclusion

I began this chapter with the New Schools Expo 2008. In a vignette from an Expo workshop, parents on both sides of the school closing/charter school issue draw on the discourse of choice. One parent has come to the event seeking support for a community struggle for a neighborhood school while Parents for School Choice are pushing markets and individual choice. Parents on both sides are, in the words of one community activist, "thirsty for change," as are teachers. The encounter reflects the complex cultural politics of charter schools and choice. It also suggests potential to build on the "good sense" of charter school choosers to reframe public education in line with self-determination of communities of color.

In the big picture, charter schools are another arena for capital accumulation facilitated by the cycle of racialized disinvestment, devaluation, and reinvestment in urban areas (Brenner & Theodore, 2002). They are part of the neoliberal restructuring of cities as nearly all aspects of urban life are commodified, and public goods are appropriated for private profit in the neoliberal remix of "accumulation by dispossession" (Harvey, 2003b). As I discuss in chapter 3, in Chicago, the dramatic expansion of charter schools is promoted by a high level public–private partnership (Renaissance 2010) between the mayor and powerful corporate and financial interests (Commercial Club of Chicago) who have been empowered to make decisions—without public oversight—about the education of the city's over 400,000 school children, 92% of whom are children of color and 85% low-income. This commodification of social life represents not only a capital accumulation strategy but a social imaginary of a market driven city with differentially awarded intellectual and material resources by class, race, and ethnicity based on individual competition and entrepreneurship. In this sense, charter schools are part of the re-norming and revaluing of urban social relations and subjectivities. This has real effects. As Dr. Rosen explained, the people with the least resources, the least connections, and without the necessary consumer know-how are the ones most left out of the education market. A discourse of choice masks the inequity it actually reproduces.

Powerful economic and political interests claim that public schools are failing and only the market can save them. But why are schools "failing" only in low-income communities of color? Chicago illustrates that these powerful interests have deployed enormous economic, political, and symbolic resources to undermine and/or neglect public neighborhood schools in communities of color and to promote charter schools as the only alternative. They have created the political and ideological conditions to dismantle urban public education and to demobilize collective struggle for a liberatory education (Apple, 2006). Charter schools open up education as a new arena for capital accumulation and their market ideology fits with the logics of the corporate interests and managers that are pushing them. Their political significance stretches beyond schools to legitimate marketing the public sector generally, particularly in cities, and to infuse market ideologies into everyday life.

However, the push for charter schools is materialized through the actions of parents and teachers. Looked at this way, neoliberalism is a *process* that works its way into the discourses and practices of the city through the actions of local actors, not just elites, but also marginalized and oppressed people acting in conditions not of their own making. In his study of African American school voucher parents in Milwaukee, Pedroni (2007) reads their participation in the voucher program against a background of prolonged struggles and failures to win a modicum of educational equity and respect for their children and themselves as public school parents. Pedroni argues the subject position (or identity) of educational consumer offers the prospect of greater dignity and agency than that of citizen-supplicant to a deaf and racist public school system that has never fully included African American children. Like the parents and teachers I talked with, he proposes that parents "inhabit" the subject position of education consumer in the face of a postwelfare state that offers no real alternative. Whatever the broader consequences of education markets, Pedroni (2007) proposes that African American parents' negotiated alliance with the educational voucher movement is "a manifestation of situated and subaltern agency within a moment of post-welfarism—and not naïve submission" (p. 212).

This insight opens a space to rethink the struggle for democratic public education by reframing what we mean by "public." There is no point in romanticizing public schools or other public institutions. While they have provided free universal education and been spaces where one can make claims for justice and are sometimes empowering and liberating, they have historically been raced, gendered, classed, and sexed spaces complicit in the reproduction of social inequalities (Apple, 2004, 2006; Fraser, 1997; Pedroni, 2007). Exclusionary, paternalistic, disrespectful, even brutal treatment of African American, Latino/a, and other people of color and women at the hands of public housing authorities, public hospitals, the police and the judicial system, public welfare agencies, elected officials, city agencies, and schools make public institutions deeply problematic places. So, *whose public* are we defending (Apple, 2006; Pedroni, 2009)? What of public education do we wish to defend and what must be reconstructed? Listening to the "good sense" in charter schools and paying attention to the perspectives of charter school parents and teachers is critical to build a counterhegemonic alliance organized around a new, radically democratic social imaginary of the urban public.

7

EDUCATION AND THE RIGHT TO THE CITY

Another World is Possible and Necessary

Based on the hopeful experiences in the shadows of the globalization and neoliberalization of our cities, we are proposing enthusiastically the construction of a new global urban world based on the solidarity and cooperation of human collectives in justice, democracy, and harmony with non-human nature. We emphatically defend radical and redistributive notions of social and environmental justice, equality of opportunity and rights to diversity. We understand these substantive rights to be enmeshed with the liberation of decision making processes, particularly enhancing the participation of all relevant parties in decision making and modes of collective (self) organization that avoid unjust hierarchies and discrimination. INURA sees it as its mandate to support the liberation of urban everyday life from the false demands and constrictions of neoliberal globalization. This, in other words, is fulfilling the promise of the "right to the city."

(International Network for Urban Research and Action [INURA], 2003)

Since I began researching and writing this book, the global capitalist system has plunged into the worst economic crisis since the Great Depression. This brought to a head a constellation of crises that had been accumulating over the past 30 years: vast economic inequalities, wars and militarization, dislocated populations at all geographic scales, historically unprecedented urbanization of poverty, and threats to the cultural and social existence of indigenous peoples and ways of life. An economic system and political philosophy geared to "accumulation by dispossession" (Harvey, 2003b) has plundered the world from Brazil's rainforests to the Gulf of Mexico to Black and Latino/a communities in U.S. cities and has produced potentially irreversible climate disaster. The U.S. government has exposed itself as largely the handmaiden of Wall Street, big oil, the health insurance industry, and big pharma and is seemingly thoroughly unwilling to address the distress of most everyone else. In education, as in other public institutions, there are severe cuts, teacher lay-offs, higher university tuitions, and stepped-up privatization. These hardships amplify the economic and social suffering of our students and their families: sustained unemployment, hunger, home foreclosures, deportation of migrants, and homelessness.

Crises of this magnitude are moments of immense danger but also present a historic opportunity. They bring into question social systems as a whole and make radical alternatives necessary and possible.

When I began writing this book, I envisioned that the conclusion would propose a framework for a more just education and city distilled from actual urban social struggles. A new social paradigm seemed largely visionary, beyond the reach of my discussion. But the capitalist crisis prompted me to rethink the current period, particularly the possibilities and necessities it opens up. Perhaps once in every generation there is a social conjuncture that puts fundamental social transformation on the agenda. Progressive social movements in the West did not succeed in taking advantage of that situation in the 1930s nor in the 1960s. But here we are again. In the United States, the economic crisis and the government's response have laid bare the failure of capitalism as an economic system and the political bankruptcy and corruption of a government that is largely run by the "party of Wall Street" (Harvey, 2010). Although there will be a range of stop-gap measures, it is remarkably clear that the system we have now is not working. Public distrust and frustration with government and the economy are running high. And there is no relief in sight.

Yet once again, originating particularly from the Global South, alternatives, rays of possibility, new social frameworks are emerging in broad and diverse social movements and state-led projects the aims of which are "anti-imperialist, anti-capitalist, feminist, environmentalist and socialist alternatives" (www. viacampesina.org). And in the most marginalized spaces in the United States, seeds of a democratic, cooperative way of living together are sprouting out of necessity—community gardens, producer cooperatives, community-run youth activities and arts spaces. They reflect an awakening of a new social imaginary. The conjunction of capitalist crisis and emergent alternatives represents an historic opportunity to uproot the fundamental causes of so much misery that has lasted for so long, and to work toward a new day. I have decided to write this chapter in the spirit of this opportunity.

But I have struggled with how to talk about a new social paradigm, tacking between the imperative to speak honestly and boldly and the desire not to be rhetorical or doctrinaire or simplistic. I have grappled with how to name that paradigm, how to open up a conversation about participatory economic and political democracy, communitarian socialism, socialism for the 21st century— *socialisms*—without evoking mind-closing images of the calcified authoritarian Soviet Union and Eastern European communism or knee-jerk reactions conditioned by the virulent anticommunism in which the United States is steeped. Yet this is a moment that compels us to rethink not just the neoliberal strategy but capitalism itself and to reimagine alternatives. This is essential not just to defend the public but to envision a more inclusive, democratic, robust "public" that foregrounds perspectives, interests, and self-determination of subordinated groups. Not to simply elect better representatives but to move toward a rich participatory democracy. To move beyond access and inclusion to real power in a new social order for all those who are part of the broad working class and those who have been marginalized and oppressed by dominant systems of racism, patriarchy, hetero-normativity, and other forms of systemic oppression. We are compelled to engage in serious discussion and debate about the world we wish to see, how we can move toward it at this juncture, and the role of education.

What are the possibilities of this new situation, and what kind of future should we envision? What are the implications for the city and public education? These questions, which so many are grappling with, animate my concluding thoughts.

Summing Up

The economic crisis has laid bare the effects of neoliberal economic and social policies that transferred wealth upward, consolidated capitalist class power, disinvested in social welfare and public goods, and excluded whole urban populations, particularly low-income African Americans and some Latino/as from any social contract. As unemployment has become entrenched, working class and even middle class neighborhoods are littered with foreclosed homes and shuttered shops, reminders that banks and developers made a killing on real estate speculation. All this is the context for a constellation of privatized, market-driven, socially stratifying education policies with global reach (Compton & Weiner, 2008).

In this book I have tried to show that education policy is constitutive of neoliberal urban restructuring in the interest of capital accumulation, racial containment, and the privileged lifestyles of the wealthy few who have profited enormously from the policies of the past three decades. I have argued that neoliberal education policies contribute to gentrification, the racialization of space, and the demonization of low-income communities of color. Marketizing education is another form of "accumulation by dispossession" (Harvey, 2003b). And education is a prime sector for the introduction of neoliberal ideologies and social relations as public schools are handed over to private operators, neighborhood schools are shut and replaced with boutique schools in gentrified areas or with charter schools, and competition is introduced into all aspects of education. This project is impelled by twin logics of capital accumulation and White supremacy. I have argued that the driving force for this agenda is a partnership of corporate and financial actors, the state, venture philanthropy, and the CEOs and managers who run urban school districts for the most part.

Neoliberalism is a deeply ideological project. Changing "the soul," as Thatcher so baldly put it, is key to neoliberalization. Neoliberalism gained traction, in part, because it was constructed as the only alternative to the "failed policies" of the Keynesian welfare state. In part, this is legitimated by racist ideologies that pathologize people of color as morally deficient freeloaders on the state, thus reframing structural problems as moral and behavioral. Supposedly progressive plans to reduce poverty and the "achievement gap" through modifying the behaviors of low-income people by mixing them with the middle class are instantiations of this ideology. George Lipsitz (2006b) argues that the neoliberal project reconstructs subjectivities around "a social warrant" that "asks people to place their identities as accumulators and consumers above their responsibilities as workers and citizens" (p. 455). This social warrant is a racial project that "builds a counter subversive consensus around the idea that economic stagnation and social disintegration stem from the excessive concessions made to subordinated groups as a result of the civil rights movement" (p. 455). Education policy is both shaped by this ideological process, and contributes to it, as schools, particularly "low-performing" schools in communities of color, are saturated with a culture of competition and top-down accountability and disciplined by high stakes testing, the threat of being closed, and performance management practices.

I have also shown that neoliberalism is materialized on the ground through the actions of teachers and parents. It taps into a common sense that emanates from lived experience with disinvested and deeply inequitable public schools. In this context, which can be extended to other public services, such as health and housing, the market seems to offer a space for agency, for moving beyond being a recipient of what public institutions dish out. This speaks to the need to not simply defend public schools but to transform them, to ask, what kind of public do we want? And it suggests that a counterhegemonic alliance would need to connect with the real experiences, desires, hopes, and needs of communities that see few options in disinvested and problematic public institutions (Pedroni, 2007). But to move forward, it is necessary to clarify the present social conjuncture and its implications for education and the city.

Going Forward: A New Social Conjuncture

In September 2008, Lehman Brothers, a gigantic global investment firm, went under, sending shock waves around the world. In one week in October, investors lost $2.3 trillion and the Dow Jones Industrial Average had its worst week ever. The crisis coursed through a globally intertwined economy as unsuspecting investors around the world found they were holding worthless mortgage-backed securities. The global integration of financial markets had allowed investors to make billions by virtually instant transfers of funds in a casino of currency markets, collateralized debt obligations, hedge funds, and other arcane speculative financial "products." But hyperglobalization was also the market's Achilles heel. The failure of excessive risk anywhere can quickly infect the system as a whole. And it did. The collapse of the housing bubble in the United States exposed a high level of risk from Britain to Greece. The government of Iceland, which was deeply enmeshed in the credit markets, went bankrupt. According to the IMF, the global loss in asset value by mid-2009 was at least $55 trillion, roughly equivalent to one year's global output of goods and services, with the potential for losses to soar to $400 trillion (Harvey, 2010, p. 223).

As the U.S. financial industry teetered, it became clear that only government intervention could save the U.S. and possibly the global financial system. U.S. Treasury officials and heads of state who had championed unregulated markets and government noninterference (foundational neoliberal theory) for decades led the charge to inject billions of public tax dollars to rescue financial institutions and insurance giants like AIG that had insured the risky investments. In a Washington, DC mired in political stalemate and inaction—from health care, to Hurricane Katrina, to immigration reform—U.S. Treasury officials working closely with Wall Street banks pushed through a $700 billion bailout of the banks at taxpayers' expense in a few days. Governments around the world followed suit to bail out some of the world's biggest banks. Others were absorbed by the few big banks left standing, further consolidating the global financial industry. The U.S. auto industry had to be bailed out too. The U.S. government bought up the bad debt of federally chartered mortgage institutions Freddie Mac and Fannie Mae to ensure their bond holders would be protected. As the housing market collapsed and workers lost their jobs, those with subprime mortgages lost their homes to foreclosures which reached an all-time high in the United States in the first half of 2009 with 1.9 million reported (Adler, 2009). But there were precious few bailouts for home owners who were castigated for not reading the fine print and for living above their means (apparently the reprimand did not apply to the big banks that had a ratio of up to 30:1 debt to deposits; Harvey, 2010, p. 30). Foreclosures hit people hardest who had few assets. Latino/as and Blacks were disproportionately the recipients of subprime loans (González-Rivera, 2009). African Americans, who were estimated to have lost between $71 and $93 billion in assets between 1998 and 2006 *before the crisis* due to subprime housing loans, suffered their biggest asset loss in history (Harvey, 2010), and U.S. unemployment overall also increased by over 5 million in a few months.

There might have been a different response. David Harvey, speaking at the World Social Forum in 2009, suggested, "What we should have done is to take the $700 billion and create an urban redevelopment bank to save all of those neighborhoods that were being destroyed and reconstruct cities more out of popular demand" (Harvey, 2009).

The crisis is not over. As I write this in August 2010, the economy continues to stagnate with little growth in full-time jobs. Fannie Mae and Freddie Mac guarantee $5 trillion in mortgages, many of them in trouble. All told, according to Harvey (2010), the U.S. government is guaranteeing more than $200 trillion in asset values (p. 223). If a sizable portion went bad, the result would be catastrophic. Some mainstream economists are talking about a 10-year recession. Furthermore, military solutions to declining economic dominance are further undermining the U.S. economy and its political legitimacy. Two wars of occupation in the Middle East threaten to engulf Pakistan and Iran. The cost of these wars (over $1 trillion since 2001; www.costofwar.com) is driving up the federal deficit at a time the government is bailing out the biggest financiers and drastically cutting social spending, particularly for public education, and attacking public sector unions. In the long run, this situation is politically untenable.

We have reached the point where capitalism's victims are most of humanity (Amin, 2008). This situation has engendered an array of anticapitalist social movements and alternatives at all spatial scales, from feminist and worker cooperatives, to large scale movements such as the Landless Movement in Brazil (MST) and La Via Campesina international peasant movement, to anti-neoliberal states. In 2002, Santos pointed to an emergent paradigm, "a transnational, emancipatory sub-politics, the political Geist of counter-hegemonic globalizations" (p. 1056). Across Latin America, resistance has congealed in the election of a spectrum of anti-neo-liberal to prosocialist governments energized by movements of indigenous peoples, women, cultural workers, environmentalists, farmers, workers, the landless, educators, and more (Harnecker, 2010).

Socialism, reinvigorated by diverse epistemologies and struggles, is once more on the agenda of the world's dispossessed, exploited, and alienated and those fighting to defend the earth. The Venezuelan government and, most importantly, grassroots mobilizations of the poor and disenfranchised and new left parties there, proclaim a Bolivarian revolution aimed at "socialism for the 21st century." In Bolivia, the Movement for Socialism, headed by President Evo Morales, an indigenous labor leader elected through a broad popular movement, has projected onto the world stage a socialist alternative and defense of the environment that draws from indigenous communitarian traditions. The long U.S. political domination of Latin America and the Caribbean through the Organization of American States now faces the counterweight of ALBA (Bolivarian Alliance for the Peoples of the Americas), which is comprised of Venezuela, Cuba, Bolivia, Ecuador, Nicaragua, and smaller Caribbean nations. Although there are certainly challenges, inherited contradictions, and weaknesses of these movements and prosocialist governments, and divergences in their paths, their significance cannot be underestimated on the global stage and as a challenge to the thesis that there is no alternative to capitalism.

Departing from doctrinaire and distorted "socialist" models of the 20th century, (e.g., Soviet Union and Eastern Europe), this "Modern Prince" (Gramsci, 1971) of the 21st century (diverse social movements, collective projects, worker organizations, and political parties) draws on a mix of cosmologies, models, and social visions to reinvigorate the deeply humanist meaning of socialism (Amin, 2008). It integrates economic transformation (e.g., socialist, communal, cooperative relations of production and distribution), cultural recognition (e.g., indigenous, feminist, African-rooted, LGBTQ[1] movements), democratic political participation (e.g., people's assemblies, cooperatives), ecological justice ("rights of mother earth" and rejection of growth based on Western industrialization as the only model of human progress), and multiple traditions, histories, experiences, and epistemologies (e.g., Marxist, Bolivarian, indigenous, postcolonial, feminist, gay, Africanist). Elsewhere, localized economic, political, and cultural contestations of neoliberalism (Leitner et al., 2007) are beginning to take on a new urgency and focus in the face of the economic crisis. This was evidenced in early 2010 by massive demonstrations of workers and students against structural adjustment in Greece and the victorious general strike of 65,000 students at the University of Puerto Rico against cuts in public education.

The Structural Crisis

Unbridled speculation in housing markets precipitated the crisis, but its roots are in the nature of capitalism itself (Bello, 2008; Foster & Magdoff, 2009). For capitalism to work, the surplus it generates must be reinvested in profitable economic activity. But high levels of inequality and insufficient wages hold down the ability of the masses of people to consume the goods and services they produce. The inability of consumption to keep up with capital's need to expand leads to periodic crises of relative overproduction and economic stagnation because there are insufficient outlets for profitable reinvestment. In the Great Depression the crisis deepened until enough productive capacity had been destroyed (factories shut down and farms untended) and a new outlet for investment was created—the war effort—to get the economy moving again (Foster & Magdoff, 2009). Stagnation is the normal state of mature capitalism because its enormous productivity and monopolistic pricing generate huge and expanding surpluses that surpass the economy's ability to absorb them. As a result, the system has become more dependent on waste to keep investment going (e.g., military spending, unnecessary consumption, advertising, and financialization; Foster & Magdoff).

In the 1970s capital tried "three escape routes from the conundrum of overproduction": financialization and massive expansion of credit, neoliberal restructuring, and globalization (Bello, 2008). As I discuss in chapter 1, these strategies were aimed at increasing profits by depressing wages, removing restrictions on capital flows, and creating new arenas for investment (i.e., markets where there had been none). But neoliberal restructuring did not produce a sufficient rate of growth. Even with dramatic increases in household and corporate debt, the reduction of real wages restricted demand. During the 1980s and 1990s, productivity increased but for the first time since 1945 failed to share any of the gains with workers (Dew-Becker & Gordon, 2005; Tabb, 2007). Globalization also opened up new areas to capitalist production (China is the prime example) but the increased productive capacity only exacerbated the crisis of relative overproduction. With investment in agriculture and industry yielding low rates of profit, capital flowed into the financial sector, and the gap between a stagnating real economy and an inflated financial sector grew (Foster & Magdoff, 2009). As investors made vast sums on speculation and trade in obscure financial "products" such as derivatives, credit default swaps, and collateralized debt obligations, risk intensified with little collateral backing up debt.

An economy based on financial speculation is a house of cards. A default in one sector, in this case the subprime mortgage market, can bring the whole thing crashing down. Because the globalization of financial markets globalized risk, the crisis quickly infected banks, investors, and government-owned investments in stocks, bonds, and other securities globally. Neoliberal measures, such as overextension of consumer credit and global financialization, introduced to forestall the last big structural crisis, triggered this one. Foster and Magdoff (2009) put it simply, "The economy could not live without financialization (along with other props to the system such as military spending) and it could not in the end live with it" (p. 19).

Counter to neoliberal theory of free markets and the noninterventionist state, financial risk was buttressed by the assurance that the state would be a lender of last resort. This was a green light for a casino economy of risky speculative deals. In fact, the history of crises since the 1970s has been one of government intervention to save financial institutions, prioritizing their well-being over that of the people; for example, the New York bank bailout in the mid-1970s and U.S. Treasury and IMF bailout of the 1982 Mexican debt crisis. In both cases, the state or the IMF insisted on austerity measures for the population: severe cuts in state funding for social welfare, lower wages, and privatization. To put it bluntly, "they protected the banks and destroyed the people" (Harvey, 2009). They imposed the same policy on Latin American, Eastern European, and African countries.

Structural Adjustment Comes Home

Capitalism can likely survive this crisis, but at what cost? The unfolding scenario is to socialize the losses of the investors through the imposition of social austerity measures (Harvey, 2010), as mandated by the European Union and IMF for the Greek crisis of 2010. In this scenario, the working and middle classes will be expected to endure repeated reductions in wages, reductions or loss of pensions and hard-won social benefits, drastic cuts in public services such as education, and further loss of personal assets, such as homes and other possessions. The initial, crisis-driven round of education cuts and privatizations may not be the last. For those already struggling to survive in many parts of the world, starvation is a real possibility. For the planet it will likely mean further environmental degradation as pollution controls are deemed "too costly" and disruptive to the "recovery."

In the United States, militarization and incarceration have been substituted for the provision of social welfare and jobs, particularly for young African American men (Fraser with Bedford, 2008; Gilmore, 2007a). But the imposition of austerity measures may call for more generalized political repression and police violence to suppress resistance and contain those who are "redundant." Elements in the state also support extreme right wing populist movements that have mushroomed in the crisis, as with political ascendancy of the "Tea Party" movement. The material and ideological infrastructure of repression are already in place: immigrant detention centers and legalized racial profiling (as in Arizona's law allowing police to stop anyone suspected of being an undocumented migrant), a vast complex of public and private jails and prisons, FBI investigations of political activists, surveillance and policing of communities of color, normalization of the highest incarceration rate in the world—disproportionately African American and Latino—the War on Terror, U.S. military preparation for urban warfare, deployment of technology that can track people's daily movements, and armed right wing militias.

Racialized "societal fascism"—exclusion of segments of the population from any social contract (Santos, 2002)—may intensify in a kind of state-organized survival of the fittest. In descent into barbarism, some people (e.g., African Americans, homeless people, some immigrants) are simply deemed superfluous in a world of intensified austerity and competition for scarce resources. I am haunted these days by images from Alfonso Cuarón's 2006 film, *Children of Men* (Abraham, 2006), in which immigrants, "others," are contained in cages in central London as everyone else rushes about their business in a degraded, garbage-filled city.

Structural adjustment is already coming home to the United States, with education a main target. The state of California, the sixth largest economy in the world, proposes draconian cuts in education, health, and programs for youth and the elderly. This scenario is repeating in state legislatures and city halls across the country with lay-offs and "furloughs" (pay cuts) of state employees and drastic cuts in public services and attacks on public employee unions. Cities are particularly hard hit by revenue shortfalls because of their deep reliance on property markets and investments in financial markets. Urban school districts are laying off thousands of teachers, increasing class sizes, shrinking teacher pensions, and cutting out music, gym, kindergarten, bilingual programs, after school and youth programs, and more. These are certain to hit hardest those least able to bear them, low-income schools of color where these are the very programs that offer some hope. We are also witnessing the dismantling of accessible and affordable quality public higher education in the United States. Budget shortfalls have accelerated a 25-year trend to reduce public funding and raise tuition while relying more on corporate funding and prioritizing those units that make money and are keyed to U.S. economic competitiveness: business schools, STEM disciplines (science, technology, engineering, mathematics), scientific research units—certainly not education, social work, or ethnic studies. The university is reverting to being a space for elites, reversing hard-won gains of the 1960s and 1970s for access and diversity, while teacher and administrator preparation are contracted out to for-profit providers and corporate alternatives.

In a rendition of "disaster capitalism," the crisis is opportunity and rationale to further privatize the public sphere. As Naomi Klein wrote in *The Guardian* in September 2008, "The massive debts the public is accumulating to bail out the speculators will then become part of a global budget crisis that will be the rationalization for deep cuts to social programs, and for a renewed push to privatize what's left of the public sector. We will be told that our hopes for a green future are, sadly, too costly." In a rerun of post-Katrina New Orleans, the crisis is a golden opportunity to accelerate school privatization from kindergarten through higher education, to wrest concessions from teacher unions, and to further streamline schooling to serve global "competitiveness" (Compton & Weiner, 2008). The UK's new Tory Education Minister, Michael Gove, proposed turning 1,000 of the most successful publicly funded schools into "academies," modeled on U.S. charter schools. According to the Anti-Academies Alliance, this would leave local authorities managing schools with the most difficulties, with diminishing budgets (Peterson, 2010). JPMorgan Chase's $325 million investment in charter school expansion in the United States is another example of the current trend (JP Morgan, 2010).

The Obama administration seized on the fiscal crisis of cities and states to further restructure public education along neoliberal lines. The Department of Education offered $4.35 billion in competitive federal economic stimulus funds, and laid out terms for favorable bids that further the market agenda. Just to be sure, the Gates Foundation awarded technical assistance grants to states to help them prepare their proposals on condition they follow market-centered criteria. Competition for the funds pushed cash-strapped states to hastily pass laws lifting charter school caps and exacting concessions from teacher unions. In one stroke, the Obama administration changed national policy, before even awarding the money.

When Arne Duncan was appointed Secretary of Education, his first official act was to fly to Detroit to tell the mayor and governor that the federal government could provide millions of dollars for the city's struggling school system—if Detroit would follow the Chicago example. As I describe in chapter

3, Duncan made it plain that mayoral takeover of the school district, closing failing schools, expanding charters, and tying teacher evaluations to student test scores were the terms on which the federal government would look kindly on Detroit. Robert Bobb, the state appointed Chief Financial Officer of the Detroit Public Schools, followed up with a proposal to close 44 schools as part of an "academic plan" to expand a market of charter schools, introduce mandatory "no social promotion" policies, evaluate teachers based on student performance, and put the mayor in charge of the schools—all without consulting Detroit's elected school board. Duncan began with Detroit, one of the most economically devastated cities in the country.

A Crisis of Legitimacy

On February 18, 2010, Joseph Stack, a 54-year-old computer software engineer, crashed his small plane into an office building in Austin, Texas, hitting an Internal Revenue Service office, killing an employee, and committing suicide. Stack left behind a manifesto describing his decades of failed attempts to be treated equitably by the U.S. tax system, to be heard by his elected officials, and to find economic security. He recalled the elderly wife of a retired steel worker in Pennsylvania forced to live on cat food when her husband's retirement benefits were stolen by the steel corporation. Stack denounced government support for corporate greed and profiteering: "Why is it that a handful of thugs and plunderers can commit unthinkable atrocities (and in the case of the GM executives, for scores of years) and when it's time for their gravy train to crash under the weight of their gluttony and overwhelming stupidity, the force of the full federal government has no difficulty coming to their aid within days if not hours?" After a long accounting of all the abuse and injustice he had seen and experienced at the hands of the U.S. political and economic system, he declared he had "had enough," hoping his act would spur others to "fight for freedom." Stack ended the manifesto by saying: "The communist creed: From each according to his ability, to each according to his need. The capitalist creed: From each according to his gullibility, to each according to his greed" (Stack, 2010).

Stack's manifesto was ridiculed in the press and his suicide dismissed as the act of a crackpot. But Stack fingered a political and economic system that works only for the rich. As an ecological catastrophe of unfathomable proportions has unfolded resulting from the BP oil spill in the Gulf of Mexico, once again the arrogance of Big Oil is displayed along with the unbridled power of the fossil fuel industries enmeshed with government agencies that are supposed to regulate them. While one in eight people in the United States relies on food banks for food and groceries, an increase of 46% over 2006 (Mathematica, 2010), Wall Street bankers and investment brokers continue to rake in millions in bonuses. Nearly every move Congress makes reveals its ties to the corporate and banking oligarchy. The operator of a now-devastated seafood company off the coast of Louisiana told *Democracy Now* host Amy Goodman on June 2, 2010,

> I know if I spill two gallons of oil in the water, they're going to give me a $150,000 fine, you know, and a $150,000 fine is like about two cents to BP compared to what it is to me, you know? And it's just a shame that the United States of America has two standards: one for the regular people and one for big corporations. You know, that's not—how did we get to this point, you know? That's got to stop. That's got to stop now.

In short, the state faces a serious crisis of legitimacy, one that could tip in different directions—a rapidly growing right wing anti-big-government movement, political cynicism, perhaps a new New Deal. In education, as the punishing effects of 8 years of No Child Left Behind and the disastrous consequences of closing schools are being felt nationally, a hopeful counterdiscourse to accountability and privatization has begun to emerge in the mainstream of society. This is reflected in proposals for equitable opportunity to learn standards and a community-grounded, democratic process of school transformation coming from established national civil rights organizations and a national coalition of community organizations (Civil Rights Framework, 2010; Communities for Excellent Public Schools, 2010). In the rest of this chapter I argue this moment of economic and political crisis is an opportunity and necessity to consider solutions rooted in a new educational and social paradigm.

Another World Is Possible and Necessary

> Progressives should boldly aspire, once again to paradigms of social organization that unabashedly aim for equality and participatory democratic control of both the national economy and the global economy as prerequisites for collective and individual liberation, and one must add, ecological stabilization.
>
> (Bello, 2009)

A realistic assessment of our situation makes it clear that another world is both possible and necessary. Capitalism is not working. According to Harvey (2010), to get back to a 3% growth rate, which most mainstream economists argue is necessary for a healthy capitalist economy, would have required finding new investment opportunities to the tune of $1.6 trillion in 2010, rising to $3 trillion by 2030. This contrasts with the $0.15 trillion needed in 1950 (p. 216). He argues that leaving aside constraints of nature (global warming) and potential political resistance, there may be no spaces left, no new lines of production, to absorb the expanded capital. There may be no way out apart from new forms of financial speculation, a new bubble (maybe education?), another crash not far down the road, and more austerity. Even more profoundly, the survival of the planet is incompatible with the capitalist imperative for profit-driven growth (Speth, 2008), a conclusion echoed by the April 2010 World Peoples' Summit on Climate Change and Rights of Mother Earth in Tiquipaya, Bolivia.

Speaking to the World Social Forum in Porto Alegre, Brazil in January 2010, Harvey said, "At some point quantitative changes lead to qualitative shifts and we need to take seriously the idea that we may be at exactly such an inflexion point in the history of capitalism. Questioning the future of capitalism itself as an adequate social system ought, therefore, to be in the forefront of the current debate" (p. 217). This is an important opportunity to stretch beyond tinkering at the edges of a dysfunctional economy and encrusted inequalities and injustices and to harness collective wisdom and political will toward fashioning a sustainable, democratic, socially just alternative. We need the courage and clarity to name the problem we face and to work together for a new social vision that fundamentally transforms the present economic, political, and social order and propels a revolution in values. Capitalism, held in place by White supremacist and patriarchal ideologies and structures, is the fundamental problem. If there ever was a time to name it, it is now.

One of the lessons of the rise of Thatcherism is the power of ideas of an organized, relatively small group to capture a crisis and put forward a solution. Imagination and vision, conceptions of social justice, play an indispensable role in motivating and inspiring us toward an alternative world. Brown and Lauder (2001) describe it well: "the great ethical hope at the beginning of the twenty-first century lies in the development of social solidarity based on the reflexivity of individuals who recognise that their quality of life depends on co-operation with others rather than relentless competition..." (p. 284). This is a social paradigm aimed at "unleashing all human potential" and grounded in the premise that the full development of each requires the full development of all as "rich human beings" with "rich human needs" (Lebowitz, 2006, p.13, paraphrasing Marx). Thus it necessarily requires integral struggle against racism—including support for the right to self-determination—patriarchy, heterosexism, colonial and imperial relations, and so on in the process of working for a socially just alternative.

Various political frameworks, particularly in the Global South, coalesce around this broad common vision; for example, the Bamako Appeal (Amin, 2008) and the Declaration of the Assembly of Social Movements at the World Social Forum (2009). There are various names for a society based on economic cooperation and participatory democracy, each shaped by its own context: radical economic and political democracy, "socialism for the 21st century" (the goal of the Bolivarian revolution), "another communism" (Harvey, 2010), "communitarian socialism" (Movement for Socialism, Bolivia), eco-socialism, "*el buen vivir*"—life lived in harmony with oneself, others and the world around (indigenous movements of Latin America). I am not much concerned right now with the name or the shades of difference, but I am not talking about the institutional "communism" of the Soviet Union—nor was Marx. The essence is a new social imaginary of a deeply ethical and humanizing society driven by the logics of democracy, justice, self-determination, harmony with the earth, economic cooperation, and solidarity. It thoroughly rejects logics of domination and exploitation. It is infused with indigenous, eco-feminist, Marxist, postcolonial, racial liberation perspectives and more—what Samir Amin (2008) calls a "convergence of diversity" that greatly expands the scope and meaning of emancipation. In the words of the Document of the Bolivarian Alternative for the Peoples of Our Americas (ALBA) at the 5th Summit of the Americas, April 17, 2009:

> The global economic, climate change, food and energy crises are products of the decadence of capitalism that threatens to put an end to the existence of life and the planet. To avoid this outcome it is necessary to develop an alternative model to that of the capitalist system. A system based on:
>
> Solidarity and complementarity and not competition;
> A system in harmony with our Mother Earth rather than the looting of our natural resources;
> A system based on cultural diversity and not the crushing of cultures and imposition of cultural values and lifestyles alien to the realities of our countries:
> A system of peace based on social justice and not on imperialist wars and policies;
> In synthesis, a system that restores the human condition of our societies and peoples rather than reducing them to simple consumers or commodities.

In the United States, such a social system seems distant, particularly because of the hold of competitive individualism, racism, and consumerism. But social visions and political manifestos such as the ALBA document gel through social struggle. Referencing one of Marx's central insights, economist Michael Lebowitz (2006), writing from the vantage point of participating in, and theorizing about, the movement toward socialism in Venezuela, writes, "In the struggle to realize the vision of a new society, we not only change the old society, we also change ourselves, and as Marx commented, make ourselves fit to create the new society" (p. 10). The struggle of thousands of (victorious) university students in Puerto Rico (May 2010) to defend public education offers a powerful illustration of this unfolding dialectic:

> The Puerto Rican students who have occupied the campus of the Universidad de Puerto Rico for weeks, surrounded by armed forces, are doing urban agriculture, collective cooking, environmentally sustainable practices, art, music … in brief, they are striving to build the elements of a different society. The student movement has shown a deep understanding of

the challenges faced by public education in our days. But their commitment goes beyond a restricted catalogue of demands, or the defense of a fixed ideal. Their struggle arises as an ongoing search for a different order of things. As they declared on the first emission of Radio Huelga after ten days of strike: "We are not the same. This process is part of our aims. We are being transformed day by day, and we have started seeing things in another way. This strike contains the desire of another world, which is possible if we construct it in the process. Making it from within." While developing strategies to enable a negotiation with the administration, an active calendar of academic and cultural activities has been organized with the support and solidarity of professors, artists, farmers, and many others. This includes: daily lectures on a wide variety of topics, poetry readings, film screenings, traditional bomba dance workshops, and even a communal garden with lettuce, tomatoes, plantains, basil, and other crops which they plan to maintain after the strike is over. Five major concerts have taken placed at the campuses of Río Piedras, Humacao, Cayey, Arecibo, and Mayagüez, with the participation of some of the most recognized Puerto Rican musicians of different styles and generations. They celebrated Mother's Day cooking together and inviting their families to the University's gateways.

(Sassen, 2010)

The Right to the City Is a Call for a New Society

French sociologist and philosopher Henri Lefebvre popularized the slogan "Right to the City" in 1968 (see Lefebvre, 1968/1996) as both a "cry and a demand, a cry out of necessity and a demand for something more" (Marcuse, 2009, p. 190). It is the right to remake the city and in the process change our selves and how we live together, to create qualitatively different urban social relationships. For Lefebvre this means transforming the power relations that produce urban space in its multiple dimensions—the material space people encounter in daily life (perceived space), representations of space (conceived space), and how people actually experience space (lived space) (Purcell, 2002). As I have shown in this book, the present situation was created by a powerful constellation of economic and political forces that have appropriated the city as their own.

Cities are strategic locations for capital accumulation and thus a key locus for opposition to its logics. The urban and metropolitan housing/real estate sector has been a critical stabilizer of the economy by absorbing huge amounts of surplus capital in suburbanization, gentrification, downtown development, and housing construction at wider and wider geographic scales (Harvey, 2008). A prime example is the urbanization of China in the last decade which accounted for half of the world's cement since 2000 and boosted the economies of Brazil,

Argentina, Australia, and Chile with its demand for raw materials (p. 37). Debt financing of urbanization has been a prime outlet for surplus capital, which helps explain why the collapse of the housing bubble hit cities and metropolitan regions particularly hard. The result has been the dispossession of hundreds of thousands of urban dwellers: "The planet as building site collides with the 'planet of slums'" (p. 37).

Urban space in the United States (and elsewhere) is racialized and White supremacy is central to the production of an urban landscape of inflated property values and private ownership (Lipsitz, 2007). In the United States, the spatial structuring and restructuring of cities has served racial containment and domination from the earliest days of slavery, through major waves of immigration, Black migrations to the North, suburbanization and White flight, deindustrialization and disinvestment of inner cores, and neoliberal urban redevelopment. Thus the right to the city necessitates a struggle against racism, ideologically and materially including the right for people of color to determine their own institutions.

For Lefebvre, the city's vitality is its diversity of people, ways of living, and perspectives—and thus its potential as a creative space of vibrant democratic dialogue and debate. This potential unity in difference is the basis of a counterhegemonic coalition of those struggling for survival and access to the city and those who are superficially integrated but whose creativity and aspirations are stifled, who are discontented with the lack of meaning and solidarity (Marcuse, 2009). The bourgeois city as private property valorizes urban space as a site to invest surplus and make profit, a space of exclusions. In contrast, Lefebvre argued for the "right of appropriation" of the city's use value, the right to take back the city as a commons for the whole of society (Purcell, 2002) rather than for capital accumulation. In this sense, the right to the city is radically democratic and fundamentally anticapitalist. It is a call for a wholly different city and society, "socialism" by whatever name (Marcuse).

Education and the Right to the City

Education is integral to a movement to reclaim the city. It is a demand for all those locked out of equitable access to public education and dispossessed of their schools, a demand for public schools that are not exclusionary (racist, homophobic, discriminatory) and for all those simply desperate to find a "good school" for their children. It is also a cry for education that develops our human potential, that prepares us to be subjects of history—to read and write the world (Freire, 1994). In the words of the indispensable radical education journal, *Rethinking Schools*, (www.rethinkingschools.org) an education that is critical, multicultural, antiracist, projustice, hopeful, joyful, kind, and visionary.

Secretary of Education Arne Duncan, speaking at Dr. Martin Luther King's church on King's 81st birthday, said "If Dr. King were here today, he would call on a new generation of leaders to build upon his work by doing the most important thing each of you can do: get an education, learn to think, learn to compete, and learn to win" (Duncan Speaks, January 15, 2010). But Dr. King, at the end of his life, had this to say: "We must rapidly begin the shift from a 'thing-oriented' society to a 'person-oriented' society. When machines and computers, profit motives and property rights, are considered more important than people, the giant triplets of racism, extreme materialism, and militarism are incapable of being conquered" (Washington, 1986, p. 240). I doubt that Dr. King would have endorsed Duncan's interpretation. Duncan is voicing a vision rooted in values of competition and self-serving individualism that permeate the neoliberalized city. More in line with Dr. King's vision, a transformative education would envision a society reaching toward the full development of human beings as part of the shift to a person–oriented society grounded in radical political and economic democracy. How might education move toward this new social paradigm?

Duncan articulates a vision of education that has become common sense through an extended process of framing schooling in neoliberal terms. Neoliberals, richly funded, have marshaled the full apparatus of the corporate media and think tanks to rearticulate education equity and quality as individualistic, competitive, and market-led. Over a couple of decades, they coalesced a wide range of social groups under this hegemonic umbrella—parents fed up with the failures of urban schools and their lack of resources, teachers seeking freedom to teach outside the constraints of public schools, managers, technicians, and testing companies for whom the accountability/managerial turn has been an employment and business boom, corporate philanthropists, charter school operators, community organizations wanting community-based schools, and neoconservatives who want government out of education (see Apple, 2006). The economic crisis alone will not galvanize a movement for social transformation. In fact, it has spawned a right wing movement. The sitiuation calls for what Gramsci termed a "war of position," strategically unravelling consent for the dominant agenda and coalescing a new coalition (or counterhegemonic social bloc) around Dr. King's vision is our task.

From Resistance to Proactive Education Politics

In the past few years, a multifaceted education movement has emerged in the United States. There is a boom in social justice teaching and social justice-oriented schools within the public system, freedom schools and popular education projects outside public education, and community-based youth programs. This boom is reflected in the proliferation of books and other publications on liberatory education and the rapid growth of local and national critical education conferences.[2] There are also emergent networks of educators centered on teaching for social justice, and organizations of activist teachers and community educators in a number of cities have joined together in a national network of teacher activist organizations.[3] Youth organizations are blossoming. These groups have joined parents in coalitions to stop school closings and privatization, prevent mayoral takeovers of urban school districts, defend undocumented students, and challenge high stakes testing.

In a highly significant development, progressive caucuses are in the leadership of both the Los Angeles and Chicago teacher unions. The Caucus of Rank and File Educators (CORE), swept the June 2010 election of the Chicago Teachers Union (CTU), the third largest teachers' union in the country (30,000 members), on a platform of democratic unionism and opposition to privatization and Ren2010 in alliance with parents, youth, and communities. The CTU has the potential to influence the direction of the American Federation of Teachers nationally and be a real force to defeat budget cuts and challenge Chicago's neoliberal education agenda.

This education movement as a whole is largely a response to neoliberal privations and comprises many efforts to create liberatory spaces in schools. But it is not yet organized around a coherent philosophy or program. To move from resistance to proactive education politics requires (among other things) a sophisticated understanding of the complex system we are up against and a multifaceted vision of the world we wish to see. As homes, jobs, and futures disappear and public education is privatized and cut back, we need forums and other opportunities where we can debate and summarize our own experiences, connect seemingly disparate problems, diagnose systemic causes, and explore alternative social paradigms (Gilmore, 2008). In the many small and large skirmishes, those who can "connect the dots" between immediate issues and larger systems of oppression and exploitation play a crucial leadership role in moving the education movement toward a systemic analysis and strategic orientation. The voices of these "organic intellectuals" (Gramsci, 1971) need to be magnified to bring to the forefront critical inquiries into the roots of the crises we face and the formulation of transformative solutions. Here there is much to learn from the important role of teachers outside the United States, for example in Oaxaca, Honduras, and British Columbia.

Reframing

Reframing the neoliberal education discourse is a critical aspect of fracturing the hegemonic alliance that supports it. How issues are framed sets the parameters of possible solutions, defines who is responsible, and embodies the sort of society we wish to have. An example is the July 2010 proposal by a coalition of civil rights organizations (Civil Rights Framework, 2010). While one might argue it is limited in certain ways,[4] the Framework is powerful because it shifts the discourse from outputs (test scores) to inputs (equitable resources), from dictating to communities (centralized accountability) to community engagement, from closing schools to transforming them (see also Communities for Excellent Public Schools, 2010), from competition for resources to education as a civil right for all. The Framework begins with a strong recognition of the crisis facing urban schools, rupturing the neoliberal trope that opposition means supporting the status quo, but critiques school closings and charter schools as unproven quick fixes when what is needed is systemic change to improve public education. Rearticulating neoliberal measures to a progressive agenda requires taking seriously the perspectives of parents, educators, and others who are drawn to school closings, corporate takeovers, the market, and top-down accountability out of frustration with the status quo and proposing an alternative that addresses their deep concerns.

Alliances with Urban Social Movements

The crisis has created an imperative for those concerned about education to ally with those opposing gentrification and evictions and foreclosures, people defending public health clinics, and campaigns for living wage jobs, an end to violence, and so on. Many of us realize that students' potential is limited by poverty, hunger, lack of health care, lack of adequate housing, and violence, and these hardships are likely to intensify as the economic crisis continues. We cannot work for equitable education without also challenging these conditions (Anyon, 2005). Conversely, a rich, problem-posing education (Freire, 1970/1998a) is integral to sustainable democratic communities and a strategic part of preparing young people to be part of fighting for a community needs. Thus education is integrally linked to the struggle for the right to the city. Building alliances across issues helps forge solidarities across lines of race, ethnicity, gender, class, and other boundaries and clarifies the interconnectedness of urban issues and the need for systemic solutions.

Nonreformist Reforms

There is clearly a need for reforms to meet needs now. But what kind of reforms? The distinction between "reformism" and "nonreformist reforms" is helpful. A strategy of reformism may win immediate gains but can also further entrench and obscure the ideologies and structures of the present economic and political system, leaving the hegemonic coalition that supports them intact, and moving us farther from a solution. In contrast, nonreformist reforms build the capacity of working class and other people to fundamentally challenge power. They help clarify the structural and ideological roots of the problems we face, and envision aspects of the society we wish to have (Bond, 2008). They reframe educational issues in line with a progressive vision and resonate with parents and teachers drawn to neoliberal solutions as a way out. The Right to the City Alliance conveys this strategy:

> The fight for reforms can be a part of the process of building power for a longer-term transformative struggle; in this sense, reform fights are part

of a pedagogical process that can help reveal the actual composition of the power structure and clarify the power that working-class people have to challenge that structure. By combining these reform fights with agitation around more transformative visions for social change and radical political education programs, these organizations are working to ensure that their reform fights do not fall into reformism.

(Goldberg, 2008)

Figuring out what this looks like in education is part of moving from defending public education to organizing to transform it. Some philosophical principles are beginning to coalesce from the emergent education movement. These four, drawn from education and community activists, might be a starting point for further discussion:

1. *Participatory democracy*: Schools should be spaces where children, youth, educators, parents, and community members participate in democratic discussion and decisions about what goes on there and about school improvement and transformation.
2. *Education for full development*: All children should have an intellectually and socially rich, culturally relevant, hopeful, and joyful education that develops their full potential through academic subjects, arts, athletics, and connections with their community and the environment.
3. *Equitably funded free public education*: All children and adults should have equal access to richly funded and resourced free public education, pre-K through higher education, with the first step being to redress the education debt owed African Americans, Native people, Latino/as and others historically denied equitable education.
4. *Education as a tool for liberation*: Public education should be antiracist, antisexist, antiheterosexist, and fully inclusive of all people. It should teach oppressed people's true histories and draw on their communities' cultures, languages, experiences, and social contributions and support their self-determination. Education should develop critical consciousness that is global in scope and prepare students to participate in transforming injustice and defending the environment.

These principles are in line with the pages of Rethinking Schools, the many social justice classrooms and freedom schools around the United States, and the dialogues of education activists. For example, the Grassroots Education Movement (GEM), a community–teacher coalition in Chicago, developed the following platform:

GEM supports the ideals of equitable, quality public education available to all residents of the City of Chicago. GEM is committed to democratic principles in the governance, pedagogy, and culture of our public schools. The GEM believes that every child has a constitutional civil and human right to a high quality, equitably funded, public education based on participatory democratic principles, community empowerment, a challenging comprehensive and enriched curriculum, respect for cultural diversity, and Universal Human Rights. The GEM believes that education should prepare students to deeply understand the roots of inequality and be prepared to act to change the world.

(July 11, 2009; available from author)

Global Connections

Globally interconnected neoliberal institutions and policies are dialectically related to the possibility and necessity for global solidarity and reciprocal learning and the creation of global institutions "from below." Strengthening transnational education alliances such as the Tri-National Coalition in Defense of Public Education formed in 1993 by educator/activists from Mexico, Canada, and the United States may be particularly critical as the crisis legitimates further privatization. The Tri-National promotes education based on democratic principles, social justice, and human rights and fosters collaboration in action, research, and information sharing (Kuehn, 2008). Global connections are an opportunity to more deeply understand the capitalist roots of the crisis and to share perspectives on alternatives. They hold the potential to deparochialize social paradigms and epistemologies, in particular for North Americans, by engaging perspectives from the Global South (Lingard, 2007).

Reimagining Public Education by Building It Now

Part of reimagining society is creating alternative spaces where we can experiment with new visions, new ways of living together, and what Dr. King (Washington, 1986) called "a revolution in values"—a new social imaginary. These spaces provide an alternative form of agency to the individualized consumer agency offered by the market, one that previews the kind of society we wish to have. There are many such projects in the United States: worker run factories, producer cooperatives, urban community gardens, cooperatively owned housing. In education, theories and practices of liberatory education have long provided an alternative education model, but primarily at the margins, except in periods of broad social movements, such as the Freedom Schools of the Civil Rights Movement of the 1960s. Today critical, culturally relevant educational spaces are thriving in localized classrooms, schools, and education projects[5] and through organizations such as Brotherhood/Sister Sol in New York and Freedom Schools, social justice oriented public schools, and teacher–educator activist organizations in cities across the United States.

These projects concretely reconceptualize public education for a new society. They are spaces where adults and children together can develop counterdiscourses and formulate oppositional interpretations of their needs, identities, and interests (Fraser, 1990); for example, African-centered, Raza, feminist, LGBTQ education spaces. We need to study, theorize, and propagate our knowledge about these alternatives to invigorate the conversation about the education and society we wish to have.

Critical pedagogy plays an important role in helping children and youth develop tools of critical consciousness and social practice to enable them to participate fully in movements for social transformation (Freire, 1970/1998a). Critical classrooms are spaces where students learn to interrogate their social realities and examine the root causes of the many crises facing their communities, explore solutions, build solidarities, and develop global perspectives. They are humanizing spaces that enable children to work democratically and see themselves as subjects of history. That educators create these spaces in public schools, often under difficult limitations, indicates the potential for critical education to engender hope and resistance despite the constraints of oppressive education policies and the oppressive conditions faced by low-income urban communities of color (e.g., Andrade & Morrell, 2008; Camangian, 2008; Camangian & Yang, 2006; Christensen, 2000, 2009; Gutstein, 2006a, b).

The seeds of alternative social visions are also evident in campaigns of teachers, youth, displaced families, and parents who insist on full participation in the educational decisions which affect them, recognition of their knowledge, and a just distribution of resources. In Chicago, the Committee for Safe Passage, a group of African American parents in the Altgeld Gardens housing project, fought to take back a neighborhood public high school in their community. They wanted more than access to a public school; they wanted a school to "develop young leaders who can work for the environmental rights of community residents, as well as for the needs of society as a whole" (Committee for Safe Passage Newsletter, March 2010, available from author). Their vision was a democratic school that would help sustain and develop a community of youth and adults—the Hazel Johnson School for Environmental justice, named for a 48-year resident of the Gardens who founded and led the community's campaign for environmental justice. A national exemplar of environmental racism, Altgeld Gardens is located in the center of a "toxic doughnut," surrounded by dozens of toxic sites. The community is afflicted with innumerable health issues and has high unemployment. The campaign for the Hazel Johnson School brought together the community's 30-year struggle for environmental justice, participatory democracy, and their desire for their children to have a meaningful, humane, liberatory education that also prepares them for productive work. It is a vision that links education with housing, economic development, a healthy environment, and resistance to racism and imagines a democratic and flourishing community.

The right to the city is both concrete and a metaphor for the transformation of oppressive and exploitative economic, political, and cultural arrangements and a new social imaginary that gives full play to the full development of human beings in relationships of mutuality, respect, solidarity, collective well-being, and joy. We are at a decisive moment when our survival may depend on developing that vision together and working to make it real. The design of the future can't be spelled out in advance except in broad brushstrokes. It is only in the process of getting there that we become clearer, more precise about the society we wish to have, and more fit to live in it.

One thing is clear. What we have now is not working. We need a fundamental rejection of neoliberal policies and of the capitalist system and its grounding in racial oppression in the United States and a new social vision seeded, in part, by an education movement in the making. In *Freedom Dreams,* Robin D.G. Kelley (2003), reminds us that "Progressive social movements do not simply produce statistics and narratives of oppression. The best ones do what great poetry always does: transport us to another place, compel us to imagine a new society" (p. 9).

NOTES

Chapter 1

1   Actual unemployment hovered around 4% and higher among people of color and some sectors of the White working class.
2   Most big labor leaders sided with elements of the state in the anticommunist witch hunts of the 1950s which drove out, and in some instances jailed, communist and militant union leaders as well as progressive journalists, film makers, teachers, and others.
3   Leaders of organized labor collaborated with a racialized and gendered dual-labor market by failing to organize low-wage industries in which people of color, immigrants, and women were concentrated, such as agriculture, domestic labor, and clerical work. It took the struggles of the Civil Rights and women's movements and independent organizing by farm workers and women outside the American Federation of Labor to win gains for some of these workers.
4   See *A Grin Without a Cat*, Chris Marker's 1978 film-essay on the political wars of the 60s and 70s.
5   The first experiment was the U.S. engineered military coup against the democratically elected socialist government of Salvadore Allende in Chile in 1973, the forced privatization of the economy and the public sector, and brutal repression of social movements.
6   Some analysts attribute this defeat in Western Europe to the conciliatory ideology of social democracy and the privileged position of a sector of labor leaders (see Marker, 1978). In the United States, the benefits accrued from the capital–labor social compact and the alliance of much of the labor movement with imperialist policies and structural racism were critical obstacles to organized opposition (Ranney & Wright, 2004).
7   Examples are minimum sentencing laws, California's "three-strikes" life sentences, and detention of undocumented immigrants.

Chapter 2

1   This developed over the next two decades through contention between old forms of state regulation and new forms of deregulation.
2   Cities in Africa and Latin America were hardest hit by structural adjustment and became

trapped in a cycle of falling wages, unemployment, loss of revenues, and impoverishment (Davis, 2006), while deregulation of international commodity markets allowed powerful economies to flood weaker ones with agricultural and manufactured products, driving out local manufacturing and farming (Bello, 2002).

3 For example, possible imposition of state regulation of financial markets in the present financial crisis.

4 See Weber (2002) for a full discussion.

5 Weber (2002, p. 526) notes that even though buildings in the African American South Side were not as old as in other areas of the city, the city more frequently categorized them as unfit or substandard.

6 For extensive coverage of Chicago TIFs see *The Reader TIF Archive*. Retrieved from http://www.chicagoreader.com/tifarchive/.

7 According to Rachel Weber (2009), Chicago's complex risk management strategy involves calculation and allocation of risks among various financial instruments and across a range of interdependent practices. Its goal is to "calculate and allocate risks in such a way that capital flows, development occurs, and the local state's legitimacy to facilitate such activities is not challenged ."

8 Weber's (2003) analysis of the impact of TIF on school finance in Illinois reveals that TIF depletes local property tax revenues for schools, making local school districts more reliant on state funding and shifting responsibility for funding schools most in need to the state level (in this case Illinois).

9 According to the conservative Reason Foundation, this set off a national discussion about privatizing U.S. toll roads (Samuel, 2005).

10 These included People's Coalition for Educational Reform, United Neighborhood Organization (UNO), Hispanic Dropout Taskforce, Aspira, State Senator Miguel del Valle, and other Latino/a grassroots groups.

11 Teachers at one high school refused to give a new standardized test pushing the district to withdraw it, and students at another high school boycotted the test. Communities and teachers also organized protests.

12 See, for example, Chicago Public Schools (2004c).

Chapter 3

1 Juan Gonzalez, cohost of *Democracy Now* (www.democracynow.org), used this term to describe the corporate takeover of public institutions and gentrification of New Orleans following Hurricane Katrina.

2 Illinois state law limits the number of charter schools that can be created in Chicago. Contract schools are a way to get around this; they function similarly to charter schools but, by contracting directly with CPS, avoid the state limitations. Some charter school operators spin off multiple schools to bypass state limits.

3 The irrationality of these categorizations was exemplified when Illinois State Achievement Test (ISAT) results reported in the Spring of 2004 converted some Chicago schools from "models" that students were scrambling to get into, to "failing schools" that students could transfer out of—all by a tenth of a percentage point on the school's test scores (Cholo & Little, 2003).

4 Four Ren2010 small high schools publicly disavowed this affiliation. They were won as neighborhood public schools through a community hunger strike, not created through Ren2010.

5 Eight of 10 students displaced by school closings transferred to schools that ranked in the bottom half of the system on standardized tests (Gwynne & de la Torre, 2009).

6 The RSF is headed by the Chairs of McDonald's Corporation and Northern Trust Bank, a partner in a leading corporate law firm, the CEO of Chicago Community Trust (a major

local corporate/banking foundation), the retired Chair of the Tribune Corporation, and top CPS officials.

7 Under NCLB, schools that do not make Annual Yearly Progress (AYP) for 5 years are subject to state takeover.

8 In 2008, the Academy for Urban School Leadership, advertised on its Web site all teacher positions at Morton and Howe Elementary Schools, with a February 20 application deadline. This was before the Board met on February 27 and finalized the turnover of these schools to AUSL (document available from author).

9 LSCs have the power to hire principals and approve the school's discretionary budget and school improvement plan.

10 Contract and performance schools designated "alternative" or "small schools" (categories that provide flexibility in relation to some CPS mandates), are not governed by LSCs for the first 2 years of operation. After 2 years, the school may *request* of the Board to have an LSC. If it does not, the policy stipulates only that "the *majority* of the members of any ['alternative' or 'small' school] governing body shall reside in the *district* [emphasis added]" (Chicago Public Schools, 2004a, Section 302.7, p. 3). Charter schools, after one year in operation, are to be run by an unelected Board of Directors.

11 The progress and challenges of LSCs since the 1988 Reform have been chronicled in *The Catalyst*, a local publication that has followed school reform in Chicago since the 1988 reform.

12 These are two of the indicators developed by the Nathalie P. Vorhees Center for Neighborhood and Community Improvement. Interpreting Neighborhood Change in Chicago. Retrieved from http://www.uic.edu/cuppa/voorheesctr/Gentrification%20Index%20Site/Main%20Neighborhood%20Change%20Revised.htm,

13 Legends South—Formerly Robert Taylor will consist of "794 public housing, 666 affordable and 434 market-rate rental units in addition to 494 affordable homeownership units" (Michaels). The original Robert Taylor Homes consisted of 2 miles of high-rise buildings—28 in all, containing 4,321 public housing units (Michaels). Thus Legends South will provide public housing for just 18.3% of the former residents. Based on an estimate of 2,700 residents (Venkatesh, 2004), over 2,200 will not have housing in Legends. "Affordable" is for families earning between 80% and 120% of Chicago's median annual income, or from $36,000 to $54,000.

14 Over 3 years of operation, the first two "showcase" turnarounds, operated by the Academy of Urban School Leadership, posted test scores comparable to those of four public schools proposed for turnaround in 2009, and in some instances, lower scores. One turnaround's student mobility is also up while its attendance has trended down (Fleming, et al, 2009).

15 Before 2006, an average of 10 to 15 public school students were fatally shot each year. That soared to 24 in the 2006–2007 school year, 23 deaths and 211 shootings in 2007–2008, and 34 deaths and 290 shootings in 2008–2009 (Hawkins, 2009). In the first 9 months of 2009, there were 33 murders of Black and Latino youth in Chicago (Hawkins, 2009).

Chapter 4

1 This is reflected in Chicago forums and symposia that bring together housing and school officials with corporate foundations and local political actors; for example, Building Successful Mixed Income Communities: Education and Quality Schools, Invitational forum co-sponsored by the MacArthur Foundation, and Metropolitan Planning Council in coordination with the Chicago Housing Authority, November 17, 2005.

2 HOPE VI was a product of the National Commission on Severely Distressed Public Housing. See: The Final Report of the National Commission on Severely Distressed Public Housing (1992). U.S. Department of Housing and Urban Development. http://www.hud.gov/offices/pih/programs/ph/hope6/about/#4

3 Kahlenberg cites a mix of methodologically rigorous studies and opinions and position papers from partisan think tanks. He also misconstrues equivocal findings as definitive evidence for his arguments; for example, Rusk (1998) who found moving to a middle class school was effective for some students in a Texas study, but Kahlenberg highlights this study summarizing the results as being universally beneficial (p. 28). His evidence also conflates race and class (e.g., Rumberger & Willms, 1992).

4 CPS's enrollment:capacity ratios did not account for how school space was actually being used, and even more severely underenrolled schools were not affected (Greenlee et al., 2008).

5 Nonexempt heads of household must work a minimum of 30 hours per week and all other nonexempt family members between ages of 18 and 61 must also work 30 hours per week or be in qualified alternative activities (e.g., enrollment in an education program, training, verified job search, etc.). In contrast, in the Henry Horner project PFT in Chicago, residents succeeded in winning real participation in the project's redevelopment and set a more flexible and resident-directed set of criteria. An estimated 90% of residents were able to remain in the development (Wilen & Nayak, 2006).

6 See for example, films such as *Dangerous Minds* (J. M. Smith, 1995), *Lean on Me* (Avildsen, 1998), *Freedom Writers* (LaGravenese, 2007).

7 These include: equalizing financial resources ("opportunity to learn" standards), changes in curriculum and testing (ending tracking to differentiate curriculum and reforming assessments and their use to focus on improving teaching rather than sorting students), investing in good teaching for all students (strengthening the knowledge base for teaching and ensuring that students have equal access to competent, caring, and supported teachers).

Chapter 5

1 These include closing schools based on testing, standards, and accountability; turnaround partners and management; and labor "flexibility," (Turnaround Challenge, 2007).

Chapter 6

1 In Illinois, charter school operators are required to be nonprofits but they can subcontract with for-profit companies.

2 A school board member in a small Massachusetts school district explained that charter schools, unlike public schools, are allowed to keep all excess funds. Management organizations get a 6% management fee and 6% licensing fee off the top and keep 100% of excess funds at the end of each academic year. As schools lose public funds that follow students to charter schools, public schools are disinvested disproportionately to their decline in enrollment. For example, loss of some students does not necessarily change the number of teachers or amount of transportation a school needs (Field notes, Saving Our Schools conference, University of Massachusetts, Amherst, March 27, 2010).

3 In schools I observed, teachers were encouraged to perform educational triage, focusing on those students just at the point of meeting state test score targets (Lipman, 2004). This practice is widely acknowledged as focusing on the "bubble kids."

4 Greater charter school accountability is a stipulation for states to win federal Race to the Top funds in 2010.

5 To apply students must have test scores in the top stanines, strong attendance records and grades.

6 Autonomous Management Performance schools (AMP) are an elite tier of CPS schools that are awarded limited autonomy from district regulations because of their high test scores.

7 Individual Education Plan for students designated as having special needs.

Chapter 7

1 Lesbian, gay, bisexual, transgender, queer.

2 For example, conferences of Teachers 4 Social Justice Bay Area; Association of Raza Educators California; Teachers for Social Justice Chicago; New York Collective of Radical Educators; Educators Network for Social Justice Milwaukee; Literacy for Social Justice St. Louis; Free Minds, Free People Conference sponsored by the Education for Liberation network; and Creating Balance in an Unjust World Conference on Math Education and Social Justice.

3 The Teacher Activist Groups (TAG) includes New York Collective of Radical Educators, Association of Raza Educators (California), Teachers4Justice (San Francisco), Teachers for Social Justice (Chicago), Educators Network for Social Justice (Milwaukee), Literacy for Social Justice (St. Louis), Teacher Activst Group (Philadelphia), and Education for Liberation Network.

4 The Framework proposes a market discourse of system of incentives for equitable resource allocations and does not challenge testing as a form of assessment.

5 See, for example, reports in *Rethinking Schools Journal* and book publications (www.RethinkingSchools.org), the curriculum archives of the Education for Liberation Network (www.edliberation.org), and the many curriculum displays and workshops at local conferences of teacher activists.

REFERENCES

Abdi, A. A., Puplampu, K. P., & Sefa Dei, G. J. (Eds.). (2006). *African education and globalization.* Lanham, MD: Rowman & Littlefield.

Abraham, M. (Producer), & Cuarón, A. (Director/Writer). (2006). *Children of men* [Motion picture]. United States: Universal Studios.

Abu-Lughod, J. (2005). Commentary: What is special about Chicago? *City and Society, 17*(2), 289–303.

Adler, L. (2009, July 16). Foreclosures at record high in first half 2009 despite aid. *Reuters News Service.* Retrieved from http://www.reuters.com/article/domesticNews/idUSTRE56F0XK 20090716?sp=true

Affordable housing conditions and outlook in Chicago: An early warning for intervention. (2006, March). Nathalie P. Vorhees Center for Neighborhood and Community Improvement, College of Urban Policy and Planning, University of Illinois-Chicago. Retrieved from http://www.uic.edu/cuppa/voorheesctr/publications.html

Alexander, M. (2007). Reinventing a broken wheel? The fight to reclaim public education in New Orleans. *Social Policy, 37,* 18–23.

Allen, R. L. (1969). *Black awakening in capitalist America.* Garden City, NY: Doubleday.

Almaca, J. (2005, September 4). A new catalog: Investments, redevelopment bring buyers to North Lawndale. *Chicago Tribune,* Sect. 1, p. 1.

Amin, S. (1997). *Capitalism in the age of globalization.* London: Zed.

Amin, S. (2008). *The world we wish to see.* New York: Monthly Review Press.

Anderson, G. L. (2010). *Advocacy leadership: toward a post-reform agenda in education.* New York: Routledge.

Anderson, J. D. (1988). *The education of blacks in the South, 1860–1935.* Chapel Hill: University of North Carolina Press.

Anderson, L. M., St. Charles, J., Fullilove, M., Scrimshaw, S. C., Fielding, J. E., & Normand, J. (2003). Providing affordable family housing and reducing residential segregation by income: A systematic review. *American Journal of Preventive Medicine, 24*(3), 47–67

Andrade, J. D., & E. Morrell. (2008). *The art of critical pedagogy: Possibilities of moving from theory to practice in urban schools.* New York: Lang.

André-Bechely, L. (2005). *Could it be otherwise? Parents and the inequities of public school choice.* New York: Routledge.

Anyon, J. (1980). Social class and the hidden curriculum of work. *Journal of Education, 162*(1), 67–92.

Anyon, J. (2005). *Radical possibilities*. New York: Routledge.

Apple, M. W. (1996). *Cultural politics and education*. New York: Teachers College Press.

Apple, M. W. (2003). *The state and the politics of education*. New York: Routledge.

Apple, M. W. (2004). *Ideology and curriculum* (3rd ed.). New York: Routledge..

Apple, M. W. (2006). *Educating the "right" way: Markets, standards, God, and inequality*. New York: Routledge Falmer.

Apple, M. W., Kenway, J., & Singh, M. (Eds.). (2005). *Globalizing education: Policies, pedagogies, and politics*. New York: Lang.

Applied Research Center (ARC). (2007). *Facing race: Legislative report card on racial equity*. Chicago, IL: Author.

Are we home yet? Creating real choice for housing choice voucher families in Chicago. Nathalie P. Vorhees Center for Neighborhood and Community Improvement, University of Illinois-Chicago. Retrieved from http://www.uic.edu/cuppa/voorheesctr/publications.html

Assembly of Social Movements. (2009). *Declaration*. World Social Forum. Retrieved from http://www.globalresearch.ca/index.php?context=va&aid=12160

Avildsen, J. G. (Director). (1998). *Lean on me*. United States: Warner Brothers Pictures.

Ball, S. J. (1990). *Politics and policy making in education*. London: Routledge.

Ball, S. J. (1994). *Education reform: A critical and post-structural approach*. Buckingham, England: Open University Press.

Ball, S. J. (2001). Global policies and vernacular politics in education. *Currículo sem Fronteiras, 1*(2), xxvii–xliii. Retrieved from www.curriculosemfronteiras.org

Ball, S. J. (2003). *Class strategies and the education market: The middle classes and social advantage*. London: RoutledgeFalmer.

Ball, S. J. (2004). Performativities and abrications in the education economy: Towards the performative society. In S. J. Ball (Ed.), *The RoutledgeFalmer reader in sociology of education* (pp. 143–155). London: RoutledgeFalmer.

Ball, S. J., Bowe, R., & Gewirtz, S. (1995). Circuits of schooling: A sociological exploration of parental choice of school in social class contexts. *The Sociological Review, 43*(1) 52 –78.

Barlow, A. L. (2003). *Between fear and hope: Globalization and race in the United States*. Lanham, MD: Rowman & Littlefield.

Barrett, M. S. (2002, March 25). *Marshaling public will to transform the CHA*. Metropolitan Planning Council. Retrieved from http://www.metroplanning.org/newsroom/resourceCenter/opinions.asp?objectID=970&authorID=1&tools=yes

Barett/Doyle Deposition, Wisconsin State Legislature. (2009, Sept. 10). Available from author.

Bell, D. (2004). *Silent covenants: Brown v. Board of Education and the unfulfilled hopes for racial reform*. Oxford, England: Oxford University Press.

Bello, W. (2002). *Deglobalization: Ideas for a new world economy*. New York: Zed.

Bello, W. (2008, October 18). Afterthoughts: A primer on the Wall Street meltdown (update). Focus on the Global South. Retrieved from http://focusweb.org/afterthoughts-a-primer-on-the-wall-street-meltdown.html?Itemid=92

Bello, W. (2009, March 20–21). *Capitalism's crisis and our response*. Speech delivered at the Conference on the Global Crisis sponsored by Die Linke Party and Rosa Luxemburg Foundation, Berlin. Retrieved from http://waldenbello.org

Bennett, L. (1998). Do we really want to live in a communitarian city? *Journal of Urban Affairs, 20*(2), 99–116.

Bennett, L. (2006). Downtown restructuring and public housing in contemporary Chicago. In L. Bennett, J. L. Smith, & P. A. Wright (Eds.), *Where are poor people to live? Transforming public housing communities* (pp. 282–300). Armonk, NY: M. E. Sharpe.

Bennett, L., Hudspeth, N., & Wright, P. A. (2006). A critical analysis of the ABLA redevelopment plan. In L. Bennett, J. L. Smith, & P. A. Wright (Eds.), *Where are poor people to live? Transforming public housing communities* (pp.185–215). Armonk, NY: M. E. Sharpe.

Bennett, L., & Reed, A., Jr. (1999). The new face of urban renewal: The Near North Redevelopment Initiative and the Cabrini-Green neighborhood. In A. Reed, Jr. (Ed.), *Without justice for all* (pp. 175–211) Boulder, CO: Westview Press.

Bennett, L., Smith, J. A., & Wright, P. A. (Eds.). (2006). *Where are poor people to live? Transforming public housing communities.* Armonk, NY: M. E. Sharpe.

Bennett, M. (2006). The rebirth of Bronzeville: Contested space and contrasting visions. In J. P.. Koval, L. Bennett, M. I. J. Bennett, F. Demissie, R. Garner, & K. Kiljoong (Eds.), *The new Chicago: A social and cultural analysis* (pp. 213–220). Philadelphia, PA: Temple University Press.

Berliner, D. C., & Biddle, B. J. (1997). *The manufactured crisis: Myths, fraud, and the attack on America's public schools.* White Plains, NY: Longman.

Betancur, J. (2005). *Gentrification before gentrification? The plight of Pilsen in Chicago* (White paper). Retrieved from Nathalie P. Voorhees Center for Neighborhood and Community Improvement, University of Illinois-Chicago. http://www.uic.edu/cuppa/voorheesctr/Publications/Gentrification%20before%20Gentrification.pdf

Betancur, J. J., & Gills, D. C. (2000). The restructuring of urban relations. In J. J. Betancur & D. C. Gills (Eds.), *The collaborative city: Opportunities and struggles for Blacks and Latinos in U.S. cities* (pp. 17–40). New York: Garland.

Bezalel, R., & Ferraro, A. (Producers/Directors). (n.d.). *Voices of Cabrini: Remaking Chicago's public housing* [Video]. Retrieved from www.voicesofcabrini.com/index.html

Biddle, B. J., & Berliner, D. C. (2002). Unequal school funding in the United States. *Educational Leadership, 59*(8), 48–59.

Bluestein, B. (2005). A new business plan for Chicago. Executive Agenda, First Quarter, 2005. A.T. Kearney. Retrieved April 12, 2005, from www.atkearney.com/main.taf?p=5,1,1,110,6

Board closes 8 child–parent centers, converts some to Head Start. (2004, September). *Catalyst: Voices of Chicago School Reform, 16*(1), 25. (Chicago: Community Renewal Society).

Body-Gendrot, S. (1993). Migration and the racialization of the postmodern city in France. In M. Cross & M. Keith (Eds.), *Racism, the city and the state* (pp. 77–92). London: Routledge.

Bond, P. (2008). Reformist reforms, non-reformist reforms and global justice: Activist, NGO and intellectual challenges in the World Social Forum. *Societies Without Borders, 3*, 4–19.

Bonilla-Silva, E. (2003). *Racism without racists.* Lanham, MD: Rowman & Littlefield.

Boyd, M. (2000). Reconstructing Bronzeville: Racial nostalgia and neighborhood development. *Journal of Urban Affairs, 22*(2), 107–122.

Boyd, M. (2005). The downside of racial uplift: The meaning of gentrification in an African American neighborhood. *City & Society, 17*(2), 265–288.

Brantlinger, E. (2003). *Dividing classes: How the middle class negotiates and rationalizes school advantage.* New York: RoutledgeFalmer.

Brenner, N., & Theodore, N. (2002). Cities and the geographies of "actually existing neoliberalism." *Antipode, 34*(3), 349–379.

Brophy, P. C., & Smith, R. N. (1997). Mixed income housing: Factors for success. *Cityscape, 3*(2), 3–31

Brown, E. R. (2007). The quiet disaster of No Child Left Behind. In K. J. Saltman (Ed.), *Schooling and the politics of disaster* (pp. 123–140). New York: Routledge.

Brown, J., Gutstein, E., & Lipman, P. (2009). The Chicago success story: Myth or reality? *Rethinking Schools, 23*(3), 10–14.

Brown, L., & Gutstein, E. (2009, February). *The charter difference: A comparison of Chicago charter and neighborhood high schools.* Retrieved from http://www.uic.edu/educ/ceje/

Brown, M. K., Carnoy, M., Currie, E., Duster, T. Oppenheimer, D. B., Shultz, M. M., et al. (2003). *White-washing race; the myth of a color-blind society.* Berkeley: University of California Press.

Brown, P., & Lauder, H. (2001) *Capitalism and social progress: The future of society in a global economy.* Basingstoke, England: Palgrave.

Bryk, A. S., Sebring, P. B., Kerbow, D., Rollow, S., & Easton, J. Q. (1998). *Charting Chicago school reform: Democratic localism as a lever for change.* Boulder, CO: Westview Press.

Buras, K. L. (2007). Benign neglect? Drowning yellow buses, racism, and disinvestment in the city that Bush forgot. In K. J. Saltman (Ed.), *Schooling and the politics of disaster* (pp. 1103–1122). New York: Routledge.

Buras, K. L., Randels, J., Salaam, K. Y., & Students at the center. (Eds.). (2010). *Pedagogy, policy, and the privatized city: Stories of dispossession and defiance.* New York: Teachers College Press.

Burch, P. (2009). *Hidden markets: The new education privatization.* New York: Routledge.

Butler, T., with Robson, G. (2003). *London calling: The middle classes and the re-making of inner London.* Oxford, England: Berg.

Call for Participation: The City from Below Conference Baltimore, MD. (2009, March 27–29). Program note.

Camangian, P. (2008). Untempered tongues: Teaching performance poetry for social justice. *English Teaching: Practice and Critique, 7*(2), 35–55.

Camangian, P., & Yang, K. W. (2006, March 30). *Transformative teaching and youth resistance.* Talk given at DePaul University, Chicago, IL.

Cammarota, J., & Fine, M. (2008). *Revolutionizing education: Youth participatory action research in motion.* New York: Routledge.

Catalyst. (1990, February). Voices of Chicago school reform, I(1).

Catalyst Chicago. (2007, February) Special report: School autonomy all over the map. Retrieved from http://www.catalyst-chicago.org/news/index.php?item=2141&cat=23

Center for Research on Education Outcomes, Stanford University (CREDO). (2009). *Multiple choice: Charter school performance in 16 states.* Stanford, CA: Author. Retrieved from http://credo.stanford.edu

Chicago Housing Authority (CHA). (2000). CHA plan for transformation. Retrieved from www.thecha.org

Chicago Public Schools. (CPS). (2004a, September). *CPS policy manual. Establish renaissance schools.* Retrieved from http://policy.cps.k12.il.us/documents/302.7.pdf

Chicago Public Schools. (CPS). (2004b, June 8). Daley announces Renaissance 2010. Press release. Retrieved from www.cps.k12.il.us/AboutCPS/PressReleases/June_2004/Renaissance2010.html

Chicago Public Schools. (CPS). (2004c, September 13). Draft policy released for opening new schools under Renaissance 2010. Press release. Retrieved from www.cps.k12.il.us/AboutCPS/PressReleases/September_2004/draft_policy.htm

Chicago Public Schools. (CPS). (2004d, September 22). Chicago Board of Education approves policy for opening new schools under Renaissance 2010. Press release. Retrieved from www.cps.k12.il.usAboutCPS/PressReleases/September_2004/2010_policy_approval.htm

Chicago Public Schools. (CPS). (2007). Policy Manual: Establish Renaissance Schools, Section: 302.7. Board Report: 07-0627-PO4 Date Adopted: June 27, 2007. http://www.ren2010.cps.k12.il.us/potential.shtml

Cholo, A. B. (2005, February 23). Businesses help new schools. *Chicago Tribune.* Retrieved from www.chicagotribune.com

Cholo, A. B., & Little, D. (2003, August 10). Some schools left behind by fine print. *Chicago Tribune,* Sect. 4, pp. 1, 6.

Christensen, L. (2000). *Reading, writing, and rising up: Teaching about social justice and the power of the written word.* Milwaukee, WI: Rethinking Schools.

Christensen, L. (2009). *Teaching for joy and justice: Re-imagining the language arts classroom.* Milwaukee, WI: Rethinking Schools.

Civic Committee of the Commercial Club of Chicago. (2009, June). *Still left behind: Student learning in Chicago public schools.* Chicago: Author.

Civil rights framework for providing all students an opportunity to learn through reauthorization of the Elementary and Secondary Education Act. (2010, July 26). Retrieved from http://

www.otlcampaign.org/resources/civil-rights-framework-providing-all-students-opportunity-learn-through-reauthorization-el

City of Chicago Announces Parking Meter Changes as Part of Long-term Agreement. (2009, February). News Release, February 11, 2009. Department of Revenue, City of Chicago.

Clarke, J., & Newman, J. (1997). *The managerial state*. London: Sage.

Clavel, P., & Kleniewski, N. (1990). Space for progressive local policy: Examples from the United States and the United Kingdom. In J. R. Logan & T. Swanstrom (Eds.), *Beyond the city limits: Urban policy and economic restructuring in comparative perspective* (pp. 199–236). Philadelphia, PA: Temple University Press.

Cohen, R. (2007). *Strategic grantmaking: Foundations and the school privatization movement.* Washington, DC: National Committee for Responsive Philanthropy.

Coleman, J. S., Campbell, E., Hobson, C., McPartland, J., Mood, F., Weinfield, F., et al. (1966). *Equality of educational opportunity.* Washington, DC: U.S. Government Printing Office.

Commercial Club of Chicago. (1984). *Make no little plans: Jobs for metropolitan Chicago.* Chicago, IL: Author.

Commercial Club of Chicago, Civic Committee, Education Committee. (2003). *Left behind.* Chicago, IL: Author.

Commercial Club of Chicago, Civic Committee. (2004, November 12). Academic achievement of Chicago public schools. Retrieved from www.commercialclubchicago.org/civiccommittee/initiatives/education/student_achievement.html

Communities for Excellent Public Schools (CEPS). (2010, July 28). *Our communities left behind: An analysis of the administration's school turnaround policies.* Retrieved from http://www.ceps-ourschools.org/

Compton, M., & Weiner, L. (Eds.). (2008). *The global assault on teaching, teachers, and their unions.* New York: Palgrave.

Cucciara, M. (2008). Re-branding urban schools: Urban revitalization, social status, and marketing public schools to the upper middle class. *Journal of Education Policy, 23*(2), 165–180.

Dale, R. (1989–1990). The Thatcherite project in education: The case of the City Technology Colleges. *Critical Social Policy, 9*, 4–19.

Dale, R. (2000). Globalization and education: Demonstrating a "common world educational culture" or locating a "globally structured educational agenda." *Educational Theory, 50* (4), 427–448.

Dale, R., & Robertson, S. (2004). Interview with Boaventura de Sousa Santos. *Globalization, Societies and Education, 2*(2), 147–160.

Daley seeks broad strategy to create "High Schools of Tomorrow." (2005, May 19). Gates Foundation. Press release. Retrieved from http://www.gatesfoundation.org/press-releases/Pages/improving-chicago-schools-050519.aspx

Danns, D. (2002). Black student empowerment in Chicago: School reform efforts in 1968. *Urban Education, 37*(5), 631–655.

Darcy, M., & Smith, J. L. (2008, September). *Social mix and social inclusion: Rhetoric and reality in Sydney and Chicago.* Paper presented at a meeting of the International Sociology Association Forum of Sociology, Barcelona, Spain.

Darling-Hammond, L. (2004). What happens to a dream deferred? The continuing quest for equal educational opportunity. In J. A. Banks (Ed.), *Handbook of research on multicultural education* (2nd ed, pp. 607–630). San Francisco, CA: Jossey-Bass.

Davis, M. (2006). *Planet of slums.* London: Verso.

Dell'Angela, T. (2004, July 12). South Side faces school shake-up: Residents skeptical of city's plan. *Chicago Tribune*, Sect. 1, pp. 1, 16.

Dell'Angela, T., & Washburn, G. (2004, June 26). Daley set to remake troubled schools. *Chicago Tribune*, Sect. 1, pp. 1, 22.

Demarrais, K. (2006). "The naves and the have mores": Fueling a conservative ideological war on public education (or tracking the money). *Educational Studies, 39*(3), 201–240.

Demissie, F. (2006). Globalization and the remaking of Chicago. In J. P. Koval, L. Bennett, M. I.

J. Bennett, F. Demissie, R. Garner, & K. Kiljoong (Eds.), *The new Chicago: A social and cultural analysis* (pp.19–31). Philadelphia, PA: Temple University Press.

Dew-Becker, I., & Gordon, R. J. (September, 2005). *Where did the productivity growth go? Inflation dynamics and the distribution of income.* Paper presented at the 81st meeting of the Brookings Panel on Economic Activity, Washington, DC.

Dillon, S. (2004, July). Chicago has a nonunion plan for poor schools. *The New York Times.* Retrieved from http://www.nytimes.com/2004/07/28/education/28chicago.html

Dingerson, L. (2008, August 26). New Orleans schools 3 years later. Center for Community Change. Retrieved fromhttp://www.communitychange.org/our-projects

Duffrin, E. (2006). Promise of new schools not met Neediest students may be left out as middle class edges in. *Catalyst: Chicago, XVII*(6), 11.

Duggan, L. (2003). *The twilight of inequality? Neoliberalism, cultural politics and the attack on democracy.* Boston: Beacon Press.

Duncan, A. (2009a, March 31). Mayors should run schools. NBC Chicago. Retrieved from http://www.nbcchicago.com/news/local/arne-duncan-mayors-schools-033109.html

Duncan, A. (2009b, May 18). Duncan vows funding to make DPS change happen. Interview. Retrieved from *Detroit News* http://www.detnews.com/article/20090518/SCHOOLS/905180349

Duncan, A. (2009c, June 22). Turning around the bottom five percent. Press release. U.S. Department of Education. Retrieved from http://www2.ed.gov/news/speeches/2009/06/06222009.html

Duncan speaks at Dr. King's church on 81st birthday of the legendary civil rights leader. (2010, January 15). Press release. U.S. Department of Education. Retrieved from http://www2.ed.gov/news/pressreleases/2010/01/01152010.html

Emihovich, C. (2005). Fire and ice: Activist ethnography in the culture of power. *Anthropology & Education Quarterly, 36*(4), 305–314.

Fainstein, S. S., & D. R. Judd.(Eds.). *Cities and visitors: Regulating people, markets, and city space.* Oxford, England: Blackwell.

Feagin, J. R. (1998). *The new urban paradigm: Critical perspectives on the city.* Lanham, MD: Rowman & Littlefield.

Ferguson, A.A. (2001). *Bad boys: Public schools in the making of black masculinity.* Ann Arbor: University of Michigan Press.

Field, J. (2005, May 5). Renaissance 2010 off-track? Chicago Public Radio, Eight Forty-Eight.

Finkel, E. (2006). Suder's old students shut out. *Chicago Catalyst, XVII*(6), 12-13.

Fleming, J., Greenlee, A., Gutstein, E., Lipman, P., & Smith, J. (2009, February). *Examining CPS' plan to close, consolidate, turn-around 22 schools. Data and Democracy Project: Investing in Neighborhoods* (Research Paper Series, Paper 2). Collaborative for Equity and Justice in Education and Nathalie P. Voorhees Center for Neighborhood and Community Improvement, University of Illinois-Chicago. Retrieved from http://www.vic.educ/ceje/resources.html

Foley, D. (2008). An introductory note on "activist educational anthropology." *Anthropology & Education Quarterly, 39*(1), 1–2.

Ford, B. (2005). The significance of charter schools and the privatization of standards: Holding the wolf by the ears. *Policy Futures in Education, 3*(1), 16–29.

Foster, J. B., & Magdoff, F. (2009). *The great financial crisis.* New York: Monthly Review Press.

Foundation Center. (2010). Growth and giving estimates: Current Outlook. New York: Author. Retrieved from http://www.foundationcenter.org

Foundation Center Statistical Services. (2006). *Top 50 U.S. foundations awarding grants for elementary and secondary education, circa 2006.* New York: Foundation Center.

Frankenberg, E., Siegel-Hawley, G., & Wang, J. (2010). *Choice without equity: Charter school segregation and the need for civil rights standards.* Retrieved from Civil Rights Project/Proyecto Derechos Civiles at UCLA, http://www.civilrightsproject.ucla.edu/

Fraser, N. (1990). Rethinking the public: A contribution to the critique of actually existing democracy. *Social Text, 25/26,* 56–80.

Fraser, N. (1997). *Justice interruptus: Critical reflections on the "postsocialist" condition.* New York: Routledge.

Fraser, N. (2007). Re-framing justice in a globalizing world. In T. Lovell, (Ed.), *(Mis)recognition, social inequality and social justice* (pp. 17–35). New York: Routledge.

Fraser, N., with Bedford, K. (2008). Social rights and gender justice in the neoliberal moment: A conversation about welfare and transnational politics. *Feminist Theory, 9,* 225–245.

Fraser, N., & Naples, N. (2004). To interpret the world and to change it: An interview with Nancy Fraser. *Signs: Journal of Women in Culture and Society 29,* 1103–1124.

Freire, P. (1994). *Pedagogy of hope: Reliving pedagogy of the oppressed* (R. R. Barr, Trans.) New York: Continuum.

Freire, P. (1998a). *Pedagogy of the oppressed* (M. B. Ramos, Trans.). New York: Continuum. (Original work published 1970)

Freire, P. (1998b). *Pedagogy of freedom.* Lanham, MD: Rowman & Littlefield.

Friedman, M. (1962). *Capitalism and freedom.* Chicago, IL: University of Chicago Press.

Fukuyama, F. (1992). *The end of history and the last man.* London: Penguin.

Fuller, E., with Orfield, G. (Eds.). (1996). *Who chooses, Who loses? Culture, institutions, and the unequal effects of school choice.* New York: Teachers College Press.

Fullilove, M. T. (2005). *Root shock: How tearing up city neighborhoods hurts America, and what we can do about it.* New York: One World Books.

Fung, A. (2004). *Empowered participation: Reinventing urban democracy.* Princeton, NJ: Princeton University Press.

Fyfe, N. (2004). Zero tolerance, maximum surveillance? Deviance, difference and crime control in the late modern city. In L. Lees (Ed.), *The emancipatory city? Paradoxes and possibilities* (pp. 40–56). London: Sage.

Gandin, L. A., & Apple, M. W. (2003). Educating the state, democratizing knowledge: The citizen school project in Porto Alegre, Brazil. In M. W. Apple (Ed.), *The state and the politics of knowledge* (pp. 193–219). New York: Routledge.

Gates Foundation (2006). *Annual report.* Retrieved from http://www.gatesfoundation.org/nr/public/media/annualreports/annualreport06/index.htm

Gates Foundation. (2007, June 13). Coalition of local community organizations to support innovative student involvement in Chicago high school reform. Press release. Retrieved from gatesfoundation.org

Gates Foundation. (2009a). 2009 Annual Report. Author. Retrieved from http://www.gatesfoundation.org

Gates Foundation. (2009b). College ready education plan. Retrieved from http:// www.gatesfoundation.org

Gates, W. (2005, March 1). What's wrong with American high schools? Retrieved from *LA Times* http://articles.latimes.com/2005/mar/01/opinion/oe-gates1

Gates, W. (2009). Annual letter from Bill Gates. Retrieved from http://www.gatesfoundation.org

Gewirtz, S. (1997) Post-welfarism and the reconstruction of teachers' work in the UK. *Journal of Education Policy, 12*(4), 217–231.

Gewirtz, S. (2002). *The managerial school: Post-welfarism and social justice in education.* London: Routledge.

Gewirtz, S., Ball, S. J., & Bowe, R. (1995). *Markets, choice and equity in education.* Buckingham, England: Open University Press.

Gewirtz, S., Mahony, P., Hextall, I., & Cribb, A. (Eds). (2009). *Changing teacher professionalism: International trends, challenges and ways forward.* London: Routledge.

Gill, S. (2003). *Power and resistance in the new world order.* New York: Palgrave Macmillan.

Gillborn, D. (2008). *Racism and education: Coincidence or conspiracy.* New York: Routledge.

Gilmore, R. W. (2007a). *Golden gulag: Prisons, surplus, crisis, and opposition in globalizing California.* Berkeley: University of California Press.

Gilmore, R. W. (2007b). In the shadow of the state. In Incite! Women of Color Against Violence (Eds.), *The revolution will not be funded: Beyond the non-profit industrial complex* (pp. 41–52). Cambridge, MA: South End Press.

Gilmore, R. W. (2008). Forgotten places and the seeds of grassroots planning. In C. R. Hale (Ed.), *Engaging contradictions: Theory, politics, methods of activist scholarship* (pp. 31–61). Berkeley: University of California Press.

Glover, R. L. (2005, October 12). *Making a case for mixed-use, mixed-income communities to address America's affordable housing needs.* Presentation to Center for American Progress. Retrieved from http://www.americanprogress.org/kf/glover.pdf

Gold, E., Simon, E., Cucchiara, C. Mitchell, M., & Riffer, M. (2007). *Building civic capacity in a privatizing system.* Philadelphia, PA: Research for Action.

Goldberg, D. T. (1993). "Polluting the body politic": Racist discourse and urban location. In M. Cross & M. Keith (Eds.), *Racism, the city and the state* (pp. 45–60). London: Routledge.

Goldberg, H. (2008). Building power in the city: Reflections on the emergence of the Right to the City Alliance and the National Domestic Workers' Alliance. *Journal of Aesthetics and Protest: In the middle of a whirlwind.* Retrieved from http://inthemiddleofthewhirlwind.wordpress.com/building-power-in-the-city/

Goldberg, H., & Mananzala, R. (2008). Right to the city: A cry and a demand for a new urban struggle (Document of U.S. Social Forum). Available from author.

Goldsmith, W. W. (2002). From the metropolis to globalization: The dialectics of race and urban form. In S. S. Fainstein & S. Campbell (Eds.), *Readings in urban theory* (2nd ed., pp. 129–149). Oxford, England: Blackwell.

González-Rivera, C. (2009, August). *People of color hardest hit by the foreclosure crisis* (Issue brief).. Retrieved from Greenline Institute http://www.greenlining.org/resources/pdfs/foreclosuresandpocbrief.pdfsn

Goodman, A. (2010). Interview. *Democracy Now.* Retrieved from http://www.democracynow.org/2010/6/2/democracy_now_travels_across_bayous_and

Gottlieb, A. (2002). Mixed income schools through choice gaining favor in Denver. *The Term Paper, 3,* 1. (Piton Foundation)

Grace, G. (1984). Urban education: Policy science or critical scholarship. In G. Grace (Ed.), *Education and the city: Theory, history and contemporary practice* (pp. 3–59). London: Routledge & Kegan Paul.

Gramsci, A. (1971). *Selections from the prison notebooks.* New York: International.

Grantmakers for Education. (2008). *Benchmarking 2008: Trends in education philanthropy.* Portland, OR: Author. Retrieved from http://www.foundationcenter.org

Gray, C. (2005, September 17). Storm's fury a mixed bag for schools. Knight Ridder Newspapers..Retrieved from http://seattletimes.nwsource.com/html/nationworld/2002500877_katschools17.html

Greenbaum, S. (2006). Commentary on Katrina. *City & Community, 5*(2), 105–209.

Greenberg, M. (2000). Branding cities: A social history of the urban lifestyle magazine. *Urban Affairs Review, 36*(2), 228–263.

Greenlee, A., Hudspeth, N., Lipman, P., Smith, D. A., & Smith, J. (2008). *Examining CPS' plan to close, consolidate, turn-around 18 schools* (Data and Democracy Project: Investing in Neighborhoods, Research Paper Series, 1). Collaborative for Equity and Justice in Education and Nathalie P. Voorhees Center for Neighborhood and Community Improvement, University of Illinois-Chicago. Retrieved from http://www.vic.educ/ceje/resources.html

Grossman, R., & Leroux, C. (2006). The unmaking of a ghetto. *Chicago Tribune Magazine,* January 29, 11–16, 26–29.

Guilhot, N. (2007). Reforming the world: George Soros, global capitalism and the philanthropic management of the social sciences. *Critical Sociology, 33,* 447–477.

Gulson, K. (2005). Renovating educational identities: Policy, space and urban renewal. *Journal of Education Policy, 20*(2), 141–158.

Gulson, K. (2007). Repositioning schooling in inner Sydney: Urban renewal, an education market and the "absent presence" of the "middle classes." *Urban Studies, 44*(7), 1377–1391.

Gulson, K. N. (2008). Urban accommodations: Policy, education and a politics of space. *Journal of Education Policy, 23,*153–163.

Gutstein, E. (2006a). "So one question leads to another": Using mathematics to develop a pedagogy of questioning. In N. S. Nasir & P. Cobb (Eds.), *Increasing access to mathematics: Diversity and equity in the classroom* (pp. 51–68). New York: Teachers College Press.

Gutstein, E. (2006b). *Reading and writing the world with mathematics: Toward a pedagogy for social justice.* New York: Routledge.

Greenbaum, S. (2006). Commentary on Katrina. *City & Community, 5*(2),105–209.

Grotto, J., Cohen, L., & Olkon, S. (2008). Public housing limbo. *Chicago Tribune,* A1, A22–23.

Gwynne, J., & de la Torre, M. (2009). When schools close: Effects on displaced students in Chicago Public Schools. Consortium on Chicago School Research.

Hackworth, J. (2007). *The neoliberal city: Governance, ideology, and development in American urbanism.* Ithaca, NY: Cornell University Press.

Hale, C. R. (Ed). (2008). *Engaging contradictions: Theory, politics and methods of activist scholarship.* Berkeley: University of California Press.

Harnecker, M. (2010). Latin America and 21st century socialism: Inventing to avoid mistakes. *Monthly Review, 62*(3), 1–78.

Harris, R. (2008, May/June). Pushing "big picture" reform: A new grassroots coalition wants to create models for district-community partnerships. *Catalyst Chicago.* Retrieved from http://www.catalyst-chicago.org/news/index.php?item=2418&cat=30

Harvey, D. (1973). *Social justice and the city.* London: Arnold.

Harvey, D. (1989) From managerialism to entrepreneurism: The transformation in urban governance in late capitalism. *Geografiska Annaler, 71B,* 3–17.

Harvey, D. (2001). *Spaces of capital: Towards a critical geography.* London: Routledge.

Harvey, D. (2003a). The right to the city. *International Journal of Urban and Regional Research, 27*(4), 939–941.

Harvey, D. (2003b). *The new imperialism.* Oxford, England: Oxford University Press.

Harvey, D. (2005). *A brief history of neoliberalism.* Oxford, England: Oxford University Press.

Harvey, D. (2008). The right to the city. *New Left Review, 53,* 23–40.

Harvey, D. (2009, January 29). *Reclaiming spaces: Habitat and crisis.* Opening speech at the Urban Reform Tent, World Social Forum. Retrieved from http://www.reclaiming-spaces.org/crisis/archives/245

Harvey, D. (2010). *The enigma of capital and the crises of capitalism.* London: Profile Books.

Hassel, B. C., & Way, A. (2005). Choosing to fund school choice. In F. Hess (Ed.), *With the best of intentions: How philanthropy is shaping K-12 education.* Cambridge, MA: Harvard Education Press.

Hawkins, K. (2009, October 6). Chicago teen deaths, violence tied to school reform plan? Huffington Post. http://www.huffingtonpost.com/2009/10/06/chicago-teen-deaths-viole_n_311877.html

Haymes, S. N. (1995). *Race, culture and the city.* Albany, NY: SUNY Press.

Heartland Alliance. (2006). *2006 Illinois poverty summit.* Chicago, IL: Author.

Henderson, T. J. (2001, November/December). Socioeconomic school integration. *Poverty & Race.* Retrieved from Poverty & Race Research Action Council, http://www.prrac.org/full_text.php?text_id=740&item_id=7782&newsletter_id=59&head

Hess, G. A. (1991). *School restructuring Chicago style.* Newbury Park, CA: Corwin Press.

Hill, P., & Hannaway, J. (2006). *The future of public education in New Orleans after Katrina: Rebuilding opportunity and equity into the "New" New Orleans.* Washington, DC: Urban Institute.

Howell, S. (2010, April 2). Interview. *Democracy Now* radio. Retrieved from http://www.democracynow.org

Hursh, D. (2007). Assessing No Child Left Behind and the rise of neoliberal education policies. *American Educational Research Journal, 44*(3), 493–518.

Hursh, D. (2008). *High-stakes testing and the decline of teaching and learning.* Lanham, MD: Rowman & Littlefield.

Imbroscio, D. (2008). "United and actuated by some common impulse of passion": Challenging the dispersal consensus in American housing policy research. *Journal of Urban Affairs, 30*(2), 111–130.

Incite! Women of Color Against Violence. (Eds.). (2007). *The revolution will not be funded: Beyond the non-profit industrial complex.* Cambridge, MA: South End Press.

International Network for Urban Research and Action (INURA). (2003, January). An alternative urban world is possible: A declaration for urban research and action. Retrieved from http://www.inura.org/INURA%20declaration.html/declaration.html

Irvine, J. J. (1991). *Black students and school failure: Policies, practices, and prescriptions.* New York: Praeger.

Jackson, A. (2004, May 20). http://financialservices.house.gov/pr052004.html

Jehl, J., & Payzant, T. W. (1992). Philanthropy and public school reform: A view from San Diego. *Teachers College Press, 93*(3), 472–487.

JPMorgan Chase creates $325 million funding initiative for high-performing charter schools. (2010, May 4). Press release. JP Morgan Chase. Retrieved from http://www.jpmorgan.com/cm/cs?pagename=JPM_redesign/JPM_Content_C/Generic_Detail_Page_Template&cid=1273099225083&c=JPM_Conten

Johnson, E. (1998, November). *Chicago metropolis 2020: Preparing metropolitan Chicago for the 21st century: Executive Summary.* Chicago, IL: Commercial Club of Chicago.

Johnson, S. M., & Landman, J. (2000). Sometimes bureaucracy has its charms: The working conditions of teachers in deregulated schools. *Teachers College Record, 102*(1), 85–124.

Jomo, K. S., & Baudot, J. (Eds.). (2007). *Flat world, big gaps: Economic liberalization, globalization, poverty and inequality.* New York: Zed/United Nations.

Jones, M., & Ward, K. (2002). Excavating the logic of British urban policy: Neoliberalism as the "Crisis of Crisis-Management." In N. Brenner & N. Theodore (Eds.), *Spaces of neoliberalism* (pp.126–147). Oxford, England: Blackwell.

Joravsky, B. (2008, May 29). The mystery of the construction obstructionist. Retrieved from http://www.chicagoreader.com/chicago/the-mystery-of-the-construction-obstructionist/Content?oid=1109707

Joravsky, B. (2009, March 19). Show us the money. Retrieved from http://www.chicagoreader.com/chicago/show-us-the-money/Content?oid=917926

Joravsky, B., & Dumke, M. (2009, October. 22). The shadow budget. *The Reader.* http://www.chicagoreader.com/chicago/the-chicago-shadow-tif-budget/Content?oid=1218391

Joseph, M. L. (2008). Early resident experiences at a new mixed-income development in Chicago. *Journal of Urban Affairs, 30*(3), 229–257.

Judd, D. R. (2003). Visitors and the spatial ecology of the city. In L. M. Hoffman, S. S. Fainsein, & D. R. Judd (Eds.), *Cities and visitors: Regulating people, markets, and city space* (pp. 23–38). Oxford, England: Blackwell.

Kahlenberg, R. D. (2001). *All together now: The case for economic integration of the public schools.* Washington, DC: Brookings Institution Press.

Karier, C. J. (1972). Testing for order and control in the corporate state. *Educational Theory, 22*, 159–180.

Karp, S. (2002, Spring.). Let them eat tests. *Rethinking Schools.* Retrieved from http://www.rethinkingschools.org/special reports/bushplan/Eat164/shtml

Karp, S. (2009, October 27). Chicago schools plan to combat violence: kinder, gentler security guards, disciplinarians. *Catalyst Chicago.* Retrieved from http://www.catalyst-chicago.org/notebook/

Karp, S. (2010, Summer). A revolving door. *Catalyst Chicago.* Retrieved from http://www.catalyst-chicago.org/issue/index.php?issueNo=156

Katz, M. B. (1992). Chicago school reform as history. *Teachers College Record, 94*(1), 56–72.

Katz, M. (1989). *The undeserving poor: From the war on poverty to the war on welfare.* New York: Pantheon Books.

Katz, M., Fine, M., & Simon, E. (1997). Poking around: Outsiders view Chicago school reform. *Teachers College Record, 99*(1), 117–157.

Keating, L. (2000). Redeveloping public housing: Relearning urban renewal's immutable lessons. *Journal of the American Planning Association, 66*(4), 384–397.

Keith, M. (1993). From punishment to discipline? Racism, racialization and the policing of social control. In M. Cross & M. Keith (Eds.), *Racism, the city and the state* (pp. 193–209). London: Routledge.

Keith, M., & Pile, S. (1993). Place and the politics of identity. In M. Cross & M. Keith (Eds.), *Racism, the city and the state* (pp. 22–40). London: Routledge.

Kelley, R. D. G. (2003). *Freedom dreams: The Black radical imagination*. Boston, MA: Beacon Press.

Kerbow, D. (1996). Patterns of urban student mobility and local school reform. *Journal of Education of Students Placed At-Risk, 1*(2), 147–169.

Kerbow, D., Azcoitia, C., & Buell, B. (2003). Student mobility and local school improvement in Chicago. *Journal of Negro Education, 72*(1), 158–164.

King, J. E. (2005a). A declaration of intellectual independence for human freedom. In J. E. King (Ed.), *Black education: A transformative research and action agenda for the new century* (pp. 19–42). Mahwah, NJ: Erlbaum.

King, J. E. (2005b). Preface. In J. E. King (Ed.), *Black education: A transformative research and action agenda for the new century* (pp. xxi–xxx). Mahwah, NJ: Erlbaum.

Klein, N. (2008, September 19). Free market ideology is far from finished. *The Guardian*. Retrieved from http://www.guardian.co.uk/commentisfree/2008/sep/19/marketturmoil.usa

Klonsky, M., & Klonsky, S. (2008). *Small schools: Public school reform meets the ownership society*. New York: Routledge.

Knapp, M. S., & Woolverton, S. (2004). Social class and schooling. In J. A. Banks & C. A. M. Banks (Eds.), *Handbook of research on multicultural education* (2nd ed., pp. 656–681). San Francisco, CA: Jossey-Bass.

Kovacs, P. (2007). The schools are failing: Think tanks, institutes, foundations, and educational disaster. In K. Saltman (Ed.), *Schooling and the politics of disaster* (pp. 159–175). New York: Routledge.

Kozol, J. (1992). *Savage inequalities*. New York: Perennial.

Kuehn, L. (2008). The education world is not flat: Neoliberalism's global project and teacher unions' transnational resistance. In M. Compton & L. Weiner (Eds.), *The global assault on teaching, teachers, and their unions* (pp. 53–72). New York: Palgrave.

Kumashiro, K. (2008). *The seduction of common sense: How the right has framed the debate on America's schools*. New York: Teachers College Press.

Kyle, C. L., & Kantowicz, E. R. (1992). *Kids first–Primero los niños: Chicago school reform in the 1980s*. Springfield, IL: Sangamon State University Press.

Ladson-Billings, G. (1994). *Dreamkeepers: Successful teachers of African American students*. San Francisco, CA: Jossey-Bass.

Ladson-Billings, G. (1995). But that's just good teaching! The case for culturally relevant pedagogy. *Theory into Practice, 34*(3), 195–202.

Ladson-Billings, G. (2005). From the achievement gap to the education debt: Understanding achievement in U.S. schools. *Educational Researcher, 15*(7), 3–12.

LaGravenese, R. (director). (2007). *Freedom writers*. United States: Paramount Pictures.

Lauder, H., Brown, P., Dillabough, J., & Halsey, A. H. (Eds.). (2006). *Education, globalization and social change*. Oxford, England: Oxford University Press.

Lebowitz, M. A. *Build it now: Socialism for the twenty-first century*. New York: Monthly Review Press.

Lees, L. (2008). Gentrification and social mixing: Towards an inclusive urban renaissance? *Urban Studies, 45*, 2449–2470.

Lefebvre, H. (1996). *Writings on cities* (E. Kofman & E. Labas, Trans. & Ed.) London: Blackwell. (Original work published 1968)

Leitner, H., Peck, J., & Sheppard, E. S. (2007). Squaring up to neoliberalism. In H. Leitner, J. Peck, & E. S. Sheppard (Eds.), *Contesting neoliberalism, urban frontiers* (pp. 311–327). New York: Guilford Press.

Leitner, H., Sheppard, E. S., Sziarto, K., & Maringanti, A. (2007). Contesting urban futures, decentering neoliberalism. In H. Leitner, J. Peck, & E. S. Sheppard (Eds.), *Contesting neoliberalism: Urban frontiers* (pp. 1–25). New York: Guilford Press.

Lens, L., & Poinsett, A. (1991, June). 2 out of 3 council members likely to run again. *Catalyst: Voices of Chicago school reform, II*(9), 2–7.

Leonardo, Z. (2009). *Race, whiteness, and education*. New York: Routledge.

Lewis, O. (1966). *La vida: A Puerto Rican family in the culture of poverty*. New York: Random House.

Lingard, B. (2000). It is and it isn't: Vernacular globalization, educational policy, and restructuring. In N. C. Berbules, N. C. Torres, & C. A. Torres (Eds.), *Globalization and education: Critical perspectives* (pp. 79–108). New York: Routledge.

Lingard, B. (2007). Deparochializing the study of education: Globalization and the research imagination. In K. N. Gulson & C. Symes (Eds.), *Spatial theories of education: Policy and geography matters* (pp. 233–250). New York: Routledge.

Lipman, P. (1998). *Race, class, and power in school restructuring*. Albany, NY: SUNY Press.

Lipman, P. (2002). Making the global city, making inequality: The political economy and cultural politics of Chicago school policy. *American Educational Research Journal, 39*(2), 379–422.

Lipman, P. (2004). *High stakes education: Inequality, globalization, and urban school reform*. New York: Routledge.

Lipman, P. (2005a). Educational ethnography and the politics of globalization, war, and resistance. *Anthropology and Education Quarterly, 36*, 315–328.

Lipman, P. (2005b). Whose city is it—anyway? *AREA Chicago, Arts. Education. Activism, 1*. Stockyard Institute, Chicago.

Lipman, P. (2008a). Mixed-income schools and housing: Advancing the neoliberal urban agenda. *Journal of Education Policy, 23*(2), 119–134.

Lipman, P. (2008b). Linking Ren2010 and the Plan for Transformation. *AREA Chicago: Arts. Education. Activism, #6*. Stockyard Institute, Chicago.

Lipman, P. (2011). Contesting the city: Neoliberal urbanism and the cultural politics of education reform in Chicago. *Discourse: Studies in the Cultural Politics of Education, 32*(2).

Lipman, P., & Haines, N. (2007). From education accountability to privatization and African American exclusion—Chicago Public Schools' "Renaissance 2010." *Educational Policy, 21*(3), 471–502.

Lipman, P., & Hursh, D. (2007). Renaissance 2010: The reassertion of ruling-class power through neoliberal policies in Chicago. *Policy Futures in Education, 5*(2), 160–178.

Lipman, P., Person, A., & Kenwood Oakland Community Organization. (2007). *Students as collateral damage? A preliminary study of Renaissance 2010 school closings in the Midsouth*. Chicago, IL: Kenwood Oakland Community Organization. Retrieved from http://www.uic.edu/educ/ceje/index.html.

Lipsitz, G. (1998). *Possessive investment in whiteness: How White people profit from identity politics*. Philadelphia, PA: Temple University Press.

Lipsitz, G. (2006a). The culture of war. *Critical Survey, 18*(3), 83–91.

Lipsitz, G. (2006b). Learning from New Orleans: The social warrant of hostile privatism and competitive consumer citizenship. *Cultural Anthropology, 21*(3), 451–468.

Lipsitz, G. (2007). The racialization of space and the spatialization of race: Theorizing the hidden architecture of landscape. *Landscape Journrnal, 26*(1), 10–23.

Liveable Places. (n.d.). Retrieved from http://www.livableplaces.org/policy/documents/mixedincomedowntownfinal_001.pdf

Lofland, J., & Lofland, L. H. (1995). *Analyzing social settings* (3rd ed.). Belmont, CA: Wadsworth.

Logan, J. R., & Molotch, H. L. (1987). *Urban fortunes: The political economy of place*. Berkeley: University of California Press.

Lupton, R., & Turnstall, R. (2008). Neighbourhood regeneration through mixed communities: A "social justice dilemma"? *Journal of Education Policy, 23*(2), 105–118.

MacArthur Foundation. (2005, Spring). Revitalizing Bronzeville: Mixed-income housing is key to community strength. *MacArthur Foundation Newsletter*. Retrieved from http://www.macfound.org

MacLeod, G. (2002). From urban entreneurialsim to a "Revanchist City"? On the spatial injustices of Glasgow's renaissance. In N. Brenner & N. Theodore (Eds.), *Spaces of neoliberalism* (pp. 254–276). Oxford, England: Blackwell.

Mahony, P., & Hextall, I. (1998). Social justice and the reconstruction of teaching. *Journal of Education Policy, 13*(4), 545–558.

Marcuse, P. (2009). From critical urban theory to the right to the city. *City: Analysis of urban trends, culture, theory, policy, action, 13*(203), 185–197.

Marcuse, P., & Van Kempen, R. (Eds.). (2000). *Globalizing cities: A new spatial order?* Oxford, England: Blackwell.

Martin, E. (n.d.). Brochure. Renaissance schools fund: Investing in excellence. (available from author).

Massey, D. S., & Denton, N. A. (1993). *American apartheid: Segregation and the making of the underclass.* Cambridge, MA: Harvard University Press.

Mathematica Policy Research, Inc. (2010). *Hunger in America.* Retrieved from http://feedingamerica.org/faces-of-hunger/hunger-in-america-2010/hunger-report-2010.aspx

McGrath, D. J., & Kuriloff, P. J. (1999). They're going to tear the doors off this place: Upper-middle-class parent school involvement and the educational opportunities of other people's children. *Educational Policy, 13*(5), 603–629.

McNeil, L. M. (2000). *Contradictions of school reform: Educational costs of standardized testing.* New York: Routledge.

Mehan, H. (2008). Engaging the sociological imagination. *Anthropology & Education Quarterly, 39*(1), 77–91.

Meier, D. (1996). *The power of their ideas: Lessons for America from a small school in Harlem.* Boston, MA: Beacon Press.

Metropolitan Planning Council. (2004). *CHA plan for transformation: Progress report.* Retrieved from https://www.metroplanning.org/ourwork/

Meyer, J. (2009, October 27). DPS evaluates school remedies. *The Denver Post.* Retrieved from http://www.denverpost.com/news/ci_13647717#ixzz0hoWh4y8T

Michaels Development Corporation. (n.d.). *The Michaels Development Co. portfolio—Michael Taylor homes.* Retrieved from http://www.michaelsdevelopmentcompany.com/portfRobertTaylor.html

Midsouth: Education Plan/Renaissance 2010 Fact Sheet (2004). Kenwood Oakland Local School Council Alliance. Chicago. Retrieved from www.teachersforjustice.org/pages/R2010factsheet.html.

Miller, B. (2007). Modes of governance, modes of resistance. In H. Leitner, J. Peck, & E. S. Sheppard (Eds.), *Contesting neoliberalism: Urban frontiers* (pp. 223–249). New York: Guilford Press.

Minneapolis Family Housing Fund. (1998). *Kids mobility project.* Minneapolis, MN: Author.

Mitchell, D. (2003). *The right to the city: Social justice and the fight for public space.* New York: Guilford.

Mitchell, K. (2001). Transnationalism, neo-liberalism, and the rise of the shadow state. *Economy and Society, 30*(2), 165–189.

Molnar, A. (1996). *Giving kids the business: The commercialization of America's schools.* Boulder, CO: Westview Press.

Mountz, A., & Curran, W. (2009). Policing in drag: Giuliani goes global with the illusion of control. *Geoforum, 40*(6), 1033–1040.

Moynihan, D. P. (1965). *The negro family: The case for national action.* Washington, DC: Office of Policy Planning and Research United States Department of Labor.

Myers, J. (2008, April). *Anyone want a turnaround?* Chicago, IL: Catalyst Chicago. Retrieved from www.catalyst-chicago.org.

Myerson, D. L. (2001, October 18–19). *Sustaining urban mixed-income communities: The role of community facilities* (ULI Land Use Policy Forum Report). The ULI/Charles H. Shaw Annual Forum on Urban Community Issues, Washington, DC: Urban Land Institute.

National Assessment of Educational Progress (2003, 2005, 2007, 2009). National Center for Education Statistics, U.S. Department of Education. Washington, DC. http://nces.ed.gov/nationsreportcard/

National Commission on Excellence in Education. (1983). *A nation at risk: The imperative for educational reform.* Washington, DC: Government Printing Office.

Neighborhood Capital Budget Group. (2006). *Modern schools across Chicago: Will the mayor's plan for financing school construction work?* Chicago, IL: Author.

Ng, J. C., & Rury, J. L. (2006) Poverty and education: A critical analysis of the Ruby Payne phenomenon. *Teachers College Record.* Retrieved from http://www.tcrecord.org/Content. asp?contentid=12596

No Child Left Behind Act of 2001. US Public Law 107-110. 107th Congr., 1st sess., 8 January 2002.

Novak, T., & Fusco, C. (2009, May 16). Maxwell Street's $750 million makeover. *Chicago Sun Times.* Retrieved from http://www.suntimes.com/news/metro/1577377,CST-NWS-maxwell17.article

Nyden, P., Edlynn, E., & Davis, J. (2006). *The differential impact of gentrification on communities in Chicago.* Chicago, IL: Loyola University Chicago Center for Urban Research and Learning.

Oakes, J., Wells, A. S., Jones, M., & Datnow, A. (1997). Detracking: The social construction of ability, cultural politics, and resistance to reform. *Teachers College Record, 98*(3), 482–510.

Obama, B. (2010, July 29). Remarks by the President on education reform at the National Urban League Centennial Conference. Retrieved from http://www.whitehouse.gov/the-press-office/remarks-president-education-reform-national-urban-league-centennial-conference

Olivio, A. (2004, May 6). Englewood rebirth plan brings hope and anxiety. *Chicago Tribune,* Sect. 1, p. 1.

Olszewski , L., & Sadovi,, C. (2003, December 19). Rebirth of schools set for South Side. *Chicago Tribune,* Sect. 1, p. 1.

Orfield, G. (1990). Wasted talent, threatened future: Metropolitan Chicago's human capital and Illinois public policy. In L. B. Joseph (Ed), *Creating jobs, creating workers: Economic development and employment in metropolitan Chicago* (pp. 129–160). Chicago, IL: University of Chicago Center for Urban Research and Policy Studies.

Orfield, G. (2001, November/December). Response. *Poverty & Race.* Poverty & Race Research Action Council. Retrieved from http://www.prrac.org/full_text.php?text_id=711&item_id=7761&newsletter_id=58&head

Parenti, C. (1999). *Lockdown America: Police and prisons in the age of crisis.* London: Verso.

Parenti, M. (2005). How the free market killed New Orleans. Znet commentary. Retrieved from http://www.zmag.org/sustainers/content/2005-09/03parenti.cfm

Patillo, M. (2007). *Black on the block.* Chicago, IL: University of Chicago Press.

Payne, R. K. (2005). *A framework for understanding poverty* (4th ed.). Highlands, TX: RFT. (Original work published 1998)

Peck, J., Brenner, N., & Theodore, N. (2008, June 7). City as lab. *AREA Chicago, Art/Research/ Education/Activism,* 6. Retrieved from http://www.areachicago.org/p/issues/city-as-lab/ city-policy-lab/

Peck, J., & Tickell, A. (2002). Neoliberalizing space. In N. Brenner & N. Theodore (Eds.), *Spaces of neoliberalism: Urban restructuring in North America and Western Europe* (pp. 33–57). Oxford, England: Blackwell.

Peck, J., & Tickell, A. (2007). Conceptualizing neoliberalism, thinking Thatcherism. In H. Leitner, J. Peck, & E. S. Sheppard (Eds.), *Contesting neoliberalism: Urban frontiers* (pp. 26–50). New York: Guilford Press.

Pedroni, T. C. (2007). *Market movements: African American involvement in school voucher reform.* New York: Routledge.

Pedroni, T. C. (2009, April).Whose public? *Learning from subaltern critiques of the public sphere.* Paper presented at Annual Meeting of the American Educational Research Association, Denver, Colorado.

Pedroni, T. C. (2011). Neoliberal urban restructuring, education, and racial containment in the post-industrial, globally compelled city. *Discourse: Studies in the Cultural Politics of Education,32*(2).

Perry, T. (2003). Up from the parched earth: Toward a theory of African American achievement. In T. Perry, C. Steele, & A. Hilliard, III (Eds.), *Young gifted and Black: Promoting high achievement among African-American students* (pp. 1–108). Boston, MA: Beacon Press.

Perry, D. C., & Wiewel, W. (2005). *The university as urban developer.* Armonk, NY: M. E. Sharpe.

Peterson, B. (2010, June 5). 1,000 English schools to become academies (Charters)? [Electronic mailing list Rethinking Schools message]. RS critical teach listserve. Retrieved from rs@criticalteach.org

Pew Center on the States. (2008). *One in one-hundred: Behind bars in America 2008.* Report of Pew Charitable Trust.

Pink, W. F., & Noblit, G.W. (Eds.). (2008). *International handbook of urban education.* Dordrecht, Netherlands: Springer.

Pitcoff, W. (1999, March/April). New hope for public housing? Shelterforce online, #104. Piton Foundation. Retrieved from http://www.nhi.org/online/issues/104/pitcoff.html.

Points for how the Chicago Board of Education failed Ralph J. Bunche School! (2004, March 1). Unpublished document. Available from author.

Polet, F. (2001). Some key statistics. In F. Houtart & F. Polet (Eds.), *The other Davos: The globalization of resistance to the world economic system* (pp. 3–6). New York: Zed.

Popen, S. (2002). Democratic pedagogy and the discourse of containment. *Anthropology & Education Quarterly, 33*(3), 283–294.

Popkin, S. J. (2006). The HOPE VI program: What has happened to the residents? In L. Bennett, J. L. Smith, & P. A. Wright (Eds.), *Where are poor people to live? Transforming public housing communities* (pp. 68–92). Armonk, NY: M. E. Sharpe.

Popkin, S. J., Cunningham, M. K., & Woodley, W. (2003). Residents at risk. Urban Institute. Retrieved from http://www.urban.org/url.cfm?ID=310824

Popkin. S. J., Katz, B., Cunningham, M., Brown, K., Gustafson, J., & Turner, M. (2004). *A decade of HOPE VI: Research findings and policy challenges.* Washington, DC: Urban Institute and Brookings Institution.

Potter, J. (2008, September). Perspectives and urban prep charter schools dump "failing" students back into public high schools? *Substance News.* Retrieved from http://www.substancenews.net/articles.php?page=560&section=Article

Purcell, M. (2002). Excavating Lefebvre: The right to the city and its urban politics of the inhabitant. *GeoJournal, 58,* 99–108.

Quality Housing and Work Responsibility Act of 1998. Office of Public and Indian Housing. U. S. Department of Housing and Urban Development. Washington DC: U.S. Government. http://www.hud.gov/offices/pih/pha/.pdf

Quigley, B. (2006, April 26). Eight months after Katrina. Retrieved from http://www.truthout.org

Raffel, J. A., Denson, L. R., Varady, D. P., & Sweeney, S. (2003). *Linking housing and public schools in the HOPE VI public housing revitalization program: A case study analysis of four developments in four cities.* Retrieved from http://www.udel.edu/ccrs/pdf/LinkingHousing.pdf

Ranney, D. (2004). *Global decisions, local collisions: Urban life in the new world order.* Philadelphia, PA: Temple University Press.

Ranney, D. C., & Wright, P. A. (2004). Chicago's South Side: Revisiting the South Loop and South Armour Square, 2001. (*Democracy, Governance and Human Rights Programme,* Paper Number 15). Geneva, Switzerland: United Nations Research Institute for Development.

Rast, J. (1999) *Remaking Chicago: The political origins of urban industrial change.* DeKalb, IL: Northern Illinois University Press.

ravis@sarai.net. (2001). *Discussing the public domain* (Sarai Reader, 1). Retrieved from http://www.sarai.net/publications/readers/01-the-public-domain/viii-009%20(enter).pdf

Renaissance Schools Fund. (2008). *Creating a new market of public education.* Chicago, IL: Author.

Reynolds, A. J., & Walberg, H. J. (1992). A process model of mathematics achievement and attitude. *Journal for Research in Mathematics Education, 23*(4), 306–328.

Rivlin, G. (1992). *Fire on the prairie: Chicago's Harold Washington and the politics of race.* New York: Henry Holt.

Rivlin, G. (2005, September 29). A mogul who would rebuild New Orleans. *New York Times,* pp. C1, C4.

Rizvi, F., & Lingard, B. (2009). *Globalizing education policy.* New York: Routledge.

Robbins, C. G. (2008). *Expelling hope: The assault on youth and the militarization of schooling.* Albany, NY: SUNY Press.

Robertson, S. (2007). *"Remaking the world": Neo-liberalism and the transformation of education and teachers' labour.* Bristol, England: Centre for Globalisation, Education and Societies, University of Bristol. Retrieved from http://www.bris.ac.uk/education/people/academicStaff/edslr/publications/17slr/

Robertson , S., Bonal, X., & Dale, R. (2002). GATS and the education service industry: Scale and the politics of territorialisation. *Comparative Education Review, 46*(4), 472–496.

Robertson, S., & Dale, R. (2003, June). *Changing geographies of power in education: The politics of rescaling and its contradictions.* Paper presented to the Joint BERA/BAICE Conference on Globalization, Culture and Education, Bristol, England.

Roelofs, J. (2007). Foundations and collaboration. *Critical Sociology, 33*, 479–504.

Rofes, E., & Stulberg, L. M. (Eds.). (2005). *The emancipatory promise of charter schools.* New York: SUNY Press.

Rosenkranz, T. (2002). *2001 CPS Trend Review: Iowa tests of basic skills.* Chicago, IL: Consortium on Chicago Research.

Rossi, R. (2004a, November 23). 52 applicants seek to create public schools. *Chicago Sun Times,* Sect. News , p. 19.

Rossi, R. (2004b, November 30). Civic leaders donating $50 million want accountability from schools. *Chicago Sun Times.* Retrieved from http://wwwsuntimes.com/output/news/cst-nws-renai30.htmlt

Rubinowitz, L. S., & Rosenbaum, J. E. (2002). *Crossing the class and color line: From public housing to white suburbia.* Chicago, IL: University of Chicago Press.

Rumberger, R. W., & Larson, K. A. (1998). Student mobility and the increased risk of high school dropout. *American Journal of Education, 107*, 1–35.

Rumberger, R. W., & Wilms, J. D. (1992). The impact of racial and ethnic segregation on the achievement gap in California high schools. *Educational Evaluation and Policy Analysis, 14*(4), 377–396.

Rury, J. R., & Mirel, J. E. (1997). The political economy of urban education. *Review of Research In Education, 22*, 49–110.

Rushing, K. (2009). Giuliani should not be a role model for Camden Police. *Advancement Project.* Retrieved from http://www.justdemocracyblog.org/?p=804.

Rusk, D. (1998). To improve public education, stop moving money. *Abell Report, 11*, 1–8.

Saito, L. (2009). *The politics of exclusion: The failure of race-neutral policies in urban America.* Stanford, CA: Stanford University Press.

Saltman, K. J. (2005). *The Edison schools.* New York: Routledge.

Saltman, K.J. (2007). *Capitalizing on disaster: Taking and breaking public schools.* Boulder, CO: Paradigm.

Saltman, K.J. (2009). The rise of venture philanthropy and the ongoing neoliberal assault on public education: The Case of the Eli and Edythe Broad Foundation. *Workplace, 16*, 53–72.

Samuel, P. (2005). Should states sell their toll roads? Reason Foundation. Retrieved from http://reason.org/files/59b301a5d83b89790d404020d4e4da9c.pdf

Sanbonmatsu, L., Kling, J., Duncan, G., & Brooks-Gunn, J. (2006). *Neighborhoods and academic achievement: Results from the moving to opportunity experiment.* Cambridge, MA: National Bureau of Economic Research Working Paper no. 11909.

Santos, B. S. (2002). Cultural and post-colonial critiques in LatCrit thoery: Nuestra America: Reinventing a subaltern paradigm of recognition and redistribution. *Rutgers Law Review, 54*, 1049–1086.

Sassen, S. (2004). A global city. In C. Madigan (Ed.), *Global Chicago* (pp. 15–34). Urbana: University of Illinois Press,

Sassen, S. (2006). *Cities in a world economy* (3rd ed.). Thousand Oaks, CA: Pine Forge Press.

Sassen, S. (2010, May 22). Beyond protests: Students making the pieces of a different society. *Huffington Post*. Retrievedfrom http://www.huffingtonpost.com/saskia-sassen/beyond-protests-students_b_586138.html

Schmidt, G. N. (2009, March 24). Chicago Bulls to help resegregation, gentrification of West Side. *Substance News*. Retrieved from http://www.substancenews.net/articles.php?section=Article&page=665

Schwartz, A., & Tajbakhsh, K. (1997). Mixed income housing: Unanswered questions. *Cityscape, 3*(2), 71–92.

Scott, J. (2009). The politics of venture philanthropy in charter school policy and advocacy. *Educational Policy, 23*(1), 106–136.

Selden, S. (1999). *Inheriting shame: The story of eugenics and racism in America*. New York: Teachers College Press.

Shipps, D. (1997). Invisible hand: Big business and Chicago school reform. *Teachers College Record, 99*, 73–116.

Shipps, D. (2006). *School reform, corporate style: Chicago, 1880–2000*. Lawrence: University Press of Kansas.

Shipps, D., Kahne, J., & Smiley, M. A. (1999). The politics of urban school reform: Legitimacy, city growth, and school improvement in Chicago. *Educational Policy, 13*(4), 518–546.

Siddle-Walker, V. (1996). *Their highest potential: An African American school community in the segregated South*. Chapel Hill: University of North Carolina Press.

Sieber, R. T. (1982). The politics of middle-class success in an inner-city public school. *Journal of Education, 164*(1), 30–47.

Sirin, S. R. (2005) Socioeconomic status and academic achievement: A meta-analytic review of research. *Review of Educational Research, 75*(3), 417–453.

Slater, T. (2009). Missing Marcuse: On gentrification and displacement. *City, 13*(2–3), 293–311.

Small, M. L. (2009). "How many cases do I need?" On science and the logic of case selection in field-based research. *Ethnography, 10*(1), 5–38.

Smith, A. (2007). Introduction: The revolution will not be funded. In Incite! Women of Color Against Violence (Eds.), *The revolution will not be funded: Beyond the non-profit industrial complex* (pp. 1–8). Cambridge, MA: South End Press.

Smith, J. L. (2000). The space of local control in the devolution of U.S. public housing policy. *Geografiska Annaler, 82B*(4), 221–233.

Smith, J. L. (2002). HOPE VI and the New urbanism: Eliminating low-income housing to make mixed-income communities. *Planners Network*.. Retrieved March 15, 2006, from http://www.plannersnetwork.org/publications/mag_2002_2_spring.html

Smith, J. L. (2006). Mixed-income communities: Designing out poverty or pushing out the poor? In L. Bennett, J. L. Smith, & P. A. Wright (Eds.), *Where are poor people to live? Transforming public housing communities* (pp. 282–300). Armonk, NY: M. E. Sharpe.

Smith, J. L. (2009a). Integration, solving the wrong problem. In. C. Hartman & G. D. Squires (Eds.), *The integration debate: Competing futures for America's cities* (pp. 229–245). New York: Routledge.

Smith, J. L. (2009b). Are we making the third ghetto? Power point presentation. Nathalie P. Vorhees Center for Neighborhood and Economic Improvement. (available from author).

Smith, J. M. (Director). (1995). *Dangerous minds* [motion picture]. United States: Hollywood Productions.

Smith, N. (1996). *The new urban frontier: Gentrification and the revanchist city*. New York: Routledge.

Smith, N. (1998). Giuliani Time: The revanchist 1990s. *Social Text, 57*(4), 1–20.

Smith, N. (2002). New globalism, new urbanism: Gentrification as global urban strategy. *Antipode, 34*(3), 427–450.

Smith, J. L., & Stovall (2008). 'Coming home' to new homes and new schools: Critical race theory and the new politics of containment. *Journal of Education Policy, 23*(2), 135–152.

Smith, S. J. (1993). Residential segregation and the politics of racialization. In M. Cross & M. Keith (Eds.), *Racism, the city and the state* (pp. 128–143). London: Routledge.

Smyth, J. (2001). *Critical politics of teachers' work: An Australian perspective.* New York: Lang.

Soja, E. W. (1999). Indifferent spaces: The cultural turn in urban and regional political economy. *European Planning Studies, 7*(1), 65–75.

Speth, J. G. (2008). *Bridge at the edge of the world: Capitalism, the environment, and crossing from crisis to sustainability.* New Haven, CT: Yale University Press.

Squires, G. D., Bennett, L., McCourt, K., & Nyden, P. (1987). *Chicago: Race, class, and the response to urban decline.* Philadelphia, PA: Temple University Press.

Stack, A. J., III. (2010, February 18). Manifesto of Austin, Texas crash pilot Andrew Joseph Stack III. Retrieved from http://www.disinfo.com/2010/02/the-manifesto-of-austin-texas-crash-pilot-joseph-andrew-stack/

Stanfield, R. (2002). Chicago's child-parent centers. Annie E. Casey Foundation. Retrieved June 5, 2006, from http://www.aecf.org/publications/advocasey/spring2002/chicago.htm

Stulberg, L. M. (2008). *Race, schools, and hope.* New York: Teachers College Press.

Swyngedouw, E., Moulaert, F., & Rodriguez, A. (2004). Neoliberal urbanization in Europe: Large-scale urban development projects and the new urban policy. In N. Brenner & N. Theodore (Eds.), *Spaces of neoliberalism* (pp. 195–229). London: Blackwell.

Tabb, W. (2007). Wage stagnation, growing insecurity, and the future of the U.S. working class. *Monthly Review, 59*(2), 20–30.

Taylor, C. (2003). *Modern social imaginaries.* Durham, NC: Duke University Press.

Teachers Network. (2007, April). Survey reveals that only 1% of teachers Find No Child Left Behind an effective way to assess the quality of schools and 69% report It's pushing teachers out of the profession [press release]. Retrieved April 3, 2007, from http://www.teachersnetwork.org/

Thatcher, M. (1987, October 31). Interview. *Women's Own Magazine.*

Traver, A. (2006). Institutions and organizational change: reforming New York City's public school system. *Journal of Education Policy, 21*(5), 497–514.

Turnaround Challenge (2007). Mass Insight Education. Retrieved from http://www.massinsight.org/stg/research/challenge/

United Nations Development Programme. (2005). *Human development report, 2005.* New York: Author.

U.S. Department of Education. (2009a, June 22). Press release. Retrieved from www.ed.gov

U.S. Department of Education. (2009b, June 25). Press release. Retrieved from www.ed.gov

U.S. Department of Education, Office of Innovation and Improvement. (2008). A commitment to quality: National charter school policy forum report. Washington, DC: Author. Retrieved from http://www.ed.gov/admins/comm/choice/csforum/report.pdf)

Valenzuela, A. (Ed.) (2005). *Leaving children behind.* Albany, NY: SUNY Press.

Valle, V. M., & Torres, R. D. (2000). *Latino metropolis.* Minneapolis: University of Minnesota Press.

Valli, L., & Buese, D. (2007). The changing roles of teachers in an era of high-stakes accountability. *American Educational Research Journal, 44*(3), 519–558.

Varady, D. P., & Raffel, J. A. (1995). *Selling cities: Attracting homebuyers through schools and housing programs.* Albany, NY: SUNY Press.

Varady, D., Raffel, J. A., Sweeney, S., & Denson, L. L. (2005). Attracting middle-income families in the HOPE VI public housing revitalization program. *Journal of Urban Affairs, 27*(2), 149–164.

Venkatesh, S. A., Celimli, I., Miller, D., Murphy, A., & Turner, B. (2004, February). *Chicago public housing transformation: A research report.* New York: Center for Urban Research and Policy, Columbia University.

Wacquant, L. (2001). The penalization of poverty and the rise of neo-liberalism. *European Journal of Criminal Policy and Research, 9*(4), 401–412.

Wacquant, L. (2008). The place of the prison in the new government of poverty. In M. L. Frampton, I. Haney López, & J. Simon (Eds.), *After the war on crime: Race, democracy and a new reconstruction* (pp. 23–36). New York: New York University Press.

Walker, N. (2010, April 2). Interview. *Democracy now*. Retrieved from www.democracynow.org

Washington, J. M. (Ed.). (1986). *A testament of hope: The essential writings and speeches of Martin Luther King, Jr.* New York: HarperCollins.

Watkins, T. J. (1997). Teacher communications, child achievement, and parent traits in parent involvement models. *Journal of Educational Research, 91*(1), 3–14.

Watkins, W. (2001). *The White architects of Black education: Ideology and power in America, 1865–1954.* New York: Teachers College Press.

Weber, R. (2002). Extracting value from the city: Neoliberalism and urban redevelopment. In N. Brenner & N. Theodore (Eds.), *Spaces of neoliberalism: Urban restructuring in North America and Western Europe* (pp. 172–193). London: Blackwell.

Weber, R. (2003). Equity and entrepreneurialism: The impact of tax increment financing on school finance. *Urban Affairs Review, 38*(5), 619–644.

Weber, R. (2009). *Financialized urban policy and the"risk management state*. Unpublished manuscript.

Wells, A. S., Scott, J. T., Lopez, A., & Holme, J. J. (2005). Charter school reform and the shifting meaning of educational equity: Greater voice and greater inequality? In J. Petrovich & A. S. Wells (Eds.), *Bringing equity back: Research for a new era in American educational policy* (pp. 219–243). New York: Teachers College Press.

Wells, A. S., Slayton, J., & Scott, J. (2002). Defining democracy in the neoliberal age: Charter school reform and educational consumption. *American Educational Research Journal, 39*(2), 337–361.

Wenglinsky, H. (1998). Finance equalization and within-school equity: The relationship between education spending and the social distribution of achievement. *Educational Evaluation and Policy Analysis, 20*(4), 269–283.

Whitty, G., Power, S., & Halpin, D. (1998). *Devolution and choice in education: The school, the state and the market*. Buckingham, England: Open University Press.

Wilen, W. P., & R. D. Nayak. (2006). Relocating public housing residents have little hope of returning: Work requirements for mixed-income public housing developments. In L. Bennett, J. L. Smith & P. A. Wright (Eds.), *Where are poor people to live? Transforming public housing communities* (pp. 239–258). Armonk, NY: M. E. Sharpe.

Williams, R. (1978). *Marxism and literature*. Oxford, England: Oxford University Press.

Williams, R. (1989). *Resources of hope*. New York: Verso.

Williams, R. Y. (2004). *The politics of public housing*. Oxford, England: Oxford University Press.

Wilson, D. (2006). *Cities and race: America's new black ghetto*. London: Routledge.

Wilson, D., Wouters, J., & Grammenos, D. (2004). Successful protect-community discourse: Spatiality and politics in Chicago's Pilsen neighborhood. *Environment and Planning*, A, 36, 1173–1190.

Wilson, E. (2001). The invisible flaneur (rev. ed.). In E. Wilson (Ed.), *The contradictions of culture: Cities, culture, women* (pp. 72–89). London, Sage.

Wilson, W. J. (1987). *The truly disadvantaged*. Chicago, IL: University of Chicago Press.

Winfield, A. G. (2007). *Eugenics and education in America: Institutionalized racism and the implications of history, ideology and memory*. New York: Lang.

Wolch, P. (1990) *The shadow state: Government and the voluntary sector in transition*. New York: The Foundation Center.

Wolff, E. N. (2002). *Top heavy: The increasing inequality of wealth in America and what can be done about it* (2nd ed.). New York: New Press.

Wong, K. K. (2009). Mayoral accountability as governance redesign in urban districts.*Teachers College Record*. Retrieved from http://www.tcrecord.org ID Number: 15687.

Wong, K. K., Shen, F., Anagnostopoulos, D., & Rutledge, S. (2007). *The education mayor: Improving America's schools*. Washington, DC: Georgetown University Press.

Woods, P., & Jeffrey, B. (2002). The reconstruction of primary teachers' identities. *British Journal of the Sociology of Education, 23*(1), 89–106.

Wood, D., Halfon, N., Scarla, D., Newacheck, P., & Nessim, S. (1993). Impact of family relocation on children's growth, development, school function, and behavior. *Journal of the American Medical Association, 270,* 1334–1338.

Woodson, C. G. (1933/1990). *The mis-education of the Negro.* Trenton, NJ: Africa World Press.

Wright, P. (2006). Community resistance to CHA transformation. In L. Bennett, J. L. Smith, & P. A. Wright (Eds.), *Where are poor people to live? Transforming public housing communities* (pp. 125–167). Armonk, NY: M. E. Sharpe

Wrigley, J. (1982). *Class politics and public schools: Chicago 1900–1950.* Piscataway, NJ: Rutgers University Press.

Zhang, Y., & Weisman, G. (2006). Public housings' Cinderella: Policy dynamics of HOPE VI in the mid-1990s. In L. Bennett, J. L. Smith, & P. A. Wright (Eds.), *Where are poor people to live? Transforming public housing communities* (pp. 41–67). Armonk, NY: M. E. Sharpe.

Zukin, S. (2002). Whose city? Whose culture? In S. S. Fainstein & S. Campbell (Eds.), *Readings in urban theory* (pp. 325–334). Oxford, England: Blackwell.

INDEX